CHANTING THE NAMES OF MAÑJUŚRĪ

BUDDHIST TRADITION SERIES

VOLUME 38

CHANTING THE NAMES OF
Mañjuśrī

The Mañjuśrī-Nāma-Saṃgīti
Sanskrit and Tibetan Texts

Translated, with Annotation & Introduction by
ALEX WAYMAN

MOTILAL BANARSIDASS PUBLISHERS PRIVATE LIMITED • DELHI

2nd Reprint: Delhi, 2018
First Indian Edition: Delhi, 1999
First Published: USA, 1985

ISBN: 978-81-208-1653-4

MOTILAL BANARSIDASS
41 U.A. Bungalow Road, Jawahar Nagar, Delhi 110 007
1 B, Jyoti Studio Compound, Kennedy Bridge, Nana Chowk, Mumbai 400 007
203 Royapettah High Road, Mylapore, Chennai 600 004
236, 9th Main III Block, Jayanagar, Bengalure 560 011
8 Camac Street, Kolkata 700 017
Ashok Rajpath, Patna 800 004
Chowk, Varanasi 221 001

Printed in India

by RP Jain at NAB Printing Unit,
A-44, Naraina Industrial Area, Phase I, New Delhi–110028
and published by JP Jain for Motilal Banarsidass Publishers (P) Ltd,
41 U.A. Bungalow Road, Jawahar Nagar, Delhi-110007

HOMAGE TO MAÑJUŚRĪKUMĀRABHŪTA

Instead of dirt and poison, we have rather chosen to fill our hives with honey and wax, thus furnishing mankind with the two noblest of things which are sweetness and light.

—Swift, *The Battle of the Books*

Devoted to Names are the Verses.
Nāmasannissitā gāthā

—*Samyutta-nikāya*, i, 39

Nāmasanniśritā gāthā

—*Abhidharmakośa-bhāṣya*, Chapter II

Mañjuśrī not a production
'Jam dpal skye ba med
is a term of the Tathāgatas.

—*Jñānālokālamkāra-sūtra*

Foreword

As I mentioned in the Introduction, in Spring 1970, while in Dharamsala, north India, the learned Lama Geshe Rabten had recommended that I meditate on Mañjuśrī. Later, Geshe Rabten and his disciple Gonsar Rinpoche established a Tibetan center in Switzerland. The more obvious manner in which I carried out that Lama's recommendation was in preparing this work *Chanting the Names of Mañjuśrī.*

Less obvious is the Tibetan tradition of the Gelugapa sect, founded by Tsong-kha-pa, that this founder is the incarnation of Mañjuśrī. The present writer spent many years studying and translating works by Tsong-kha-pa. I put out the last part of the *Lam rim Chen mo* under the title *Calming the Mind and Discerning the Real,* which was published by Columbia University in the U.S.A. and later by Motilal Banarsidass in India; later published my translation of the Bodhisattva section of that same Tibetan work. I prepared my rendition of this author's work on Buddhist Logic as the last work in my *A Millennium of Buddhist Logic,* Vol. One. In my works on Buddhist Tantra, occasionally I have cited Tsong-kha-pa's tantric survey called *Sṅags rim chen mo,* since I transcribed every single quotation of this work on individual sheets kept in notebooks.

That shows that I indeed followed Geshe Rabten's meditation advice, and I am pleased to have an Indian edition of *Chanting the Names of Mañjuśrī* issued by Motilal Banarsidass.

ALEX WAYMAN

CONTENTS

PART ONE

Introduction

UPON PRESENTING this remarkable work, to be called "Chanting the Names of Mañjuśrī," the present writer should explain the origin of this project and what the final result amounts to. In Spring of the year 1970, at Dharamsala, H.P., India, I had the good fortune to meet and consult with Geshe Rabten and his disciple Gonsar Rinpoche, who in recent years have been in Switzerland. The learned Geshe told me I should meditate on Mañjuśrī. I was indeed impressed with this advice, but my nonritual devotion is in taking pains to solve problems, both in the language of a text and in its associated ideas.

During my tantric studies, resulting in several published works, I long ago learned about the importance of the *Mañjuśrī-nāma-saṃgīti* to all Tibetan sects. My own library has the Peking Sanskrit-Tibetan blockprint of this text, originally procured in Peking by my teacher F. D. Lessing, as well as a copy of P. Minaeff's Sanskrit edition, St. Petersburg, 1885. Some of my published articles utilize the Smṛti commentary in its Tibetan version. Conceiving the plan of a volume of "minor" tantric texts, including the *Mañjuśrī-nāma-saṃgīti*, I made draft translations of this and some other texts that had commentaries to aid the project. This plan was interrupted by other projects in recent years. In 1982 I decided that such important texts (whether or not called "minor" by length) should not remain in manuscript and set to work first on the *Mañjuśrī*, but then found the supporting material so multiplying that a separate work was indicated.

My library has long had duplicates of two Yogatantra commentaries on the *Mañjuśrī* from the Tibetan Tanjur—those by Candrabhadrakīrti and by Smṛti. In order to balance these, I obtained the commentary by Narendrakīrti in the Kālacakra section of the Tanjur. It turned out that Narendrakīrti wrote the most intellectual commentary, Smṛti the most learned, and Candrabhadrakīrti the most intuitive and speculative. For reasons only partially clear to me, these commentaries proved individually superior for certain chapters of the text. While these commentaries sufficed, for a few places I consulted some other commentaries, both in the Yogatantra and the Kālacakra sections of the Tanjur. The commentaries furnished extra meanings, sometimes fascinating, for this and that; and also clarified the structure of the text, but did not reveal why this text was so popular, indeed, why their authors were moved to write commentaries. To explain this paramount role of the *Mañjuśrī-nāma-saṃgīti*, I have prepared several introductory chapters.

In Chapter 1, on background, I attempt to trace Mañjuśrī's emergence from obscurity in early centuries A.D. to an identification with Prajñāpāramitā (Perfection of Insight or of Wisdom), eventually to become the Primordial Buddha (*ādibuddha*). Chapter 2, on the citations in Nāro-pā's commentary on the *Hevajratantra*, has all fifty-three of his quotations of the *Mañjuśrī* in the order of the *Hevajratantra* chapters. This shows the importance of the *Mañjuśrī* in the cult that uses both the *Kālacakratantra* and the *Hevajratantra*. Chapter 3 on the seven *maṇḍalas* of the *Mañjuśrī-nāma-saṃgīti*, associates chapters of this text with cults of Mañjuśrī by way of iconographical forms, of which a full list is furnished from Jaya Paṇḍita. In Chapter 4, remarks on the Tibetan text, I set forth the makeup of the Sanskrit text and its brilliant Tibetan translation by Rin-chen-bzaṅ-po, considerations which bring out the meaning of Mañjuśrī's "names" and also affect the translation into English. Chapter 5 on "the six cycles of praise" presents a translation of the prose insertion of some *Mañjuśrī-nāma-saṃgīti* editions. These six paragraphs extol the recitation of the *Mañjuśrī* and contemplation of the deity Mañjuśrī, and so help the reader into a frame of mind agreeable with the text and translation of the *Mañjuśrī-nāma-saṃgīti* that immediately follow.

Certain scholarly aids are appended: an index of the Sanskrit first *pādas* (metrical feet), an index of Tibetan first lines (of the four-lined verses), along with an index to the translation and its notes by chapter and verse. The not inconsiderable labor to present this text in the proper light is the way I have meditated on Mañjuśrī.

1. Background of the *Mañjuśrī-nāma-saṃgīti*

THE *MAÑJUŚRĪ-NĀMA-SAṂGĪTI* as a text includes an enormous amount of Buddhist lore, both of the early variety as well as the later Mahāyāna, and it has traces of Hindu religious ideas. Hence, the commentators were taxed to make adequate comments. It is not practical to set forth a "message" of this text independent of its study along with the commentaries. It appears more worthwhile to show how the text came to be as it is, with its challenge to the commentators. I propose to clarify the text's background under three headings: (1) the names Mañjuśrī and Mañjughoṣa, (2) the kinds of commentary on the *Mañjuśrī-nāma-saṃgīti*, and (3) "Chanting the Names" of Mañjuśrī.

The Names Mañjuśrī and Mañjughoṣa

In the translation part of this work I have cited the commentator Smṛti on the name Mañjuśrī showing that the portion *mañju* means "smooth" because of being free from hard defilements, hence the path of rejecting the bad; while *śrī* means "glory" because of gaining excellent merits, hence the path of accepting the good. Thus the name Mañjughoṣa (the sound or expression of *mañju*) stresses the purification side and performance-teaching of it. Such is the message of the large ritualistic work, *Mañjuśrī-mūla-kalpa*, in its Chapter 15:[1]

> Mañjughoṣa, the youth (*kumāra*), is always pure among all creatures. As long as this instruction is in the world, he will perform the deeds of the Buddha.

The commentator Smṛti also mentions that in the "*śrāvaka* theory systems" Mañjuśrī is a youth, usually aged sixteen; in Mahāyāna, he is a Bodhisattva of the Tenth Stage; and in the special theory common to the *Mañjuśrī-nāma-saṃgīti* (hereafter: M-N-S) he has represented Buddhahood for uncountable ages. The separation into three in that manner is somewhat arbitrary, because Mañjuśrī as a youth (Sanskrit: *kumārabhūta*) is frequently paid homage to at the head of Mahāyāna scriptures, especially in their Tibetan form. Smṛti's remarks, however, do point to a situation where Mañjuśrī was becoming identified with Prajñāpāramitā (called "Mother of the Buddhas") and doing so as a "male" adolescent, and this led to a remarkable role in later Mahāyāna.

The cult of the Bodhisattva Mañjuśrī was scarcely developed in the first centuries A.D. during the early Mahāyāna formation. Mañjuśrī in time became an interlocutor in various Mahāyāna scriptures, so in the *Saptaśatikā Prajñāpāramitā*, among others.[2] An early interlocutor role is in a paramount scripture of Chinese Buddhism, the Pure Land sect, entitled *Ārya-aparimitāyurjñāna-nāma-mahāyāna-sūtra*, about the heaven of the Buddha Amitāyus.[3] Mañjuśrī appears as an interlocutor in various chapters of the celebrated *Saddharma-puṇḍarīka-sūtra*, where also Śāriputra, the early disciple foremost in insight (*prajñā*), has an important role in early chapters.[4] A number of later Mahāyāna scriptures show his name in the title: *Mañjuśrīnirdeśa*, *Mañjuśrīparipṛcchā*, *Mañjuśrībuddhakṣetraguṇavyūha*, *Mañjuśrīvikurvāṇaparivarta*, *Mañjuśrīvikrīḍita*.[5] In such titles, he appears as a Bodhisattva of the Tenth Stage as are also Avalokiteśvara, Samantabhadra, Vajrapāṇi, and so on. In this sense he is representing Buddhahood, according to Prajñāpāramitā teachings, but not Complete Buddhahood.[6] After a growing importance in Buddhist tantric works, Mañjuśrī in the M-N-S and also in the *Kālacakratan-*

tra tradition, as will be shown below, became the "primordial Buddha" (*ādibuddha*).

The identification with Prajñāpāramitā led Mañjuśrī to be considered a spiritual progenitor. Thus Lamotte cites a passage in the *Ajātaśatrurājasūtra* where the Buddha informs Śāriputra, "Mañjuśrī is the father and mother of the Bodhisattvas, and he is their spiritual friend."[7] This needs explanation. The oldest source for the idea of Prajñāpāramitā as "Mother of the Buddhas" is the *Aṣṭasāhasrikā Prajñāpāramitā* (the Eight-Thousand One), Chapter 12, "Showing the World." This scripture here treats Prajñāpāramitā as "mother" in two ways: to be honored, accordingly protected; and as the source of the Tathāgatas' "all-knowledge." The first way starts curiously, so in Conze's translation:[8] "It is as with a mother who has many children—five, or ten, or twenty, or thirty, or forty, or fifty, or one hundred, or one thousand. If she fell ill, they would all exert themselves to prevent their mother from dying. . . ." For this, one should accept that there is just one "mother" in this sense; hence the numbers, five or one thousand, do not matter. Vimalamitra, in his commentary (preserved in Tibetan) on the *Saptaśatikā Prajñāpāramitā*, treats just this first way (I incorporate in parentheses his remarks from a preceding paragraph):[9]

> It is said that they (i.e., the sons) should guard (i.e., *prajñāpāramitā*, so its contemplation will expand and not deteriorate), should protect it (so it is not harmed by others), should seclude it (so it does not stray to lower vehicles). By the example of sons who endeavour to dispel their mother's illness, it is taught that the Buddhas guard, etc. In this sense the Buddha Bhagavat is like a son; and Prajñāpāramitā is like a mother.

The second way of being a "mother" amounts to showing the world as it really is. This goes with the explanation of the title "Tathāgata"—who has understood the same way as all Buddhas have understood. But this still has not explained what is meant by being a "father." The "Eight-Thousand" scripture by calling the chapter "showing the world" indicates the way in which the "sons" are not distinguished from one another—be they five or one thousand, i.e., by the "showing" or the "viewpoint" (*darśana*). They are indeed distinguished by practice (*caryā*), hence by "vehicles" (*yāna*), whereby the "father" is the "means" (*upāya*). This point is brought out by many passages near the beginning of the Bodhisattva section of Tsoṅ-kha-pa's *Lam rim chen mo*, and cannot be dwelt upon here. In short, when there is talk of "five families" of the Tantras, as happens in tantric literature and in the present work, it took the "father"—in this sense of the word—to get different sons.

In Buddhist tantric literature there are various ways of setting forth the families. Thus, Lamotte cites the Chinese translation of the *Mañjuśrī-mūla-kalpa*, "In the Northeast direction beyond universes as numerous as the sands of the Ganges, there is a universe Saṃkusumita, and its Buddha has the name Saṃkusumitarajendratathāgata. He has a prince regent named Mañjuśrī."[10] This name Saṃkusumita was replaced in later Tantras by the name Amoghasiddhi,[11] who in the five-Buddha system heads the Karma Family. This association with *karma* in the sense of rites and proper conduct pervades the *Mañjuśrī-mūla-kalpa*. Mkhas-grub-rje's work on Tantra, the Kriyātantra section, states that the Tathāgata Family has as Lord, Bhagavat Śākyamuni; and as Master, Mañjuśrī, whose chief tantra is the *Mañjuśrī-mūla-tantra*, another name for the *Mañjuśrī-mūla-kalpa*.[12] But then the M-N-S, as the translation shows, places Mañjuśrī in the heart of each of the six Buddha "progenitors."

Mañjuśrī is prominently associated with the number "five," and two verses of M-N-S, its VI,18, and VIII,17, are devoted to this fivefold symbolism. Lamotte points out that Mañjuśrī's name Pañcacīra (in Tibetan translation meaning "having five knotted locks") might derive from the mountain chain around the Lake Anavatapta in the Himālayas. This mountain chain is crowned by five peaks (*pañcaśikha* or *pañcaśīrṣa*). He cites the Pāli commentary on the *Udāna* to the effect that this lake is surrounded by five mountain peaks, called Sudarśana, Citra, Kāla, Gandhamādana, and Kailāsa.[13] Also he mentions that the Gandhamādana is said to be frequented by the Ṛṣis and the Pratyekabuddhas and to serve as the residence of the king of the Gandharva Manjughoṣa, also named Pañcaśikha.[14]

Sculptures of the Gandharva Pañcaśikha and his retinue are found in early Buddhist art, second century B.C. on, shown making background music when Indra visited the Buddha.[15] Thus the word "Gandharva" means a celestial musician. Texts insist that Gandharva Pañcaśikha also has singing talent and fine voice quality—going well with the name Mañjughoṣa.[16] Among the Mañjuśrī types in the list given in my chapter, "The Seven Maṇḍalas of the *Mañjuśrī-nāma-saṃgīti*," there are several that emphasize the voice. Besides Mañjughoṣa, there is Vādirāja (king of speech), Vādisiṃha (lion of speech), and Dharmadhātu-Vāgīśvara (Speech Lord of the Dharmadhātu). The M-N-S especially shows this speaking side of Mañjuśrī, and by the name Mañjughoṣa, in three verses:

> Lord of speech, master of speech, skillful in speech, master over words, of limitless words; true speech, speaking the truth, preceptor of the four truths. (VI, 9).
>
> Mañjughoṣa with great sounding, whose single great sound in the three worlds is great, sounding throughout the sky expanse, best of those who are sounding. (VII, 10).
>
> The great speaker as Lord of Speech, exemplary person of speech as king of speech; excellent and outstanding among speakers, the invincible lion of speech. (VIII, 25).

Moreover, the *Mañjuśrī-mūla-kalpa* has at several places the term *mahāmudrāpañcaśikha* (great gesture with five points),[17] presumably the origin of the five-pointed *vajra*, said in certain Buddhist tantric currents to be in the heart at the time of enlightenment[18] and so associated with Mañjuśrī in the M-N-S lineage.

The Kinds of Commentary on the *Mañjuśrī-nāma-saṃgīti*

The M-N-S as a text subject to commentary may well have started out as a chapter in a kind of *Māyājāla-mahātantra*, which is named in the M-N-S, I, 13. The inclusion as a "*Gīti*" (song) chapter in a bigger work is consistent with the basic text of the M-N-S not being chapterized, e.g., in the carefully edited Dharamsala Tibetan text that I have consulted. The Peking Sanskrit-Tibetan edition of M-N-S is chapterized, but doubtless by authority of the commentaries, of which there are many in the Tibetan canon. Besides, the commentators had trouble deciding on the end of the M-N-S, Chapter VI, Pure Dharmadhātu Wisdom, and the beginning of Chapter VII, Praising the Mirrorlike Wisdom. And the fifty-three citations of the M-N-S (evincing "sweetness and light" in comparison to the others) that I traced out in Nāro-pā's commentary on *Hevajratantra* are clearly independent of chapters. The dating of the M-N-S is also dependent on the commentators. These include Candragomin; and if he is the eminent Buddhist grammarian, he has been placed in the first half of the sixth century.[19] There is more than one Candragomin; and the M-N-S commentator is reasonably to be identified with the one who wrote the commentary in the cycle of the "Twenty-one Praises of Tāra," probably in the eighth century, where is also the M-N-S commentator Vimalamitra. The M-N-S shows influence of the Tathāgatagarbha theory, specifically the three kinds of Tathāgatagarbha that are set forth in a basic scripture of this tradition, the *Śrī-Mālādevīsiṃhanāda-sūtra*, which was first translated into Chinese in the early fifth century, where it was very popular for about a century thereafter.[20] The M-N-S cannot be earlier than this popularity.

Also, it is preceded by the *Mañjuśrī-mūla-kalpa* (meaning the first two published volumes, not the later third volume devoted to legends and prophecy), which may belong to the fourth century as a kind of early Buddhist Tantra. Taking all the evidence into consideration, the M-N-S should be placed in either the sixth or seventh centuries, and I suppose that the seventh century is more realistic.

That there are two kinds of commentaries on the M-N-S was long ago called to my attention by the Tibetan author Mkhas-grub-rje.[21] Indeed, the commentaries in the Tibetan Tanjur on the M-N-S are separated into two groups—those in the Anuttarayogatantra and those in the Yogatantra section. The Anuttarayogatantra ones are in two places—among the *Kālacakratantra* commentaries and among the "Father Tantra" commentaries. It has been called to my attention that Sa-paṇ (Sākya-paṇḍita) once wrote that he had studied the six lineages of M-N-S interpretation current in his day (thirteenth century) in Tibet.[22] I believe I am able to state what these are in terms of my own use of these commentaries. The Yogatantra commentaries are of two types: (1) represented here by Smṛti's, following Līlavajra,[23] claiming that there are seven *maṇḍalas* involved and implicating the Tathāgatagarbha theory; (2) the Mañjuśrīmitra lineage, claiming there are six such *maṇḍalas* and represented here by Candrabhadrakīrti's commentary (but I employed Mañjuśrīmitra's on the "six cycles" of the M-N-S). In the Anuttarayogatantra class, the *Kālacakra* type commentaries are of two types: (1) those that also employ the *Hevajratantra*, represented here by Nāro-pā's citations of M-N-S in his commentary on the *Hevajra*; (2) those that do not use the *Hevajratantra*, among which I have much employed the Narendrakīrti one and the fascinating Padma-dkar-po commentary mainly for one important passage. Also in the Anuttarayogatantra are the "Father Tantra" texts (immediately following the Yamāri texts), but there is much difference between the Peking and Derge Tanjurs for inclusion of texts here, apparently a disputed matter. The position in the Tanjur requires (1) to be those affiliated with the angry form of Mañjuśrī called Yamāri or Yamāntaka, while (2) would be other "Father Tantra" types, mainly *Guhyasamājatantra* lineage. My work has scant representation of these two lineages. For all these lineages, I selected comments that seemed helpful, and made no attempt to carry through a particular lineage. It should be granted that whatever the comments I included, anyone who has access to other commentaries will find quite different comments.

To give a bare idea of the difference between comments drawn from the two sets of commentaries, let me take first the Yogatantra comments. These commentaries are reasonable from the M-N-S itself in literal form. Thus, the M-N-S devotes a chapter to the *Vajradhātu-maṇḍala*, which is the first section of the basic Yogatantra, the *Tattvasaṃgraha*. Chapter III, "Surveying the Six Families," was easily and convincingly commented upon by the Yogatantra commentaries while Narendrakīrti, whose intelligently written commentary in the *Kālacakra* section was extremely helpful on some other chapters, could contribute nothing of value for understanding this brief, but key chapter of the M-N-S.

To indicate some of contents one may expect to find in the *Kālacakra*-type commentaries, let us consider the one called *Amṛtakaṇika-nāma-āryanāmasaṃgīti-ṭippanī* by Sūryaśrījñāna.[24] In the M-N-S, VI, 18, the phrase "Buddha with five-body nature," is commented: "with five-body nature of waking, dream, deep sleep, the fourth, and beyond the fourth." The term "pervading lord" of the verse is explained: "because pervading the states of child, etc., with the nature of bliss." After mentioning for "five-wisdom nature" that they are the five, mirrorlike, etc., this commentary cites verses that explain the five Buddhas in terms of the five elements and use "twilight language" terms like *vola* (gum-myrrh). Then this commentary explains the five wisdoms in terms of a sexual union that gives rise to an embryo. Since the M-N-S, VIII, 17, has five's again, this commentary explains "flowers on five knotted locks" as the five states, waking, etc. (as above). On the M-N-S, X, 3, the phrase "holding the *bindu* of sixteen halved twice," this commentary is initially quite helpful, saying "half of sixteen parts is eight, and half of this is four, i.e., this generator holds the four states, waking, dream, deep sleep, and the fourth (*turiya*), which are the characteristic of body, speech, mind, and knowledge." We notice that this commentator likes to mention the four states of consciousness, and to use the Śaivitic term "beyond the fourth." Narendrakīrti, in his *Kālacakra*-type commentary, prefers to bring in the four "joys" (*ānanda*).

But it remains to be explained why the M-N-S obtained these *Kālacakratantra* lineage commentaries. When we look at the Kanjur (the translation of "revealed scriptures") and at the Tantra section (*Rgyud*), we notice in the Derge edition that the very first work is the *Mañjuśrījñānasattvasya paramārtha-nāma-saṃgīti* ("Rehearsal of the Supreme Names of Mañjuśrī the Knowledge-Being"); this is the long version of the title usually given as *Mañjuśrī-nāma-saṃgīti*. This rather brief work is followed immediately by basic scriptures of the *Kālacakra*. This suggests a tie-up, a suggestion that becomes confirmed upon investigation, as follows. The chief *Kālacakra* "revealed scripture" is entitled *Paramādibuddhoddhṛtaśrīkālacakra-nāma-tantrarāja* ("King of Tantra Called Śrī-Kālacakra Drawn from the Supreme Primordial Buddha"). This work is in five chapters: (1) Arrangement of the World-Realms (*lokadhātu*), (2) Inner Certainty (*adhyātma*), (3) Initiation (*abhiṣeka*), (4) Evocations (*sādhana*), (5) Knowledge (*jñāna*). The celebrated Tibetan savant Bu-ston, who put together the Kanjur and Tanjur, has great works on the *Kālacakra* found in the first volumes of his collected works. The very first volume contains this chief *Kālacakra* work together with Bu-ston's interlinear comments. At the end of Chapter two (the *adhyātma*), the Tantra states:[25]

> You are the mother. You are the father. You are the guru of the world. You are the friend and good companion. You are the (protective) lord (*nātha*). You are the worker, benefactor, dispeller of sin. You are endowed with the high rank. You have the isolated state and have the best state of powers. The destroyer of faults is you, indeed. You are the (protective) lord and the wish-granting gem for the lowest types (of sentient beings). In You, powerful one of victors, I take refuge.

Before the first of these "You are," Bu-ston makes the comment, "Mañjuśrī, teacher of the condensed tantra." Near the end of Chapter V (on *jñāna*), there is another flurry of "You are" sentences, concluding with another taking of refuge. Again, Bu-ston annotates the first "You are" with "Mañjuśrī." It starts: "You are the old man, entirely a youth, spiritual son of the Jina. You are from the beginning, the primordial Buddha."[26] This reminds us of the M-N-S, VIII, 5, "Whose body of youth is unique in the three worlds; elder, old man, lord of creatures. . . ." and M-N-S, VI, 17, "supreme primeval bearing the three bodies." In short, there are indications, which require more study, for which this present work of mine may well constitute the groundwork, that this *āgama* of the *Kālacakra* was composed with the M-N-S as one of the sources and with possibly an even greater role than I can now determine. This might be a reason for the set of commentaries on M-N-S in the *Kālacakra* section of the Tanjur, and a reason for Nāro-pā, who wrote a commentary on the initiation (*abhiṣeka*) part of the *Kālacakra*, to have employed the M-N-S so frequently in his commentary on *Hevajratantra*, giving the impression that he had thoroughly mastered all the verses of M-N-S. A better reason is that the M-N-S is cited by chapter in the *Vimala-*

prabhā commentary on the *Kālacakra*; and in the "Jñāna," fifth and last chapter, the entire M-N-S is referred to, with specific mention of chapters and with mention of 162 as the total number of verses. This reference to the M-N-S in such a way has probably made it a mandatory scripture to go along with *Kālacakra* study. I noticed this in the Bu-ston edition, with annotation, of the *Vimalaprabhā*, this particular passage in his collected works, Vol. 3(Ga), folio side 214, or f. 107b. Besides, the *Vimalaprabhā* (Bu-ston, Ka, *Khams le*, f. 60a-7) says: "Whoever does not know the *Nāma-saṃgīti* does not know the knowledge body of Vajradhara" (*gaṅ gis mtshan yaṅ dag par brjod pa mi śes pa des rdo rje 'dsin pa yi ye śes kyi sku mi śes so*).

"Chanting the Names" of Mañjuśrī

In the first chapter of the M-N-S, Vajrapāṇi implores the Bhagavat Śākyamuni to tell the "chanting of names" (*nāma-saṃgīti*), which has "profound meaning" and "broad meaning." The best explanation I could find was that of Smṛti's. He explains "profound" by voidness (*śūnyatā*), or by being "incomparable," and "which is good in the beginning, the middle, and the end." And he explains "broad" by way of seven *maṇḍalas* in a conventional (*saṃvṛti*) sense, and which stills defilement. Thus, the commentator Candrabhadrakīrti's claim that the "names" of Mañjuśrī are the names of deities in the *maṇḍalas* is the conventional meaning. Hence, also, the "profound" is the absolute meaning (*paramārtha*), and so the path "which is good in the beginning, the middle, and the end" must have this meaning. So in the full title of the work, as was mentioned, the words "*paramārtha-nāma-saṃgīti*" do apply to the form of the verses of the M-N-S. This use of the term *paramārtha* to apply to the path agrees with one way of allotting the two truths (conventional and absolute) to the four Noble Truths, namely, that the truths of suffering and source of suffering are conventional truth; and the truths of cessation of suffering and path leading to the cessation are absolute truth.[27]

The foregoing amounts to Nāro-pā's terminology in his commentary on the *Hevajratantra*, since he calls "provisional meaning" (*neyārtha*) the descriptions of deities in the iconographical sense as placed within a *maṇḍala*; and calls the "final meaning" (*nītārtha*) the portrayal stressing the internal reality, voidness, and the like. Hence, on the one hand, one can use the terms "broad," "names of deities," "*maṇḍala*," "conventional meaning," "provisional meaning"; and on the other hand, use the terms, "profound," "reality," "voidness," "absolute meaning," "final meaning," "path which is good in the beginning, the middle, and the end." It should be clear also that in this tradition of the two truths—conventional and absolute—there is no intention to downgrade one of these, namely, the conventional, as some would say, missing the point, "not really a truth." My chapter on the seven *maṇḍalas* represents this sense of the "broad meaning," i.e., of the praxis that stills defilement.

A commentator on the M-N-S, Mañjuśrīmitra, in his *Bodhicitta-bhāvanā-dvādaśārtha-nirdeśa*, states:[28]

> "Mañjuśrī" is the errorless comprehension of the character of *bodhicitta*, the birthplace of all the Buddhas. For this reason, he is the mother of all the Sugatas, the sole path of all the Jinas.

This then is an example of the "profound meaning."

On the other hand, when it is said of Mañjuśrī, as was previously quoted, "You are the mother. You are the father. You are the guru of the world," this, like names of deities, is an example of the "broad meaning."

But, how about the "names" of Mañjuśrī as a "chanting" (rehearsal) in the verses of the M-N-S? These are not names in the sense of epithets—which would have all amounted to "broad meaning"—as though the term *paramārtha* in the title of the M-N-S should not have been there. Indeed, the chapters that contain this rehearsal are given over to verses that fall usually in four parts (the Sanskrit *pāda*, or "foot"), and the Tibetan imitated this regular pattern insofar as possible. Thus, each of the four parts of a verse amounts to a statement of fact, whereby the word "name" (*nāma*) is employed as the character of Mañjuśrī rather than an epithet. An example of the pattern is found in the M-N-S, V,8. The first "foot" is: "Wise one, holding the great illusion." The second one: "performing the aim of great illusion." The third one: "pleased with the pleasure of great illusion." The fourth one: "using the hallucination of great illusion." Since this is the inner nature of Mañjuśrī, the "profound meaning" is expressed. However, when Smṛti, in the commentary I cited for this verse, identified each of the four with "diamond beings" in the Buddha Amoghasiddhi's family in the North and also with four of the voidnesses in the list of sixteen voidnesses—both these kinds of identifications go under the heading of "broad meaning" for purification of defilement.

In short, when the verses of the M-N-S are rehearsed or chanted, as is, they constitute the "profound meaning"; and when identifications are superimposed, they become the "broad meaning." See below, the fifth introduction section devoted to the "six cycles of praise," for an exposition of the fruits promised for a thrice-daily recitation of the M-N-S.

2. Citations of the *Mañjuśrī-nāma-saṃgīti* in Nāro-pā's Commentary

Nāro-pā is a celebrated author in his own right and also important for the eleventh century transmission of the "Six Laws of Nāro-pā" to Mar-pa, which is the foundation of the Tibetan Bka'-brgyud-pa sect. Nāro-pā, who wrote a commentary on the *Kālacakra-tantra*'s "initiation" (*abhiṣeka*) section, reveals in his commentary on the *Hevajratantra* the tie-up between the *Kālacakra* commentarial tradition, the *Hevajratantra* itself, and the M-N-S. Within the limited space of this chapter, I can only show his employment of the M-N-S in the course of his *Hevajratantra* commentary, entitled *Vajrapada-sāra-saṃgraha-pañjikā*.[1] The *pañjikā* kind of commentary does not deal with each term of the basic text, but selects terms (he calls them *vajrapada*, "diamond words") for discussion. That is why he may have much material, especially due to citations, for a quite brief chapter of the *Hevajra*, and then have less material for a much longer chapter of the Tantra.

The M-N-S citations are traceable especially with the index of Tibetan first verse lines, included in this work. The citations (I found fifty-three in all) are in the commentary on the individual chapters of the *Hevajratantra*, so it should be mentioned that this Tantra is in two parts (*brtag pa*) that can each be rendered "assembly," in each of which the chapter count may start from no. 1.[2] To clarify Nāro-pā's citations of the M-N-S, I list them in the order of citation by chapter and verse according to my translation and in combination with the respective chapters of *Hevajra's* two 'assemblies":

Nāro-pā's Citations of M-N-S in Commentary on First Assembly

The Teacher (II, 1ab; VI, 10-11ab; X, 5; VIII, 16; VI, 16; VIII, 11cd-12; IX, 17)

The Tantra (X, 14; VI, 24)

Hevajra's opening sentence (VI, 14ab; VI, 23cd-24ab; VIII, 31cd-32; VIII, 5cd-6; VIII, 21-22-23ab)

Chapter 1, The Vajra Family (VI, 20cd-21; X, 3bcd)
Chapter 2, Mantra (V, 1bcd-2ab; VI, 5-6ab; VI, 21cd-22ab)
Chapter 3, Deities (V, 9-10ab; IV, 2; VIII, 3; V, 8)
Chapter 4, Initiation (VIII, 23cd-24ab; VI, 19)
Chapter 5, Reality (VIII, 24cd; X, 4)
Chapter 6, Praxis (I, 8; IX, 24; VI, 6cd)
Chapter 7, Secret Signs (IX, 13cd-14ab; IX, 4, 5; VI, 2-3ab)
Chapter 8, Yoginī-s (VI, 20ab; X, 1cd-2ab; IX, 6-7ab; X, 3; IX, 20-21ab; VI, 5ab)
Chapter 9, Purification (VIII, 1; X, 9)
Chapter 10, Initiation in the *maṇḍala* (I, 1cd-2ab; VI, 12cd-13ab + VIII, 8 + VI, 17)
Chapter 11, Enlightenment of Vajragarbha (VIII, 13)

Nāro-pā's Citations of M-N-S in Commentary on Second Assembly

Chapter 1, Consecration (VIII, 2)
Chapter 2, Success (VIII, 27; V, 3-4-5ab)
Chapter 3, Saṃdhibhāṣa (I, 1ab)
Chapter 4, Mudrā-s (no citation)
Chapter 5, Arising of Heruka (VIII, 9cd-10ab)
Chapter 6, Making a Painting (I, 15)
Chapter 7, Feasting (VI, 7cd-8ab)
Chapter 8, Taming (no citation)
Chapter 9, Construction of Mantras (no citation)
Chapter 10, Recitation (no citation)
Chapter 11, Meaning of Together Born (IX, 18)
Chapter 12, Four Initiations (VII, 6cd)

The above distribution of M-N-S citations reveals their important role in Nāro-pā's commentary on the *Hevajratantra*. Of course, Nāro-pā cites a number of other works, especially the Prajñapāramitā scripture and the *Kālacakra* scripture, which he refers to as *Dpal dan po'i sans rgyas* (Śrī-Ādibuddha), but there is no doubt that the M-N-S is a favorite of his and that he cited his especially appreciated passages of it.

In the following I shall differentiate between Nāro-pā's naming of the M-N-S as the source of the quotation and his citing of the verse(s) without so naming. In no case did Nāro-pā refer to a chapter of the M-N-S; indeed his quotations are quite independent of the particular chapters of the M-N-S.

First Assembly Commentary

The Teacher

Nāro-pā explains that the Buddha speaks in different languages and appears in different forms appropriate to the beings being guided. Accordingly, he cites (at 2-1-1) M-N-S, II, 1ab:

> Now Śākyamuni, Bhagavat, Saṃbuddha, best of the two-footed.

"Best of the two-footed" means, best of those born through a human womb and other two-footed ones, as in the hells. In teaching other two-footed ones, the Buddha might do it through various theory-systems and to beings in various stages of spiritual development. Showing the Buddha in the role of the saint, he cites (at 2-1-5, 6) M-N-S, VI, 10-11ab:

> Irreversible, not returning, rhinoceros, solitary guide, liberated by diverse ways of deliverance; a single cause amidst the great elements. Bhikṣu, arhat, who has destroyed the fluxes, devoid of passion, his senses controlled.

These diverse appearances are the function of the Buddha's body called Nirmāṇakāya, as he cites (2-1-8), without naming the M-N-S, its X, 5:

> Who has the best of bodies in the Nirmāṇakāya, maintaining the lineage of Buddha-*nirmāṇa*; having the multifarious *nirmāṇa* in the ten directions, performing according to the aims of the living beings.

To show that the Buddha thus becomes the refuge and the protector, Nāro-pā (at 2-2-6) cites, without naming, VIII, 16:

> Having the best, one gives the best and is the chief; now the best refuge worthy of refuge; excels as enemy of the great dangers, remover of every last danger.

The Bodhisattvas, in order to follow the illustrious example must collect merit and knowledge and become "irreversible." So he cites (2-3-1, 2) without naming the M-N-S, its VI, 16:

> Having merit, whose collection of merit is great; having knowledge, whose mine of knowledge is the great knowledge; knowing what is and what is not; collected the two collections.

And to illustrate the Buddha as the paragon of such a teacher, refuge, protector, Nāro-pā (2-3-7, 8) cites, not naming the M-N-S, its VIII, 11cd-12:

> The pervading lord who bears the great wish-granting gem, having the best of all jewels. Great flowering wish-granting tree, best of great auspicious flasks, agent of performing the aim of all sentient beings, with parental affection for sentient beings when seeking their benefit.

This activity is then stated in terms of three vehicles—of the *śrāvakas* or auditors, the *pratyekabuddhas* (called in a foregoing verse "rhinoceros"), and the *bodhisattvas* of the Great Vehicle—and the one vehicle; and here Nāro-pā cites the M-N-S, IX, 17:

> By means of the rules for the various vehicles, he constructs the aims of the world; having delivered the three vehicles, he stays in the one-vehicle fruit.

The Tantra

Then Nāro-pā turns his attention to the Tantra. Now it is necessary to learn about the four "seals" (*mudrā*), and after some explanation, he refers (3-2-7) to M-N-S, its X, 14:

> Preeminent patron of Dharma, revealing the meaning of the four *mudrā*-s; best resort of living beings and of those traveling the three ways of escape.

These four are the *karma*, *jñāna*, *mahā*, and *samaya*, but not mentioned in the *Hevajra* itself. Nāro-pā summarizes: The *karma*-seal (i.e., the external woman) is the causal one, being initial, and from which there is the together-born (*sahaja*), nontransiting bliss.[3] While that is indeed a truth (*satya*), there are two truths; and it is in the conventional sense, like the mirror (reflection) as a mundane simile, but is not in the absolute sense; so one of keen faculty should not embrace the *karma*-seal. One should cultivate the *jñāna*-seal,[4] i.e., by purifying the personal aggregates (*skandha*), elements (*dhātu*), and sense bases (*āyatana*) into images of deities (*lha'i rnam pa*), as the ritual of the *maṇḍala*-circle reveals; by working them with continual friction, one ignites the fire of wisdom (*jñāna*). What is to be attained is the "great seal" (*mahāmudrā*). How is it attained? Through that fire when the HAṂ syllable is burnt (as the *Hevajratantra*, Chapter 1, last verse, states). The "great seal" is like a dream, a hallucination, and the nature of mind. One should embrace this (i.e., the "great seal") until one realizes directly the "symbolic seal" (*samaya-mudrā*), which is not a perishing thing.

He cites sources about correlating the yogin's body, speech, and mind with the Body, Speech, and Mind of the Buddha; and now he cites (3-3-4, 5) the M-N-S, its VI, 24:

> Mantrin who bears the three families, maintaining the *mantra* that is great and a pledge; chief one bearing the three jewels; teacher of the three that are best and vehicles.

Hevajra's Opening Sentence

This is the *E-vaṃ mayā śrutam* ... ("Thus by me it was heard ..."). In his discussion, overlapping my own citations (*Yoga of the Guhyasamājatantra*, pp. 105–113) in regard to the *Guhyasamājatantra*'s opening sentence, at 4-2-5, he cites without naming, M-N-S, VI, 14ab:

> Shining king of the Dharma, whose Dharma is illustrious; supreme illuminator of the world.

At 5-1-2, Nāro-pā cites M-N-S, VI, 23cd-24ab, partly as his previous quote:

> The disposer with diverse bodies, great seer worthy of offerings and worthy of esteem. Mantrin who bears the three families, maintaining the *mantra* that is great and a pledge.

He then says (5-1-3), "And it is proclaimed in the same work," namely VIII, 31cd-32:

> The master of all the world-lords, master of all *vajradhara*-s. Who has the great Mind of all Buddhas, dwelling in the heart-mind of all Buddhas; who has the great Body of all Buddhas, and has the divine Speech of all Buddhas.

And soon another citation by name, at 5-2-1, the VIII, 5cd-6:

> Bearing the thirty-two characteristics; handsome and (most) lovely in the three worlds. Excellent instructor of wisdom to the

world, confident instructor to the world; *nātha*, savior, adept of the three worlds; the refuge and protector without superior.

He cites these passages to go with the words "body, speech, and mind heart" (*kāyavākcittahṛdaya*) of *Hevajra*'s opening sentence. As though the passage points to the outcome of the whole discussion, he cites (5-3-1, 2, 3), M-N-S, VIII, 21-22-23ab:

> Unsubdued, unexampled, unmanifest, not an appearance, without "consonants"; unchanging, going everywhere, the pervader; subtle, not a seed, fluxless. Without impurity, one lacks impurity and is immaculate; having ended faults, is without shortcoming; wide-awake, has fully awakened nature; omniscient, is best at all-knowing. Having transcended the nature of perception, knowledge maintains a nontwo nature.

Immediately after this citation, Nāro-pā says (5-3-3), "Accordingly, the Bhagavat Hevajra, who has the nature of the four bodies that are free from all obscuration, Lord of the twelve stages, is teacher of the Dharma." And "teacher of the Dharma" means teacher of what is taught in the *Hevajratantra*.

Chapter 1, Vajra Family

After much discussion about this chapter, Nāro-pā at 8-2-7 mentions that the fire alluded to in the last verse of this chapter—i.e., the situation when Caṇḍālī blazes at the navel, and so forth, until the moon-HAM at the crown of the head is burnt—is alluded to in M-N-S, VI, 20cd-21:

> Born from the sky, self-born; great fire of insight-knowledge. Vairocana the great light is the light of knowledge, shining upon, the torch of knowledge that is the lamp for the world, the great brilliance, the clear light.

And then, to go with his previous discussion of sixteen parts and other multiples of four, he cites at 8-3-4, without naming the M-N-S, its X, 3bcd:

> Holding the *bindu* of sixteen halved twice; when without branches and beyond calculation, holding the pinnacle of the Fourth Dhyāna.

Nāro-pā's prior discussion and the *Hevajratantra* context show that the dividing of the *bindu* has to do with the "petals" in multiples of four that are ascribed to the *cakras* of the body. In order to get a group of four as dividing factor, Nāro-pā at 8-1-5, cites authority for adding a Mahāsukhakāya to the traditional three (Dharmakāya, Sambhogakāya, and Nirmāṇakāya) Buddha bodies. Hence, these are the four that he meant in the statement cited above that Hevajra has the nature of four bodies.

Chapter 2, Mantra

Since this is the Mantra chapter, Nāro-pā cites at 8-5-5, without naming, the celebrated passage of M-N-S, V, 1bcd-2ab:

> The Saṃbuddha arisen from A.
> A is the best of letters, of great purpose, the supreme syllable.
> The great inhalation is not a production, free from utterance by speech.

This chapter of *Hevajra*, fourth sentence, mentions that OṂ is at the beginning, and at the end there is SVĀHĀ or HŪṂ PHAṬ. Accordingly, Nāro-pā brings in the well-known Buddhist saying, "good in the beginning, good in the middle, good in the end," and at 9-3-5 he cites without naming, M-N-S, VI, 5-6ab:

> Beginningless, devoid of elaboration, pure natured and self likewise; speaks truly, as he says so he does, does not speak (anything else). Not the two, preaching there is not two; situated in the ultimate limit.

Here, "devoid of elaboration" is the OṂ that is good in the beginning; "speaks truly" is the middle part of the *mantra* that is good in the middle; and "not the two" is the SVĀHĀ or HŪṂ PHAṬ that is good in the end. "Preaching there is not two" and "does not speak (anything else)" suggests that all Hevajra's speech is *mantra* (per *Hevajratantra*, Chapter 5).

Toward the end of commenting on this chapter, Nāro-pā cites a number of passages on generalities of *mantra*, including one at 10-3-2 from M-N-S, its VI, 21cd-22ab:

> The torch of knowledge that is the lamp for the world; the great brilliance, the clear light. King of magic charms (*vidyā*) and sovereign over the best incantations (*mantra*); king of the *mantras* that work a great purpose.

It is of interest that soon after this quotation, Nāro-pā draws three citations from the *Laṅkāvatāra-sūtra*.

Chapter 3, Deities

Nāro-pā at 12-1-7, cites M-N-S, V, 9-10ab:

> Best as a great patron. Foremost bearer of great morality. Steadfast as a bearer of great forbearance. Enterprise of great striving. Dwelling in a *samādhi* of great meditation. Bearing the body of great insight.

These are of course the six perfections (*pāramitā*) of Mahāyāna Buddhism. Nāro-pā gives the "final meaning" (*nītārtha*) of them according to the *Kālacakra* ("ādibuddha"), as follows: (1) giving is dispensing jewels, (2) morality is when there is no "transit" (*'pho ba med pa*) even in the company of women, (3) forbearance is refraining from (ordinary) speech, etc., (4) striving is suppressing the passage of the "*ga*" of the wind,[5] (5) meditation is the dwelling in the "together-born bliss" (*sahaja-sukha*), and (6) insight makes all consciousness move. The six "perfections" are brought in at this point, since the six arms of the deity are so interpreted in the *Hevajratantra* itself. The fifth, meditation (*dhyāna*), and the sixth, insight (*prajñā*), were put together because they are the pair of hands with which the Lord clasps the goddess Vajraśṛṅkhalā (diamond chain). To work out the remaining to the best of my understanding, the trident in the first left hand must be "forbearance" as refraining from ordinary acts of body, speech, and mind; the bell in the second left hand should be "giving"; the *vajra* in the first right hand should be "morality" as explained with no transit, hence with no alternation; and the knife in the second right hand is the "striving" that cuts off the passage of the wind.

In speaking (12-3-8) about the fourth Buddha Body, the Mahāsukhakāya, a "pervasive" *sahajakāya*, he identifies it with the gnosis embodiment as in M-N-S, IV, 2:

> ... the gnosis embodiment stationed in the heart of the Buddhas abiding in the three times.

And after stating various ways it is referred to in scriptures, he cites (12-4-4), but without naming M-N-S, its VIII, 3 for a further description:

> Formless, of lovely form, and foremost; multiform and made of mind, glorious appearance of all forms, bearing no end of reflected images.

For an additional feature, at 12-4-7, he cites M-N-S, V, 8:

> Wise one, holding the great illusion. Performing the aim of great illusion. Pleased with the pleasure of great illusion. Using the hallucination of great illusion.

Nāro-pā at 12-4-8 refers to the *Kālacakra* ("Śrī-Ādibuddha") for an explanation that the illusory three realms are like the rainbow; that the nonarising natures are like the sky reflected in the water. Nāro-pā's point that the *sahajakāya* abides in the heart of the Buddhas agrees with my rendition of the term, namely that the "together-born body" is the body born together with the heart.

Chapter 4, Initiation

Nāro-pā, in a rather lengthy commentary considering how brief is this chapter of the *Hevajratantra*, cites M-N-S twice, first at 13-2-8, VIII, 23cd-24ab:

> Without constructive thought and without effort, performs the Buddha deeds in the three times. Buddha without beginning or end, the primordial Buddha without preceding cause.

He cites a passage about the four methods of birth, and so I believe my translation "initiation" is better than the "consecration" frequently used to translate the term *abhiṣeka*.[6] Since "birth" in its exalted sense is birth of a Buddha, he cites at 13-5-2, without naming, M-N-S, VI, 19:

> Progenitor of all the Buddhas; most excellent son of the Buddhas; womb-source for the gestation by insight; *dharma*-womb making an end to phenomenal life.

Chapter 5, Reality (tattva)

In this chapter, there is a passage about the term "Tathāgata" (an epithet of the Buddhas). In this connection, Nāro-pā at 16-1-3, cites M-N-S, VIII, 24cd:

> The unstained single eye of knowledge; Tathāgata embodiment of knowledge.

And at the very end of his comments on this chapter, while discussing some obscure verses of the *Hevajratantra*, Nāro-pā cites (16-4-7), without naming the M-N-S, its X, 4:

> Having supernormal cognition of all the *dhyāna*-branches and knowing the family and genus of *samādhi*-s; who has the best of bodies in the body arising from *samādhi*, the supremacy in the Sambhogakāya.

Hence, it seems to be Nāro-pā's interpretation of those final verses of Chapter 5, that the Sambhogakāya is meant. Thus, verse 19cd has: *maṇḍalaṃ pādalekhaḥ syān malanād maṇḍalam ucyate*, "(His) foot-print is a *maṇḍala*; it is called a *maṇḍala* due to the impression." And here we should understand that wherever the Sambhogakāya places the foot, it creates a *maṇḍala* at that place. The Sambhogakāya was, at least in the Tibetan tradition, credited with the thirty-two characteristics and eighty minor marks; and among these were certain auspicious symbols on the foot, which would be impressed in the footprint.

Chapter 6, Praxis (caryā)

At the beginning of this chapter there is a description of the Heruka-yogin, a peculiar person, to be sure! Besides wearing all the ornaments, earrings, bracelets, etc., and a tiger-skin, his food is required to be the five "ambrosias." The Tibetan author Tsoṅ-kha-pa cites this passage about them from the *Mahāmudrātilaka*:[7]

> Ratnasaṃbhava is blood, Amitābha is semen;
> Amoghasiddhi is human flesh, Akṣobhya is urine;
> Vairocana is excrement. These are the five best ambrosias.

On the surface this appears to be dreadful and disgusting conduct. However, Nāro-pā has two citations of the M-N-S with elevated sentiments to show his attitude toward this chapter of the *Hevajra*. At 16-5-4, he cites M-N-S, I, 8:

> So that all the sentient beings sunk in the bog of ignorance, their minds disturbed by defiled things, may obtain benefit and the incomparable fruit.

And at 17-1-2 he cites its IX, 24, for a different way of describing this Heruka-yogin:

> Whose incorporeal body is the foremost body, "comprehender" at the apex of bodies; who exhibiting every kind of form is the "peak jewel," the great gem.

Clearly Nāro-pā takes the *Hevajratantra* passage to indicate a non-human. He further does this in comment on the chapter's verse 6, the "lonely tree" (*ekavṛkṣa*), which is one of the places where it is good to meditate. He comments (17-1-5) that it is an unbroken bliss of the *sahajakāya*, unique, unchanging, at the "lonely tree"; that the "lonely tree" is *bodhicitta*. Hence, the tantra teaching that the *bodhicitta* as a mystic element has a *prajñā* (= female) and an *upāya* (= male) ingredient, does not require the same for the *sahajakāya*; and we shall observe below from Nāro-pā's comments on *Hevajra*, Pt. 1, Chapter 8, that he denies such an attribution to the *sahajakāya*.

The *Hevajra* verse 25 of this chapter can be rendered as follows:

> Even should a demon positively appear in front looking like Indra, he should have no fear in this case and should stroll with the form of a lion.

In this regard, Nāro-pā cites at 18-2-2, without naming, M-N-S, VI, 6cd:

> ... having the lion's roar of nonself that frightens the deer of bad heretics.

Chapter 7, Secret Signs (chomā)

Nāro-pā's first citation (at 19-1-2), but not naming the M-N-S, is IX, 13cd-14ab:

> Who stays on the path of all deliverances and teaches all deliverances. Uprooting the life of the twelvefold members, he maintains the pure twelve aspects.

He interprets the twelvefold members as dependent origination. This goes with *Hevajra*'s chapter, verse 11, mentioning twelve stages (*dvādaśa-bhūmi*), on which, according to this Tantra, one should contemplate certain male and female divinities called "heroes" and "heroines" in the sequence of places assigned to the stages. Apparently, Nāro-pā intends the M-N-S's next phrase, "he maintains the pure twelve aspects," to allude to the twelve stages in this special sense.

At the next citation (19-2-4), he names M-N-S, its IX, 4-5:

> Standing upon the pithy spot of earth, he presses down with the sole of one foot; standing on a toenail width, he presses down up to the top of Brahmā's realm. Having as single meaning the meaning of nontwo natures, the supreme that is not fearful; his object-entity of forms with diverse representation, his stream of consciousness with the [*bodhi*-] Thought and *vijñāna* [-seeds].

Nāro-pā's comments in this section show that he understands "Brahmā's realm" as the Brahmā-gate (*brahma-dvāra*), i.e., at the top of the head where the Buddha's *uṣṇīṣa* is represented. That forces the "pithy spot of earth" to be at the base of the spine. "Presses down" was previously shown (comments on *Hevajra*, Chapter 5) to create a *maṇḍala*, hence a series of *maṇḍalas* (= the *cakras* of the "subtle body") up to the "Brahmā-gate."

Then to go with the epithet "Lord of the Ten Stages" of the *Hevajra*, this chapter, Nāro-pā cites at 19-3-2, without naming, the M-N-S, VI, 2-3ab:

> Who has attained the ten perfections, whose site is the ten perfections, who is the purity of the ten perfections, who is the principle of the ten perfections. Nātha, who is lord of the ten stages, whose site is the ten stages.

Previously, in the commentary on the Tantra's opening sentence, Nāro-pā was noticed as calling Bhagavat Heruka "Lord of the twelve stages." This is a distinction of "Buddha" and "Complete Buddha" (often Saṃbuddha). The "Buddha" is the lord of the ten stages and the "Complete Buddha" lord of the twelve (compare Smṛti's solution of "twelve stages" in comments on M-N-S, Chapter IV, 2).

Chapter 8, Yoginī-s

Nāro-pā, when discussing the "solid nature," i.e., adamantine nature of the *maṇḍala*, cites at 20-3-6 without naming, M-N-S, VI, 20ab:

> Whose diamond nature has solid single essence;
> no sooner born, the master of living beings.

This quotation from M-N-S goes with the chapter's verse 3a, *dharmodayodbhavaṃ cakraṃ*, "the *cakra* (= *maṇḍala*) arisen from the Dharmodaya (source of natures);" and the words "no sooner born" go with the chapter's verses 6cd-8ab about the five Wisdoms and their "images" (*ākāra*). According to Nāro-pā at 20-4-1, the translation of the final words of the M-N-S, IX, 5 (cited in the preceding chapter commentary) should be slightly altered from their present form, which is "[*bodhi-*] Thought and *vijñāna* [-seeds]." The Sanskrit compound should be construed, "the *vijñāna* in the *citta*," where *vijñāna* is the *ālayavijñāna* ("store consciousness"), and where *citta* is the *bodhicitta*. Nāro-pā says: "The *ālayavijñāna* in the middle of the *bodhicitta* is the *gandharva-sattva*" (*byaṅ chub kyi sems kyi dbus su kun gźi'i rnam par śes pa dri za'i sems can no*).[8] And he continues (20-4-2), "Then the mirrorlike and the other Wisdoms along with their images." He gives the emanation process in this order: (1) the moon or *bodhicitta* possessed of vowels is the Mirrorlike Wisdom, Vairocana who engenders [as "image"] the personal aggregate of forms (*rūpa-skandha*); (2) the sun or menstrual blood possessed of consonants is the Sameness Wisdom, Ratnasambhava who engenders the personal aggregate of feelings (*vedanā-skandha*); (3) the *gandharvasattva* possessed of the HŪM-syllable is the Discriminative Wisdom, Amitābha who engenders the personal aggregate of ideas (*samjñā-skandha*); (4) the unification of these, the *prāṇa*-wind possessed of the HAṂ-syllable is the Procedure-of-Duty Wisdom, Amoghasiddhi who engenders the personal aggregate of motivations (*saṃskāra-skandha*); (5) the completion of all parts (*cha śas*) of the body and perception (*vijñāna*) possessed of the HAṂ-syllable is the Pure Dharmadhātu Wisdom, Akṣobhya who engenders the personal aggregate of perceptions (*vijñāna-skandha*). The merger of those (five) into one is the seed Vajrasattva. From that account, we may conclude that the M-N-S's phrase "the master of living beings" refers to the five Buddhas and their merger, Vajrasattva, as "the master."

Nāro-pā then turns to the topic of "Vajrasattva." The Tantra chapter, verse 8cd, alludes to Vajrasattva's "seat" (or, throne) as a union of vowels and consonants. In this connection, Nāro-pā at 20-5-5 cites M-N-S, X, 1cd-2ab:

> There is the nonsyllable, the birthplace of *mantras*, the three great-*mantra* families. Who generates the purposes of all *mantras*; the great *bindu* is nonsyllabled.

The quotation of the M-N-S lines here is consistent with the jurisdiction allotted to Vajrasattva in M-N-S, Chapter III, where he heads the family that retains the *mantra* (the male incantation) and the *vidyā* (the female charm). For contemplation of Vajrasattva, Nāro-pā cites at 21-1-5, M-N-S, IX, 6-7ab:

> His pleasure is in every single on-going object-entity, and his pleasure in voidness the best intelligence; having transcended the lusts of phenomenal life, his great pleasure is in the three worlds. Pure white like a white cloud and well shining like the rays of the autumn moon.

For describing the role of the goddesses of the *maṇḍala* in "final meaning," Nāro-pā launches into the meaning of the four Joys, a topic that goes from the chapter's verse 23 to 35. It is in this connection that he cites at 21-3-4, M-N-S, X, 3 (this time the entire verse):

> Having all images and lacking all, holding the *bindu* of sixteen halved twice; when without branches and beyond calculation, holding the pinnacle of the Fourth Dhyāna.

The four Joys are in an order—as Nāro-pā quotes 21-3-2—first, Joy (*ānanda*, T. *dga' ba*); second, Perfect Joy (*paramānanda*, T. *mchog tu dga' ba*); third, Joy of Cessation (*viramānanda*, T. *khyad dga'i dga' ba*); and the remainder is Together-born Joy (*sahajānanda*, *lhan cig skyes dga'*).[9] Nāro-pā explains at 21-3-5, "having all images and lacking all," consistent with his above remarks that the phenomenal images of the Buddha pentad are the personal aggregates (*skandha*), and so in the absence of this phenomenalization, the Buddhas lack them. "Beyond calculation" refers to the Together-born Joy (cf. Narendrakīrti's comment under verse X, 3 in the translation). As to the sixteen parts of the *bindu*, meaning sixteen parts of the *bodhicitta*, Nāro-pā explains them, starting 21-2-7, as the fifteen digits of the moon identified with the fifteen *yoginī*-s of this chapter, with Hevajra as the sixteenth. Thus, he says: Starting from the first lunar day in the increasing phase of the moon, the first five, Nairātmyā, etc., because they are the purity of the five personal aggregates, are the first, Joy circle. Then, going from the sixth to the tenth lunar days, Gaurī II,[10] etc., because they are the purity of the five elements (*dhātu*), are second, Perfect Joy circle. From the eleventh digit or lunar day to the fifteenth, the full moon, Śavarī, etc., because they are the purity of the five sense objects, are third, Joy of Cessation circle. At their conclusion, the sixteenth part of the *bodhicitta*, the Bhagavat Hevajra, voidness of voidness, is the Together-born Joy. And he says that this has the meaning of initiation (*abhiṣeka*). Furthermore, Nāro-pā, explaining in the above M-N-S quotation the words "without branches" at 21-3-6 says this means dwelling at the end of the fifteen parts, i.e., the Lord Hevajra. And he also says, at 21-4-1, that this is the "pinnacle of the Fourth Dhyāna."

As to the *Hevajratantra* remark in this chapter, verse 24a, *ṣaḍaṅgaṃ bhavayed yogī*, Nāro-pā at 21-4-1 begins to discuss this in the meaning of the six-membered yoga, which he treated at length in his commentary on the Abhiṣeka chapter of the *Kālacakratantra*. This is not especially germane to the M-N-S; but what is relevant is the *Hevajratantra*'s listing of six colors in verses 22cd-23, which Nāro-pā does not treat. Since these colors are the "essence of the six Tathāgatas," they can be understood by the M-N-S, Chapter IV, as Mañjuśrī in the role of six knowledge beings stationed in the hearts of the respective family progenitor. However, in order to harmonize the *Hevajratantra* colors—(1) black, (2) red, (3) yellow, (4) green, (5) blue, (6) white—with the sequence of colors mentioned under M-N-S, Chapter IV, 3, comments, one may change (1) black to blue and (5) blue to white, thus with two whites. Nāro-pā, as mentioned above, attributes the color white to Vajrasattva, and this is the usual color of Vairocana. But, significantly, the Second Assembly part of the *Hevajratantra*, Chapter 11, verses 5-7, gives colors of yogins (in the M-N-S would all be Mañjuśrī) in the Buddha families: the black "yogin" in Akṣobhya's family; the white one, Vairocana's; the deep green one, Amoghasiddhi's; the yellow one, Ratnasaṃbhava's; the red one, Amitābha's; the white one, Vajrasattva's family. Nāro-pā, in his commentary on Second Assembly, Chapter 11, while commenting on everything therein, at 39-3-6, begins his quote of the *Hevajra*, this part II, verse 1cd-4, at 39-3-8, saying, "Likewise, one should understand the yellow, white, etc., ones in this sequence." In short, Nāro-pā takes the listing of colors in this later chapter as "diamond words" worthy of comment, while in the first part of *Hevajra*, Chapter 8, his noncomment on the list there suggests that he considers the passage corrupt. This suggestion is fortified when we observe that he also did not comment on the subsequent verses of this chapter 8, especially 27d-28ab, *dvaividyaṃ sahajaṃ tataḥ/yoṣit tāvad bhavet prajñā upāyaḥ puruṣaḥ smṛtaḥ/*, "The *sahaja* ("together born") is of two kinds, on which account, to that extent *prajñā* would be a woman, and *upāya* would be a man." Nāro-pā apparently accepts a rival theory of the *Vimalaprabhā* (the great commentary on the *Kālacakra*), which he cites at length at the beginning of his comment on *Hevajratantra*, First Assembly, Chapter 5; the *Vimalaprabhā* citation, at 14-4-5, reads in part:

> Here, *prajñā* is the nature of the fifteen parts, the "white half" (= increasing phase of the moon). The deterioration of the moon, i.e., the "black half" (= decreasing phase of the moon), is *upāya*. Accordingly, the "white" is night; the "black" is day.[11] For this reason, the *sahajakāya* ("together born body") is not *prajñā*, nor is it *upāya*.[12] It is the *sahajakāya* of the Buddhas. Accordingly, it is neither the "white half" when (the moon is) present, nor is it the "black half" when (the moon is) absent with absence of on-going parts....

Nāro-pā resumes his commentary on verses of this Chapter 8, on verse 46. Then, in connection with the Tantra's line, 46c, *svasamvedyā bhavet siddhiḥ* (success [= enlightenment] is to be self-experienced), he cites at 22-1-4, M-N-S, IX, 20-21ab:

> Having eliminated the object for every idea, his object of perception creates cessation; having all sentient beings as his mind's object, he dwells in the minds of all sentient beings. Who has the minds of all sentient beings dwelling within (himself) and has realized sameness with their minds.

Repeating in part a previous citation, he cites without naming, M-N-S, VI, 5ab:

> Beginningless, devoid of elaboration, pure natured and self likewise.

Chapter 9, Purification

The opening of this chapter espouses the experiencing of reality as the way of purification, so in the case of the personal aggregates, the senses, and their objects. In his commentary Nāro-pā quotes a passage from the *Vajraśekhara*, one from the "Thusness" chapter of the *Prajñāpāramitā* scripture, and then at 22-4-1, the M-N-S, VIII, 1:

> True nonself that is thusness, true limit, and without syllables; leader of bulls who tells voidness, whose roaring is deep and far-spread.

That is to say, contemplating the personal aggregates as void of self and the celebrated Heart Scripture's identification of the personal aggregates with voidness is a way of purifying them. Another way of stating this proposition is the identification of the personal aggregates, the elements, and the sense bases with deities; and in fact this very chapter of *Hevajratantra* proceeds to do so in the case of the personal aggregates, the sense objects, and the elements of fire, etc.

In regard to verse 15, which refers to overcoming the four Māras, Nāro-pā at 23-3-2, 3 cites M-N-S, X, 9:

> The hero enemy of the Māras and tamer of the Māras, who ends the danger of the four Māras; who defeats the entire Māra army, (you) the complete Buddha, guide of the world.

Nāro-pā explains that the obscuration of body is the personal aggregate Māra; the obscuration of speech is the defilement Māra; the obscuration of mind is the death Māra; and the externalization of nescience (*phyi rol tu ma rig pa 'jug pa*) is the son-of-the-gods Māra.

Chapter 10, Initiation in the Maṇḍala

In his rich commentary on this chapter, Nāro-pā at 25-4-7, commenting on words of verse 12, *puruṣaḥ purāṇa īśvaro* (the person, ancient lord), and referring to the characteristic of the fourth Joy, the Together-born Joy, cites M-N-S, I, 1cd-2ab:

> The hero, victorious over the three worlds, lord of secrets, the adamantine lord; his eye like an opening white lotus; his face like a wide-open lotus.

Then he alludes to the same work, happening to be M-N-S, VI, 12cd-13ab; followed immediately by VIII, 8, and this by VI, 17:

> Without "mine," without "I"; abiding in the manner of two truths. Gone to the bank beyond *saṃsāra*, duty-done, standing on the dry land (VI, 12cd-13ab).
>
> Laid to rest every bit of defilement, gone to the other side of the ocean of *saṃsāra*, on the crown the gnosis initiation and decorated with the complete Buddhas (VIII, 8).
>
> Yogin ruling all, the eternal; master of the intelligent ones, being contemplated, the meditation; the nonswerving one to be introspected; supreme primeval bearing the three bodies (VI, 17).

Chapter 11, Abhisaṃbodhi of Vajragarbha

In commentary on words of verse 8, *samayaṃ bhakṣayet* (He should eat the pledge), Nāro-pā at 27-5-8 cites M-N-S, VIII, 13:

> Knowing good and evil, knowing the time, knowing the pledge, pervading lord with the pledge; knowing the faculties of sentient beings, knowing the occasion, skilled in the three liberations.

Before quoting this verse, he mentions that there are two kinds of "pledge" (*samaya*), external and internal. The yogin should guard his external pledge, i.e., on behalf of the world, by collecting merit. The yogin should guard his internal pledge, on behalf of himself, by collecting knowledge.

SECOND ASSEMBLY COMMENTARY

Chapter 1, Consecration (pratiṣṭhā)

At 28-5-8, Nāro-pā cites M-N-S, VIII, 2:

> Whose conch-shell of Dharma has a loud sound, whose gong of Dharma rings, who is in the Nirvāṇa of no fixed abode, whose large drum of the Dharma (is heard) in the ten directions.

It would be difficult to find Nāro-pā's reason for citing this passage in his comments on this chapter, unless one knows, as will be shown later in the present work, that the "conch-shell of Dharma" represents the sound of *samādhi*. He is pointing to the mental component when making the offerings and uttering the *mantras* set forth in the chapter. This is because it is basic to the Tantras that the yogin should relate to the Buddha's Mind with *samādhi*, to his Speech with *mantra*, and to his Body with *mudrā*.

Chapter 2, Success (siddhi)

Nāro-pā cites at 30-1-7 M-N-S, VIII, 27:

> Leader as best of great healers, supreme extracter of thorns; paradise tree with every single medicinal herb, great enemy of defilement-sickness.

Then near the end of this *Hevajratantra* chapter, Nāro-pā at 31-1-2 quotes M-N-S, V, 3-4-5ab:

> Great offering, great love, gratifying all sentient beings. Great offering, great hatred, great enemy of all defilement. Great offering, great delusion, driving away the delusion of deluded minds. Great offering, great fury, great enemy of great fury. Great offering, great clinging, driving away all clinging.

The point of the citation is the chapter's verses 53 and following, with characteristics of the five Buddhas, namely "great delusion" is

Vairocana; "great hatred" is Akṣobhya; "great love" is Amitābha; "great fury" according to Smṛti in his commentary on the M-N-S verse is Amoghasiddhi, while "great clinging" was commented by him as Ratnasambhava. However, the *Hevajra* appears to differ in the last two cases, taking "envy" as Amoghasiddhi, and "calumny" as Ratnasambhava.

Chapter 3, Saṃdhibhāṣa

In discussing the remarkable language of verses 29-30 of this chapter, which on the surface seems to recommend the opposite of the Buddhist layman's vows, in particular "You should slay living beings," Nāro-pā explains at 31-4-2, 3, that this signifies the training of beings difficult to train (? incorrigibles), and that one does this training by the power of *yoga*. Accordingly, he cites, without naming, M-N-S, I, 1ab:

> Now Vajradhara, *śrīmat*, supreme tamer of those hard to tame.

And in the commentary on this verse in the translation part of this work, I have cited Narendrakīrti's explanation that this training involves pain to those being trained.

Chapter 5, The Arising of Heruka

The description of Heruka with eight faces, four legs, and sixteen arms, and other details amounting to iconography, is according to Nāro-pā the provisional meaning (*neyārtha*). So also the exhortation of the goddesses for the Lord to emerge from the seminal state.[13] For the "final meaning" (*nītārtha*), starting at 34-3-1 in Nāro-pā's commentary, first there is a quotation from the great *Kālacakra* work *Vimalaprabhā*; next at 34-3-4 a citation of M-N-S, its VIII, 9cd-10ab:

> Liberated from all hindrances has attained the sameness like the sky. Having transcended all defilement and dirt, comprehends the three times and the timeless.

Chapter 6, Making a Painting

In this chapter it is advised that the painter, making a painting of Heruka, should keep the five colors in a human skull bowl, and use a brush made from the hair of a corpse. It is on this level, called "provisional meaning" that Nāro-pā cites at 36-1-5, M-N-S, I, 15:

> To dispel every bit of defilement, to eliminate every bit of ignorance, may I explain in accordance with the particular aspiration of sentient beings.

Chapter 7, Feasting

Here Nāro-pā at 36-4-8, cites M-N-S, VI, 7cd-8ab:

> Jina and Vijayi who has conquered the enemy, wheel-turner of great power. Instructor of the troop and head of the troop; lord of the troop and master of the troop, magically subduing.

According to the indication of the commentary at this point, the citation goes with verse 9 of the chapter, referring to the yogin who represents Heruka and who places the *yoginī*-s in the eight directions. He then is called "wheel-turner," "lord of the troop," etc.

Chapter 11, Meaning of Together Born

After commenting upon this chapter, with its somewhat surprising contents that afford difficulty to commentators, Nāro-pā in his concluding remarks discusses the fourth Joy, the Together born, as contrasted with the other three (see First Assembly Commentary, on Chapter 8); and to show how it follows after the third one, the Joy of Cessation, he cites at 40-3-3, M-N-S, IX, 18:

> Who having purified the realms of defilements, has made an end to the realms of *karma*; who having crossed over the ocean of floods, has emerged from the glade of praxis.

Chapter 12, the Four Initiations

As his last citation (at 40-4-3) from M-N-S, Nāro-pā picks VII, 6cd:

> Wielding all of *vajra* as *vajrin* ("*vajra* holder"), defeating the (opposing) warriors as *ekavajrin* ("unique *vajra* holder").

The quotation clearly is meant to describe the adamantine master (*vajraguru*) of the chapter, verse 1. This *guru* is implored to confer the four initiations upon the disciple.

3. The Seven Maṇḍalas of the *Mañjuśrī-nāma-saṃgīti*

THE PRESENT-DAY Western-language systemization of Mañjuśrī forms has two helpful sources, the writings of B. Bhattacharyya[1] in English and a work on Mañjuśrī iconography by de Mallmann[2] in French. For this essay, however, I needed more data than those sources could provide, and so I consulted a variety of Tibetan works and some in Sanskrit.

As to the expression "seven *maṇḍalas*," the author Smṛti, a commentator on the M-N-S, several times says this (see his comment on I, 10), disagreeing, e.g., with Candrabhadrakīrti who speaks of six. To clarify what is meant, one should acknowledge that of the thirteen chapters of the M-N-S certain chapters cannot be considered for *maṇḍala* interpretation. These disallowed chapters are the first three—"Asking for Instruction," "The Reply," "Surveying the Six Families"; and the last three—"Praise of the Five Tathāgatas," "Exhibition of Mantras," and "The Summing Up." The theory of six *maṇḍalas* is that there are six tantric families going with the remaining seven chapters, by taking Chapter IV, "Abhisaṃbodhi Sequence of the 'Net of Illusion,'" and Chapter V, "The Great Maṇḍala of Vajradhātu," as one *maṇḍala*; and by leaving the remaining chapters on the five Wisdoms to go with the remaining five families and their *maṇḍalas*. Smṛti's position is that each of the seven chapters can be interpreted as a *maṇḍala*, so there are seven. However, I have not found any of these authors willing to explain all six or all seven *maṇḍalas*. In practice, they mainly have *maṇḍala* rituals going with the Dharmadhātu-Vāgīśvara, the Arapacana group, and the Vajrabhairava cult of the fierce Mañjuśrī, in short, three *maṇḍalas*, no matter whether they think there are six or seven. But the fact that I do not find the commentators spelling out in lucid terms the details of six or seven *maṇḍalas* does not justify a solution colored by speculation. This is why considerable research has been necessary to support the correlations set forth herein.

The way to combine the indications of chapters IV and V of the M-N-S in one *maṇḍala* is the manner of Bu-ston (in his collected works, Vol. Pha).[3] This is a lengthy exposition of the *maṇḍala* Dharmadhātuvāgīśvara, relying on Mañjuśrīmitra, a voluminous commentator on the M-N-S and accompanying ritual. The chief deity is a white Mañjughoṣa, four-headed, eight-armed. The Tanjur work that Bu-ston uses, attributed to Mañjuśrīmitra, has a title, *Gaganāmalasupariśuddhadharmadhātujñānagarbha* ("Womb of the Pure Dharmadhātu Wisdom, Where [All Natures] Are Pure like the Sky"),[4] which is taken from the M-N-S, Chapter XII, "Exhibition of Mantras."

If one accepts Smṛti's position that there are seven maṇḍalas, it would be necessary to separate chapters four and five in *maṇḍala* terms, appealing to the *Niṣpannayogāvalī*,[5] a published collection of twenty-six *maṇḍalas*, including a *Dharmadhātu-Vāgīśvara-maṇḍala*, with chief deity a golden Mañjughoṣa, four-headed, eight-armed; and a *Vajradhātu-maṇḍala*, with chief deity a white Vairocana, four-headed, eight-armed. One would have to claim that these two deities should not be combined into one because their respective four heads and eight arms have differing, contrasting interpretations. The discussion could get quite complicated; and restricting ourselves to the respective four heads, we appeal to M-N-S, X, 2, "the great *bindu* is nonsyllabled," to conclude that the elaborate *maṇḍala* of

Dharmadhātu-Vāgīśvara, with a host of deities, various sets of twelves, also the planets, etc., is a wordless vision, so the four heads must stand for seeing in all directions. In contrast, the *Vajradhātu-maṇḍala*, named in the title of Chapter V, M-N-S, would represent the initial expression or teaching,[6] according to M-N-S, X, 2, "great void is five-syllabled," and here the four heads can mean the four gateways to liberation.[7]

Candrabhadrakīrti, a commentator on the M-N-S, and drawn upon for important notes to my translation, presents the six-*maṇḍala* scheme by information at the ends or beginnings of his commentary on Chapters V–X. This commentator analyzed the mantras of Chapter XII into six parts explained by six Mañjuśrī names that originally occurred in Chapter IV, verse 3, namely, Vajratīkṣṇa, Duḥkhaccheda, Prajñājñānamūrti, Jñānakāya, Vāgīśvara, and Arapacana. These six are associated with the six Buddha family heads, such as Vairocana. Five of these family heads go respectively with the five Wisdoms (providing names for Chapters VI–X), and are tabulated under VI, 18, as follows: Vairocana with the Dharmadhātu Wisdom, Akṣobhya with the Mirrorlike, Amitābha with the Discriminative, Ratnasambhava with the Sameness, and Amoghasiddhi with the Procedure-of-Duty. But the six families announced in Chapter III add a Vajrasattva family to the usual five. Candrabhadrakīrti, when detailing the Mañjuśrī names and Buddhas at the ends of the Chapters V–X, sticks to the established correlations of the Mañjuśrī names with Buddhas and their five Wisdoms. For the sixth Buddha Vajrasattva he assigns the Mañjuśrī name Arapacana and the *maṇḍala* of Chapter V, the great Vajradhātu. While it seemed reasonable for him to correlate Vairocana with the Dharmadhātu Wisdom of Chapter VI (indeed, VI, 1 even mentions "Buddha Mahāvairocana"), it happens that the Vajradhātu *maṇḍala* (of Chapter V) is well recognized by the *Niṣpannayogāvalī* and other sources to have Vairocana as its central deity, not Vajrasattva. Besides, what Candrabhadrakīrti explained, on Chapter XII, as Arapacana's *mantra*, is the very one which Mañjuśrīmitra used for the title ("Womb ...") of his work which Bu-ston expanded in the Dharmadhātu-Vāgīśvara *maṇḍala* ritual, but Bu-ston, when referring to Mañjuśrī, does not call him Arapacana. Now, this "womb" (of the pure Dharmadhātu Wisdom, ...) is expressly mentioned in Chapter VI, "The Pure Dharmadhātu Wisdom," verse 19, by the word *yoni*, which is also mentioned in terms of the Tathāgatagarbha theory, in Smṛti's comments on VI, 1. For these reasons, Arapacana should be associated with the Dharmadhātu Wisdom, not the *Vajradhātu-maṇḍala*. In short, Candrabhadrakīrti's solution in some aspects is quite suspect and signals the considerable difficulty that the commentators experienced with the M-N-S. By employing three commentators for notes to my translation, I hope to have escaped the limitations of any one of them.

In the case of Chapter III, "Surveying the Six Families," I have presented both Candrabhadrakīrti's and Smṛti's list of the Six Families. We can conclude that the sixfold correspondences did not merely add a Vajrasattva line to the fivefold ones, but caused further changes within the former fivefold scheme. Significantly, Amoghasiddhi's *karma* family was allotted to Vajrasattva, and the verse, III, 2, refers to Amoghasiddhi's family by a new name, Mahāmudrā, which Smṛti, following Līlavajra, calls Bodhicittavajra family. This altered situation of the sixfold correspondences affects the Vajrasattva, the Vairocana, and the Amoghasiddhi correlations. The other three Buddha families are kept as before, and so here Candrabhadrakīrti's correlations are quite acceptable, namely, Akṣobhya's Vajra family and the Mirrorlike Wisdom; Amitābha's Lotus family and the Discriminative Wisdom; Ratnasambhava's Jewel family and the Sameness Wisdom. The other families that Candrabhadrakīrti could not get straight have these correlations: Amoghasiddhi's Mahāmudrā (or Bodhicittavajra) family and the Dharmadhātu

Wisdom; Vajrasattva's Karma family and the Procedure-of-Duty Wisdom; Vairocana's Tathāgata family and the *Vajradhātu-maṇḍala*.

It should be useful to summarize the results in a table including the six Mañjuśrī names.

Chapter of the M-N-S	*Buddha*	*Family*	*Mañjuśrī name*
V. The Great Maṇḍala of Vajradhātu	Vairocana	Tathāgata or Triple	Prajñājñānamūrti
VI. The Pure Dharmadhātu Wisdom	Amoghasiddhi	Mahāmudrā or Bodhicittavajra	Arapacana
VII. The Mirrorlike Wisdom	Akṣobhya	Vajra or that illumines the world	Duḥkhaccheda
VIII. Discriminative Wisdom	Amitābha	Lotus or the mundane and supramundane	Vajratīkṣṇa
IX. The Sameness Wisdom	Ratnasambhava	Ratna or Mahauṣṇīṣa	Vāgīśvara
X. Procedure-of-Duty Wisdom	Vajrasattva	Karma or retaining mantra and vidyā	Jñānakāya

It is inescapable that the commentators who insisted on six *maṇḍalas* for the M-N-S must have pointed out that there are six Buddhas, six Families, and six Mañjuśrī names, so why talk of a seventh *maṇḍala*? Nevertheless, M-N-S, IV, 1, states, "accompanied by the six Mantra Kings, belonging to the Master of Speech." This sets "the Master of Speech" outside of the six; and since Dharmadhātu-Vāgīśvara means "Speech-Lord of the Dharmadhātu," this implies that the *Dharmadhātu-Vāgīśvara-maṇḍala* is additional to the six, making a total of seven *maṇḍalas*, as Smṛti insisted but did not spell out. It is known that the Mother Tantra of the Anuttarayogatantra class uses either a sixfold or a sevenfold system of correspondences. It is simple to get the seventh Buddha by adding Vajradhara (or among other names, Śrī-Heruka), the fruitional state, where Vajrasattva is the causal Vajradhara. I have also cited elsewhere the tantric author Padmavajra on how to increase the five personal aggregates (*skandha*) to seven for the sevenfold series, namely by addition of a *jñāna-skandha* and a *dharmadhātu-skandha*.[8]

Before going to the individual treatment of seven *maṇḍalas*, it will be necessary to collect some data on different Mañjuśrī forms. From the Jayapaṇḍita's Tibetan work,[9] Vol. II (Kha), f. 154b-5, I draw the following information on evocations (*sādhana*):

1. Mañjughoṣa, Sthiracakra (brtan pa'i 'khor lo), yellow, two-armed, *sādhana* by *ācārya* Bhavaskandha, translated by Paṇḍita Amoghavajra and Bari-pa.
2. Mañjuśrī, Siṃhanāda (seṅ ge'i sgra), yellow, two-armed, eleven deities in all.
3. Mañjughoṣa, Vādirāj (ṅag gi rgyal po), red-yellow, two-armed, *sādhana* by Paṇḍita Dpal-ldan Yid-bźin-nor-bu Sbyin-pa (also stated to be seated on a lion throne).
4. Ārya Mañjuśrī Vādirāj, color of molten gold (*gser źun*), two-handed, the Lord and companion (*gtso 'khor gñis*).
5. Vādirāj, yellow, two-handed, three deities.
6. Vādirāj, the treasure for expanding insight (*prajñāvardhana*), three deities, *sādhana* by Paṇḍita 'Phrog-byed-' joms-pa.

7. Vādirāj, color of purified gold (*gser btso ma*), two-handed.
8. Arapacana, white, two-handed, five gods, *sādhana* by *ācārya* Ajitakalyānamitra, tr. by Kamalagupta and the translator Rin-bzaṅ.
9. Arapacana, red, two-armed, five gods, in the work "Rje btsun 'phags pa 'jam dpal sgom pa'i man ṅag."
10. Sadyonubhava (*'phral du ñams su myoṅ ba*) Arapacana, white, two-handed, Lord and companions, five in all.
11. Mañjuśrī, white, five gods, the versified *sādhana* (no evocation permission).
12. Vajrānaṅga (*yan lag med pa'i rdo rje*), yellow, six-armed, found in the *Pañjarā*, tr. by Amoghavajra and Ratnakīrti.
13. Mañjuśrī Vajrānaṅga sādhana.
14. Dharmadhātu-Vāgīśvara, white, four-faced, eight-armed, tr. by Bari.
15. Dharmadhātu-Vāgīśvara, red, four-faced, eight-armed.
16. (Mañjuśrī) in *Sems can thams cad dbaṅ du byed pa'i tiṅ ṅe 'dsin.*
17. Dharmadhātu-Vāgīśvara, in the *samādhi* "Ocean of Dharma," white.
18. Arapacana, white, two-armed.
19. Vādirāj, red, two-armed.
20. Mañjuśrī Siddhaikavīra (*dpa' bo gcig sgrub*), white, two-handed.
21. Vādirāj, red, two-armed.
22. Mañjuśrī Mahārājalīla, yellow, two-armed.
23. Mañjughoṣamahārājalīlasādhana [Toh. No. 3654], by Dri-ma-med-pa'i lha.
24. Ārya Mañjuvajra-Siddhaikavīra.
25. Alimanmatha (*buṅ ba myos pa*), red, three-headed, six-armed, *sādhana* by Rin-chen-myu-gu.
26. Vaśyādhikāra (*lhag par dbaṅ du byed*), red, six-armed, *sādhana* by *ācārya* Dge-ba-byed-pa.

The list continues from Jaya Paṇḍita, Kha, now at f. 156a-5:

27. Mañjuśrī, red, three-faced, six-armed.
28. Saṃkṣipta-Mañjuśrī-(sādhana), white, two-handed, from the *Vidyādharapiṭaka*, translated by Amoghavajra and Bari.
29. Mañjuśrī, Prajñāvardhana, white, two-handed, also from the *Vidyādharapiṭaka*.
30. Prajñācakra, white, two-handed, that attains the highest *siddhi*, from *(Mañjuśrī)-nāmasaṃgīti-upadeśa*.
31. Dharmasaṅkhasamādhi-Mañjuśrī.
32. Nāmasaṃgīti-Mañjuśrī, red, three-faced, four-armed.
33. Mañjuvajra, yellow-red, three-faced, six-armed.

The list continues from Jaya Paṇḍita, Kha, now at 163b-4:

34. Sthiracakra, Bhagavat Mañjughoṣa, red-yellow, two-armed, by Vidyāpatra and tr. by Rin-chen-bzaṅ-po.
35. Sthiracakra, a lengthy *sādhana* tr. by Bari.
36. Arapacana, white, two-handed, lengthy, by *ācārya* Padmasambhava, tr. by Paṇḍita Amoghavajra and Bari.

37. Viśuddha-Mañjuśrī, or Mañjuśrī-vajra, yellow, three-headed, six-armed, tr. by Bari.
38. Bhagavat Mañjuśrī-vajra, red, two-armed, Lord and companions, five in number.
39. Mañjuśrī Vādirāj, two-armed, Lord and companion, two in number, tr. by Bari.
40. Mañjuśrī-rājalīla, red-yellow, two-handed.
41. Mañjuśrī, associate of *prajñā*, tr. by Bari.
42. Nāmasaṃgīti Mañjuśrī, white, three-faced, four arms.

The list concludes at Kha, f. 169b-6:

43. Ārya Mañjuśrī Vādisiṃha, red-yellow, two-handed.
44. Mañjuśrī and Sarasvatī, Yab-yum (no permission available).

Using the work by Bhattacharyya, *The Indian Buddhist Iconography*, the one by de Mallmann, *Étude iconographique sur Mañjuśrī*, and other readings in the literature, I have grouped the foregoing for the purpose of subsequent utilization and also signal those which will not be so used:

(a) Sthiracakra (1, 34, 35) and Mañjuśrī Siṃhanāda (2), for the *maṇḍala* of the "Mirrorlike Wisdom" chapter.
(b) Vādirāj (3, 4, 5, 6, 7, 19, 21, 39), for the *maṇḍala* of the "Sameness Wisdom" chapter.
(c) Arapacana (8, 9, 10, 11, 18, 36, 38), for the *maṇḍala* of the "Pure Dharmadhātu Wisdom" chapter.
(d) Alimanmatha (25, 27) and Mañjuvajra (33, 37), for the *maṇḍala* of the "Procedure-of-Duty Wisdom" chapter.
(e) Nāmasaṃgīti Mañjuśrī (32, 42), for the *maṇḍala* of the "Great Vajradhātu" chapter.
(f) Dharmadhātu-Vāgīśvara (14, 15, 17), for the *maṇḍala* of the "Net of Illusion" chapter.
(g) Vādisiṃha (43), Mañjuśrī and Sarasvatī, Yab-yum (44), and Dharmasaṅkhasamādhi (31), for the *maṇḍala* of the "Discriminative Wisdom" chapter.

Not utilized is the set of Vajrānaṅga (12, 13), Vaśyādhikāra (26), and Sems can thams cad dbaṅ du byed pa'i tiṅ ṅe 'dsin ["Samādhi of Dominating All Sentient Beings"] (16). Also not utilized is a miscellaneous group of white Mañjuśrī-s with one head and two arms, namely, Siddhaikavīra (20, 24), probably Prajñāvardhana (28, 29, 41) and Prajñācakra (30); and the yellow Rājalīla (22, 23, 40).

Maṇḍala 1. Net of Illusion: *Dharmadhātu-Vāgīśvara*

This goes with M-N-S, Chapter IV, "Abhisambodhi Sequence of the 'Net of Illusion.'" The *maṇḍala* name means "Speech-Lord of the Dharma-realm." The Lord here is named Mañjughoṣa. He is depicted as seated on a lion, legs in diamond-interlock, shining like the disk of the newly arisen sun, with golden color, with a splendid attire like sapphire, wearing gleaming ornaments, and having a jewel crest of the five Buddhas. Of his four faces, showing erotic sentiment, the basic one is yellow, right one blue, back one red, left one white. Of his eight arms, two of them make the gesture of Dharma-wheel (*dharmacakra-mudrā*); the other right ones hold a sword, an arrow, a *vajra*; and the other left ones hold a Prajñāpāramitā book, a bow, a vajra-bell. His central shrine is surrounded by four elaborate circles of deities. In the first circle, eight *uṣṇīṣa* deities, beyond them the four Buddhas (Akṣobhya, Ratnasambhava, Amitābha, Amoghasiddhi) on mounts in the cardinal directions, their four goddess associates (Locanā, Māmakī, Pāṇḍarā, Tārā) in the intermediate directions, plus four male *vajra* gate-keepers. In the second circle, in the East the twelve *bhūmis*, in the south the twelve Pāramitā goddesses, in the West the twelve Vaśitā, in the North the twelve *dhāraṇī* deities, in the gates the four Pratisamvits, and in the intermediate corners the four secret goddesses (Lāsyā, Mālā, Gītā, Nṛtya). In the third circle there are sixteen Bodhisattvas, in four groups going with the cardinal directions; the gates are occupied by the ten Krodha (furious) deities, four in the cardinal directions, four in the corners, one above ("zenith") and one below ("nadir"); in the corners there are the eight offering goddesses, two in each "right" corner and two in each "left" corner. In the fourth circle, there are the eight mundane directional deities (Indra, Yama, etc.) on their characteristic mounts. Beyond the fourth circle there is a host of Hindu and other deities, fifteen Hindu gods (Brahmā, etc.), the nine classical planets of Indian astronomy-astrology, the four headed by Balabhadra on mounts, the eight serpent gods starting with Ananta, the eight asura kings headed by Vemacitri, the eight Yakṣa kings accompanied by Hāritī, and the twenty-eight asterisms (*nakṣatra*).[10]

It is proper to wonder how such an elaborate *maṇḍala* can fit into the subject matter of the brief Chapter IV (only three verses). Notice that this chapter lists in verse 2 the twelve vowels. These go with twelvefold sets, the four such in the second circle. Besides, the first two vowels (A, Ā) and the last two (AṂ, AḤ) make up a set of four that can go with the four heads (front and back, right and left). The twelve are the prototype of the Buddhist path, said to be good in the beginning (A, Ā), good in the middle (the next eight vowels), and good in the end (AṂ, AḤ). IV, 1 states, "... whose nature is nonproduction and occurs nontwo...." This is a state obscurely pointed to in M-N-S, X, 1: "To be realized by all the Buddhas is the incomparable enlightenment of the Buddha; there is the nonsyllable, the birthplace of mantras, the three great-*mantra* families." According to this, the elaborate *maṇḍala* Dharmadhātu-Vāgīśvara could be referred to as nonproduction because it is the vision of the Buddha-eye as a "Net of Illusion." That state is called "nonsyllable" because it is wordless. In Tibetan tradition the Dharmakāya does not teach, but is the source of the teaching. So the verse X, 1, said "the birthplace of *mantras*."

In another work I have cited the tantric author Padmavajra's explanations of Buddha bodies.[11] Using his data, the *maṇḍala* description appears to fit Mañjughoṣa (as Mañjuśrī is frequently called) in the role of Dharmakāya, which Padmavajra says is the set of planets, asterism, etc.; the nonoozing ecstasy of dwelling in the Akaniṣṭha (heaven) (so the Lord's faces were said to show "erotic" sentiment) and those who have transcended the ecstasy (realizing the "Net of Illusion"); the gods dwelling in the wind and *vijñāna*, who have nonapperception. One can so describe the Dharmakāya, since it is a "*gāthā*" (metaphorically a verse) that occurs nontwo. "Nontwo" in this case indicates that the Lord Mañjughoṣa is not other than the variegated items of the *maṇḍala*. The Lord in the center of the *maṇḍala* can also be understood as the central element—the *maṇḍa*—while the surrounding gods and goddesses are the containing element—the *la*;[12] and these are nontwo.

Finally, what is the meaning of "*abhisaṃbodhi* sequence" in the title of Chapter IV? This literature sets forth five sequential *abhisaṃbodhi*, implicating the remark in M-N-S, IV, 2, "Stationed in the heart of the Buddhas abiding in the three times, am I (*aham*) the Buddha, gnosis embodiment." Mkhas-grub-rje says: "Thus, the five-pronged, white *vajra*, seen in one's own heart at the time of contemplating intensely the five Abhisaṃbodhi in sequence, is called 'first *vajra*.'"[13] Thus, it is the primordial Buddha (*ādibuddha*) dwelling in the heart, at the time of complete enlightenment.

MAṆḌALA 2. THE GREAT MAṆḌALA OF VAJRADHĀTU: *Nāmasaṃgīti Mañjuśrī*

M-N-S Chapter V has the name "Vajradhātu-maṇḍala" in its title. This *maṇḍala* is known in Sanskrit, found in the *Niṣpannayogāvalī*. My translation of Chapter V presents the elaborate notes of Smṛti and Candrabhadrakīrti identifying lines of the verses with deities of the *Vajradhātu-maṇḍala*. However, while the version in the *Niṣpannayogāvalī* has the standard thirty-seven basic deities, the M-N-S chapter has verses for 33, having no verse for the four gatekeepers, and adds the sixteen bodhisattvas of the Bhadrakalpa ("fortunate eon"), for a total of forty-nine deities. Candrabhadrakīrti calls this "the supreme horse (*paramāśva*) maṇḍala." It might have been the intention to let the thirty-three deities constitute the *maṇḍa* (essential of the *maṇḍala*), with the sixteen bodhisattvas constituting the *la* (enclosure of the *maṇḍala*). Speaking briefly, V, 2 is interpreted as the four adamantine goddesses, who are also the four syllables A, Ā, AṂ, AḤ, the four gates to liberation, respectively involved with the four Wisdoms (omitting the Dharmadhātu). Subsequent verses are explained as the five Buddhas, the sixteen adamantine beings (male), the four secret goddesses and the four offering goddesses. Then come verses intending the sixteen bodhisattvas according to the list in the *Māyājāla-mahātantrarāja*.

The central deity is Vairocana, actually Mahāvairocana as contrasted with the Vairocana in the five-Buddha correspondence system.[14] The *Niṣpannayogāvalī* version describes the main deity as seated with legs in diamond interlock, showing the five Buddhas in his crown along with a lock of matted hair. He has gleaming ornaments, is white in color. His four faces show calm sentiment (*śānta*), and are white, yellow, red, and green. He has eight arms, two main ones holding a *vajra* while exhibiting the *bodhyaṅgī* (= the Dharma wheel) gesture, while the second pair shows *dhyāna* (meditation) gesture. The other two right arms hold a rosary and an arrow; the other two left ones hold the wheel (*cakra*) and the bow.

Notice that to the Dharma-wheel gesture of the central deity in Maṇḍala No. 1, this central deity adds a *dhyāna* gesture. According to Tibetan tradition, Mahāvairocana is the Sambhogakāya with the initial teaching or expression to the sixteen bodhisattvas, although the deity is in meditative equipoise.

As to a Mañjuśrī form in Jaya Paṇḍita's list that would apply here, it has to be the one called the Nāmasaṃgīti Mañjuśrī, either red or white, with three heads (Vairocana's triple family of Body, Speech, and Mind), and four arms carrying symbols (as does Mahāvairocana here, since of his eight arms, two pairs show gestures, and four separately hold symbols). The Nāmasaṃgīti Mañjuśrī in the *Sādhana-mālā* holds the arrow and bow in the first right and left, and the sword and book in the second right and left. This agrees with the Lord's bow and arrow, and instead of the Lord's rosary there is a book; and instead of the wheel, a sword. This Mañjuśrī would be the form in which the yogin must first identify himself, preparatory to generating the Lord and retinue of the Diamond-Realm *maṇḍala*. Bu-ston suggests this in that *maṇḍala* ritual on Dharmadhātu-Vāgīśvara already mentioned. His first passage on Mañjuśrī goes (f. 3b-7), "and from the transformation, oneself becomes possessed of a body, like a full moon, of the venerable Mañjuśrī; seated with diamond interlock on a lotus and moon, holding in two right hands a sword and an arrow; in two left hands a Prajñāpāramitā book and a bow."

No mention is made of three heads, so it might be the form de Mallmann states[15] as popular in Nepal by S. Lévi's description: the four hands carry the sword, arrow, book, and bow; and there is just one face. Later in Bu-ston's text (f. 25b-4), the Mañjuśrī form is moon-white, four-headed and eight-armed, agreeing with the Dharmadhātu-Vāgīśvara form, since Bu-ston in this work combines the *maṇḍala* I count as Nos. 1 and 2.

Is there some way of justifying the Mañjuśrī name Prajñājñānamūrti (Insight-Wisdom Body)? As told in Mkhas-grub-rje's work, the Buddhas of the ten directions bestowed on Śākyamuni the third initiation (or consecration) called Prajñājñāna; then they revealed the steps of Abhisaṃbodhi. He successively dissolved the three voids, and the Clear Light of the Absolute Object came into direct view. He emerged from that Clear Light in the pure illusory body.[16] Presumably this is the meaning of "Insight-Wisdom Body." In another way of talking, Mkhas-grub-rje's work when treating the fourth Abhisaṃbodhi, says: "Thereupon, all the Buddhas of the ten directions bestowed upon the Bodhisattva Sarvārthasiddha the initiation of the name (*nāma-abhiṣeka*). Having removed the name Sarvārthasiddha, they gave in exchange the name Bodhisattva Vajradhātu. Then they bade him contemplate intensely the meaning of the mantra, '*vajrātmako 'ham*' ('I consist of *vajra*')."[17] Thus, one way of characterizing that "body" (*mūrti*) is as a "diamond body"; another way is as an "illusory body."

MAṆḌALA 3. THE PURE DHARMADHĀTU WISDOM: *Arapacana*

This *maṇḍala* is based on Chapter VI. VI, 1 contains the name Mahāvairocana, which Smṛti explains as the Dharmakāya and the Tathāgatagarbha. VI, 19, clearly refers to the Tathāgatagarbha by the word *yoni*; cf. the comments thereunder. Therefore, Mahāvairocana ("great sun"), despite appearances to the contrary, was not referred to with the implication of being the family head for the pure Dharmadhātu Wisdom. Instead, here there is the Mahāmudrā or Bodhicittavajra family headed by Amoghasiddhi. What is the meaning of "Mahāmudrā" in this case? The commentator Dombīheruka, on VI,15 (q.v.), "aim accomplished," comments, "accomplished the *paramārtha* Mahāmudrā in the manner of nondiscursive thought"; thus the name "Bodhicittavajra" must mean *paramārtha* kind of *bodhicitta* (Mind of Enlightenment). However, VI, 18, "Buddha with five-body nature" refers to the Mahāmudrā in a different usage, what the tantric commentator Padmavajra calls "Consummated Body" (cf. *Mkhas grub rje's*, p. 228, note), i.e., the Family Lord appearing with the "four seals (*mudrā*)" and attired appropriately, with ornaments and the like.

The Mañjuśrī name in the family of Amoghasiddhi is Arapacana. The five syllables may be understood in the Prajñāpāramitā scripture sense (cf. Conze, *The Large Sūtra* ..., p. 160),[18] "A" because unproduced from the beginning (*ādi-anutpanna*); "RA" because free from dirt (*rajas*); "PA" because explained in the absolute sense (*paramārtha*); "CA" because with out decease (*cyavana*) or rebirth; "NA" and to the left. Instead of Jālinīkumāra, the name Sūryaprabha may occur.[20] The principal deity and his companions are phy. It agrees with Padmavajra's explanation of the "pure Dharmadhātu Wisdom": it is the location of the other four Wisdoms as well as their object (i.e., what they know), and is the great Nirvāṇa.[19]

The very popular deity Arapacana is also called Sadyonubhava ("of sudden experience"), and is either white or yellow-red. As Bhattacharyya explains the *maṇḍala*, the principal deity originates from the first syllable "A." Of his four companions, Jālinīkumāra is from the "RA" and in front; Candraprabha is from the "PA" and behind; Keśinī is from the "CA" and to the right; Upakeśinī is from "NA" and to the left. Instead of Jālinīkumāra, the name Sūryaprabha may occur.[20] The principal deity and his companions are always represented with one head and two arms; the right hand holding the sword of insight (*prajñā*) and the left one holding against the chest an opened lotus on which is a book of scripture. To this should be added that they are seated in diamond interlock.

The collection *Rgyud sde kun btus*,[21] Vol. III, has such a *maṇḍala* ritual by Ṅor-pa Dpon-slob Ṅag-dbaṅ-legs-grub, entitled *'Jam dpa'i dbyaṅs A RA PA TSA NA lha lṅa'i dkyil 'khor*, with deity description at Arabic numeral folios 47–48. Here Mañjuśrī is white in color. The first three deities represent light in various ways, consistent with the radiant character of the pure Dharmadhātu. Thus, the body of the main deity is emitting many rays. In the East (i.e., foreground) from "RA" is the Youth with netted (light); in the West (i.e., background) from "PA" is the Youth with moon (light). All three have the sword and the book at the chest. In the South (i.e., to the right) from "CA" is She who is hairy; in the North (i.e., to the left) from "NA" is the Assistant She who is hairy. These two goddesses show in the right the "gift-giving gesture" (*varada-mudrā*), and hold in the left a (scripture) book on a lotus. These two have smiling, pretty faces and have firm, close breasts. All five deities are dressed in silk and decorated with precious ornaments, white, with feet in diamond interlock. The lotus in all cases is called *utpala*, which means the blue lotus.

The meaning of the two "hairy" goddesses is difficult, but probably related to the description of the youth Mañjuśrī, to be added to the above, that the hair of his head is in five knotted locks. It is clear that in the case of the goddesses the hair is carefully tied. The "hairiness" should point to some character of the Dharmadhātu other than the luminescent nature represented by the first three, male, deities. There is a suggestion that Mañjuśrī's head hair stands for a feminine side, i.e., when tied or knotted.[22]

This peaceful form of Mañjuśrī contrasts with the fierce form that follows in the next *maṇḍala*.

Maṇḍala 4. Mirrorlike Wisdom: *Trailokyavijaya*

Chapter VII concerns the Vajrabhairava cult, responsible for elaborate works in the Tibetan language. In the present *maṇḍala* the main deity is called Vajrahūṃkāra, whose other name is Trailokyavijaya (Victorious over the Three Worlds). There is an acute problem of where the chapter begins. My translation follows the Peking parallel Sanskrit-Tibetan blockprint, which starts with VI, 25d. Both the Narendrakīrti and Smṛti commentaries agree, because they begin their comments on Chapter 7 on the word "Vajrabhairava" of VI, 25d. However, the Candrabhadrakīrti commentary claims that Chapter 6's *maṇḍala* is complete with its verse 23. If this validly points to the ancient situation, it would obviate the strange verse partition of VI, 25. It means that Chapter VI would have twenty-three verses rather than twenty-five; and Chapter VII would have twelve verses rather than ten. So Candrabhadrakīrti at the end of his remarks on Chapter VII, at PTT ed., 8-5-8, speaks of twelve verses.

That the material of Chapter VII does begin with VI, 24 is clear from the Tibetan evocation rituals (*sādhana*, *sgrub thabs*) of Vajrabhairava. Having looked at several, I know the performer soon identifies himself with a human-appearing Mañjuśrī, with one head and two arms that carry the sword and the scripture book at his chest or upon a lotus. Among these descriptions, one by Tsoṅ-kha-pa is very well written (cited in *Rgyud sde kun btus*, Vol. 10, i.e., Tha, Arabic no. 317, or f. 3b):

> From its transformation, he becomes himself the causal Vajradhara Mañjuśrī Kumārabhūta, body colored yellow, only his

> mind angry (*yid tsam khros pa*); his right arm wielding a sword, his left arm holding the (scripture) book at his chest; his feet in the diamond interlock; adorned with the thirty-two characteristics and eighty minor marks (of the Buddha); hair of his head in five knotted locks, decorated with all ornaments. The ĀḤ in his heart becomes a solar disk. Thus he contemplates carrying the path of the Sambhogakāya of the Intermediate State (*bar do loṅs sku'i lam khyer bsgom*).

If this description be allowed to go with VI, 24, "Mantrin who bears the three families ..." then Tsoṅ-kha-pa's subsequent description would go with VI, 25, "Victorious one with unfailing noose ..." because his *sādhana* continues that rays sent out from that solar disk attract the Buddhas, Bodhisattvas, Furious Deities, and Family hosts, that are the ten directions, and so on. Thus, VI, 25, could be interpreted as four stages in this attraction, namely, (a) victorious one with unfailing noose, (b) great seizer with diamond noose, (c) diamond hook with great noose, (d) Vajrabhairava who creates fear. These four statements of M-N-S, VI, 25, may be this Tantra's way of referring to the four *mantras* JAḤ, HŪṂ, VAṂ, HOḤ that are frequently employed for the purpose. As I have translated from the *Sādhana-mālā*, "OṂ, may the diamond hook attract, JAḤ! OṂ, may the diamond noose draw in, HŪṂ! OṂ, may the diamond chain tie, VAṂ! OṂ, may the diamond bell subdue, HOḤ![23]

The Mañjuśrī name going with Akṣobhya, the Lord of the Mirror-like Wisdom, is Duḥkhaccheda (who destroys suffering), but what would be the Mañjuśrī name in Jaya Paṇḍita's list? So far, my studies of Mañjuśrī iconography reveal no other Mañjuśrī forms that would fit Tsoṅ-kha-pa's depiction than the Arapacana, already discussed, or the yellow Sthiracakra that begins Jaya Paṇḍita's list. The *Sādhana-mālā*, Nos. 44–45, are white Sthiracakra forms with insufficient description for Bhattacharyya to make a good exposition. It is significant that both mention the syllables A, RA, PA, CA, NA, but without identification with the five deities of the Arapacana *maṇḍala*. Observing that the Tibetan translation of the name Sthiracakra is *brtan pa'i 'khor lo*, Candrabhadrakīrti implicates this form with Akṣobhya in the remark, though on Chapter IX (at 10-5-5): "Akṣobhya (not disturbable) is steady (*brtan pa*), with the fury of firm mind (*brtan po'i khro bo*), and has an unpleasant form (*mi sdug pa'i gzugs*)." This carry-over of an Arapacana-like Mañjuśrī, as the one the performer should first identify himself with, agrees with the position of certain commentators on the M-N-S, e.g., Narendrakīrti, who rationalize the order of contents in the M-N-S, in the present case, from Chapters VI–VII.

As to the *maṇḍala* deities, I have already mentioned the main one, Vajrabhairava = Vajrahūṃkāra = Trailokyavijaya. Candrabhadrakīrti obviously experienced trouble in working out the *maṇḍala* retinue on the basis of the M-N-S verses themselves, while Narendrakīrti and Smṛti were even less helpful. Against what Candrabhadrakīrti says about VII,1, the first verse "foot" (*pāda*), at least, should be the description of the central deity when it says, "Six-faced, fearful Ruler of the Furies." This may account for the description in the work "Gsaṅ ldan sgrub" by Kong-sprul Blo-gros mtha'-yas (*Rgyud sde kun btus*, Vol. 10, "the Anuttara explanation of the *Mañjuśrī-nāma-saṃgīti*," Arabic No. 453, f. 10a-2,3): "The Knowledge Body becomes clearly manifested as the body of Mañjuśrī, white, six-faced, two-handed (*ye śes kyi skur gyur pa ni/'jam dpal sku mdog dkar po źal drug phyag gñis pa'i rnam pa can du gsal bar gyur/*), while one's own consciousness is bright—the mirrorlike wisdom devoid of constructive thought (*raṅ sems gsal la rtog pa med pa me loṅ lta bu'i ye śes so*)." At No. 456–457, f. 11b-6 to 12a-1, we notice this realization attributed to a *bodhi-samādhi* of the tenth (? chapter) *Māyājāla*, to wit: "From the transformation of the A-syllable on the nave of the [heart] wheel (*cakra*) [cf. the name Sthiracakra], oneself becomes in body the Bhagavat Mañjuśrī the Knowledge Being (*jñānasattva*), six-headed, two-armed, the two upper stacked heads white, basic head blue, right one yellow, back one red, left one green; the two hands in equipoise gesture (*samāpatti-mudrā*), while his right hand holds a red lotus and left a blue stem of lotus on which is a (scripture) book; and seated in diamond interlock." The three commentators on the M-N-S that I employed throughout passed over the "six eyes" of VII, 1. Probably that whole phrase "six-eyed, six-armed powerful one" refers to the three Buddha progenitors (Vairocana, Amitābha, Akṣobhya); cf. in VI, 24, which we have discussed above as possibly starting the Mirrorlike treatment, "Mantrin who bears the three families."[24] As to VII, 1c–d, the "skeleton with terrible tusks" might be a vampire (*vetāla*) mount; the "hundred faces of Halāhala" might be the demonic being that is downtrodden by the main deity Vajrabhairava.

For the remaining deities, the *Niṣpannayogāvalī*, in its Vajrahūṃkāra *maṇḍala*, gives them as the ten Krodha deities, with new names Vajradaṇḍa, Analārka, Vajroṣṇīṣa, Vajrakuṇḍalī, Vajrayakṣa, Vajrakāla, Mahākāla, Vajrabhīṣaṇa, Uṣṇīṣa, Vajrapātāla; the first four in the cardinal directions, the next four in the intermediate directions, the last two above and below. For the scheme, see *A New Tibeto-Mongol Pantheon*, Part 12, Maṇḍala No. 11.[25] The eleven deities have old names, the main deity, plus Yamāntaka, etc., for which see *Niṣpannayogāvalī*, Introduction, p. 44. Presumably this group of eleven, whether with old or new names, is intended by Jaya Paṇḍita's entry right after the Sthiracakra: Mañjuśrī Siṃhanāda, eleven deities, since the *maṇḍala* of the Mirrorlike Wisdom is the only one of the seven that has eleven deities.

MAṆḌALA 5. DISCRIMINATIVE WISDOM: *Vādisiṃha*

The commentator Candrabhadrakīrti calls the *maṇḍala* of Chapter VIII on Discriminative Wisdom, the Padmanarteśvara-*maṇḍala* (circle of the Lotus Lord who is dancing), but I have no confirmation. Here Mañjuśrī is Vajratīkṣṇa in Amitābha's Lotus (Padma) Family, the mundane and the supramundane. VIII, 25, emphasizes Amitābha's role as "Lord of Speech." Part of the explanatory tantra cycle of the Yogatantra *Tattvasaṃgraha*, namely the *Śrī-paramādya-mantra-kalpa-khaṇḍa-nāma* (PTT, Vol. 5, p. 143-1-2), tells the kind of "speech" in the Lotus Family: "The Lotus Family with the speech of *samādhi* is called 'Completely Pure Lotus.'" (The Vajra family contrasts by having the sound of the thunder-cloud; and the Jewel family by having the sound of Dharma.) And (p. 143-1-3,4), having put "self" and "what belongs to self" in front, in the Vajra family one thinks, "I shall destroy them"; in the Lotus family, "I shall purify them"; in the Jewel family, "They are all sky." Again (p. 143-2-5, 6), in the Lotus family *siddhis* (occult powers) manifest directly in *samādhi*. The emphasis in the Lotus family on purity agrees with the *upahṛdaya* (near-heart *mantra*) of Vajratīkṣṇa in M-N-S, Chapter XII: "All natures are intrinsically pure like the *abhāva* (the unsubstantial)."

The natural candidates of Mañjuśrī forms that would go with this heading are those iconographically affiliated with Amitābha. Bhattacharyya, *The Indian Buddhist Iconography*, pp. 102–103, mentions only one, called Vajrarāga, also called Amitābha Mañjuśrī, who is referred to in M-N-S, VIII, 33, "the great passion (*maharāga*) beginning with dispassion." This is in a *sādhana* of the *Sādhana-māla*, No. 64.[26] This Mañjuśrī is white in color, two-armed, one-faced, with his two hands in *samādhi* gesture. The performer should imagine on his "diamond" tongue the figure of Buddha Amitābha. Notice how this fits the kind of "speech" in the Lotus family, as mentioned above. However, that particular *sādhana* contains in the concluding title the name Dharmaśaṅkhasamādhi, which is No. 31 in Jaya Paṇḍita's list of Mañjuśrī forms. This name Dharmaśaṅkha is mentioned in VIII, 2, "whose conch-shell of Dharma has a loud sound," and this sound, according to the above indications, is the sound of *samādhi*. De Mallmann's book shows in Pl. VI, a beautiful Dharmaśaṅkhasamādhi image that is in the Musée Guimet, Paris.

However, the kind of Mañjuśrī that belongs here and can be surrounded in a way to form a *maṇḍala* is the one called Vādisiṃha, which is a principal Mañjuśrī type in the triad known as "insight promoting (*prajñāvardhana*) deities," the three being Mañjuśrī, Sarasvatī, and the White Acala. The very title of this chapter, "Discriminative Wisdom," is a terminology much associated with *prajñā* in Mahāyāna texts where the term "discriminative insight" (*pratyavekṣaṇa-prajñā*) often occurs. M-N-S, VIII, 41, mentions "great insight." The chapter begins (VIII, 1) with a stress on non-self, which Buddhism traditionally associated with *prajñā*. The name Vādisiṃha occurs in VIII, 25, "(invincible) lion of speech." I use the version in *Sgrub thabs kun btus*,[27] Vol. Two (Kha), according to the school of Pha-dam-pa Saṅs-rgyas. This is the saffron (*kuṅkum*) colored Mañjuśrī in company of Sarasvatī. In the present version, Vol. Two, Arabic no. 156, the performer generates Mañjuśrī, body colored red, decorated with precious ornaments, tied-up hair standing up; in his right hand holding the sword of insight (*prajñā*), in his left hand (stem of) blue lotus on which is the *Aṣṭasāhasrikā (Prajñāpāramitā)* book; and is seated in diamond leg position. When the performer has identified himself with this Mañjuśrī, he generates in his foreground [actually to his left foreground] Devī Sarasvatī, body colored sky blue [later described as sapphire-colored, Indranīla]; showing an angry smile (*khro 'dsum du 'dug pa*); her head-hair high blue (= sapphire) decorated on top with a gem; holding in her right and left hand the same symbols as does Mañjuśrī; placed on a lotus and moon, her body proudly disposed. The evocation includes imagining that the performer is surrounded by all the Buddhas and Bodhisattvas.

For the five Buddhas, see VIII, 8, and Narendrakīrti's comments. For the sixteen Bodhisattvas, cf. VIII, 9–16 (eight verses) with Candrabhadrakīrti's comments.

For a possible iconographic representation, cf. de Mallmann, Pl. IX, "Mañjuśrī and Prajñā," an image in the Central Handicrafts Museum, New Delhi. Here the "Prajñā" is seated partially on the left leg of Mañjuśrī. This may well be a variant of the Mañjuśrī-Sarasvatī couple.

MAṆḌALA 6. SAMENESS WISDOM: *Vādirāj*

The *maṇḍala* is based on Chapter IX, for which there is Ratnasambhava's Jewel Family; Mañjuśrī as a knowledge being is here called Vāgīśvara. In the discussion of the previous *maṇḍala* it was pointed out that the Jewel Family has the kind of speech concerned with expressing the Doctrine (Dharma as one of the three Jewels). This is borne out in the verses of Chapter IX, mentioning basic doctrines of Buddhism, the four mindfulnesses, eightfold noble path, twelve-membered dependent origination. Thus, even though *sādhanas* put Akṣobhya in the crown of Vādirāj, the emphasis in this chapter on teaching doctrine is shown in the Vādirāj *maṇḍala*, and his *mantra* includes the name Vāgīśvara, so the placement must be here.

Vādirāj is frequently shown with two companions, Sudhanakumāra and Yamāri, or just with Yamāri. De Mallmann (p. 24) points out that one *sādhana* (*Sādhana-mālā*, No. 46) puts Vādirāj at the center of a *maṇḍala*. Vādirāj is described as colored yellow, golden, yellow-red, or red, as making the gesture of explaining (the Dharma) (*vyākhyāna-mudrā*), well-ornamented, holding in his left hand a blue lotus, and seated on a lion. Sudhanakumāra, at his right, is yellow, has various ornaments and is radiant; holds at his armpits a single book with all doctrines; has his hands together in *añjali*.[28] Yamāri, at his left, is black, with distorted face, holding a mallet. Suryaprabha is in front, and Candraprabha in back. In the cardinal directions, starting from East are the four Buddhas, Vairocana, Ratnasambhava, Amitābha, Amoghasiddhi; and in the intermediate directions, the four goddesses, Locanā, Māmakī, Pāṇḍarā, and Tārā. The main deity has the *mantra*, OṂ Dharmadhātu-Vāgīśvara MUḤ SVĀHĀ.

The M-N-S commentator Mañjuśrīmitra has a little work called *Ekavīra-sādhana* (PTT, Vol. 75, p. 133-4-5, 6), where Ekavīra is described as yellow, holding the blue lotus with his right hand, and with his left making the gesture of explaining the Dharma (*chos 'chad*). One imagines oneself that way, surrounded by the six syllables, OṂ Vāgīśvara MUḤ. Ekavīra has the fuller form Siddhaikavīra, so the yellow form seems to be a variant of Vādirāj.

MAṆḌALA 7. PROCEDURE-OF-DUTY WISDOM: *Mañjuvajra*

It was previously explained that Vajrasattva heads the Karma Family in charge of *mantra* (incantation) and *vidyā* (charms) and why this "sixth" Buddha is in charge of Chapter X devoted to Procedure-of-Duty Wisdom. Mañjuśrī is now called Jñānakāya.

Here are all the three-headed, six-armed forms: Mañjuvajra, Alimanmatha, Viśuddha-Mañjuśrī of Jaya Paṇḍita's list. As to the meaning of three heads, X, 1, has "the three great mantra families"; X, 11, "three clear visions"; X, 14, "three ways of escape." For the possible meaning of the six arms, X, 2, has "*bindu* void is six-syllabled"; X, 11, "with six supranormal cognitions and the six remembrances."

The Lord Vajrasattva in the form of Mañjuvajra is red like vermilion, so also his basic face, with right face blue and left one white. His two principal hands embrace a Prajñā like himself (three-headed, six-armed, three-eyed); the other hands hold the sword, arrow, lotus, and bow. Notice X, 8, "who bears the sword of insight along with bow and arrow." This seems to be an iconographic representation of the form in which Gautama Buddha successfully faced the onslaught of the Māras. Notice X, 9, "who defeats the entire Māra army."

The *maṇḍala* is the first one in the *Niṣpannayogāvalī*. The central deity is surrounded by the ten Krodha (Fury) deities: Yamāntaka, Prajñāntaka, Padmāntaka, Vighnāntaka, in the directions E, S, W, N; Ṭakkirāja, Nīladaṇḍa, Mahābala, Acala, in the directions SE, SW, NW, NE; Uṣṇīṣacakravarti, zenith; and Sumbharāja, nadir. The four Buddhas, Vairocana, Ratnasambhava, Amitābha, and Amoghasiddhi, are in the cardinal directions, East, etc., with the four goddess consorts, Locanā, Māmakī, Pāṇḍarā, Tārā, in the intermediate directions, SE, etc. In another circle there are six adamantine sense-object goddesses, Rūpavajrā, SE; Śabdavajrā, SW; Gandhavajrā, NW: Rasavajrā, NE; Sparśavajrā, East-North; Dharmadhātuvajrā, East-South. The goddesses are in order (starting with Rūpavajrā), the adamantine form, sound, odor, taste, touch, and objects in the mind. The last two are located close together by the Eastern side of the circle, one more in the arc to the North, the other more in the arc to the South.

Thus concludes the seven *maṇḍalas* going with seven of the M-N-S's thirteen chapters.

4. Remarks on the Tibetan text of the *Mañjuśrī-nāma-saṃgīti*

THE *MAÑJUŚRĪ-NĀMA-SAṂGĪTI* in its Tibetan form, the *'Phags pa 'Jam dpal gyi mtshan yaṅ dag par brjod pa*, is probably the most revered and recited tantric text among all the Tibetan Buddhist sects. In the Derge edition of the Kanjur it is the very first work of the Tantra section (*rgyud 'bum*), just preceding the Kālacakra (*dus 'khor*) scriptures. It consists of only 160 verses (*gāthā*) plus some mantra sentences, but these cover an enormous lore, if one can believe the commentaries in the Tanjur.

The Tibetan translation is a brilliant piece of work by the great translator Rin-chen-bzaṅ-po, who has also translated an affiliated work, called in Sanskrit *Māyājāla-mahātantrarāja*. He was assisted on the *Saṃgīti* work by the Indian pandit Kamalagupta, and later the text was revised by Śoṅ Blo-gros brtan-pa, whose possible contribution to the present version will be considered below.

For my initial application to this text, I used the Sanskrit version edited by I. P. Minaeff in 1885; the Sanskrit-Tibetan in a Peking blockprint; and the Dharamsala Tibetan edition to which is appended both the method of reciting, descended from Sa-skya Paṇḍita, and a copy of the *Heart Sūtra* (*Prajñāpāramitā-hṛdaya-sūtra*), which is also recited on that occasion.[1] It was not until revising my translation with the help of three Tanjur commentaries—those by Narendrakīrti, Candrabhadrakīrti, and Smṛtijñānakīrti ("Smṛti" for short)—that I caught onto the scheme of the verses and learned why Rin-chen-bzaṅ-po had to translate in the manner he did. After making an index of the Tibetan first lines of the four-line verses, I traced out in Nāro-pā's commentary on the *Hevajratantra* fifty-three citations of the *Mañjuśrī-nāma-saṃgīti*, with or without reference by name. The translation of this Nāro-pā work was supervised by the famous Śākyaśrībhadra, a teacher of Sa-skya Paṇḍita, and a century and a half after Rin-chen-bzaṅ-po; it was later revised by a committee of four Tibetans. Most of the Nāro-pā citations in the Tibetan version are equivalent to the "official Tibetan version"—the carefully prepared Dharamsala version mentioned above can serve for this—but some citations are in partially alternate translation, to be discussed later.

The *Saṃgīti* is basically not in chapters; the commentaries divide it into chapters, and the Peking blockprint of the Sanskrit-Tibetan is so divided, as is the Derge Kanjur edition. For recitation purposes it is not in chapters, nor is it in chapters as the basis for Nāro-pā's citations. For study purposes, and my translation into English likewise, it is reasonably divided into chapters, with notes from the Tanjur commentaries so dividing. When chapters are imposed, there are thirteen. For the translation into Tibetan, these chapters are in two groups—those with the so-called "names" of Mañjuśrī and those without them. The chapters without the "names" are the first chapter, "Asking for Instruction"; the second, Śākyamuni's "Reply"; the third chapter, "Surveying the Six Families"; the fourth called "Abhisambodhi Sequence of the 'Net of Illusion'"; chapter XI, "Praise of the Five Tathāgatas"; chapter XII, "Exhibition of Mantras"; and chapter XIII, "The Summing Up." All these chapters are in verses or in mantras, where Rin-chen-bzaṅ-po could translate the verses normally. By this I mean by the usual rules imposed on the translators and responsible for the remarkable translations of the Kanjur and Tanjur. The translators were obliged to take account of all the Sanskrit words, if possible by the established Sanskrit-Tibetan equivalences, and were permitted a certain leeway of moving around in the Tibetan verse, of which the smallest and most common consists of four lines of seven syllables each. In contrast, the six chapters five through ten—the Vajradhātu (Diamond Realm) and the five Wisdoms (*jñāna*, *ye śes*)—had to be translated in a special way because they contain what the name of the work refers to, the "names" of Mañjuśrī. Now these "names" are not epithets or names in the sense of the first section of the celebrated Sanskrit-Tibetan Buddhist dictionary *Mahāvyutpatti*, giving the *paryaya-nāmāni*, i.e., the set of names of the Tathāgata, the Buddha, even though a considerable number of terms in this list do indeed appear in the M-N-S. Rather, the "names" in the *Saṃgīti* go mainly by metrical feet, of which there are four in each verse, called a *gāthā*. And these names are not what Mañjuśrī is called, in the sense of the grammatical vocative, but rather in the nominative, as the commentator Smṛti explains, intending, "You, Mañjuśrī, are" thus and thus. Hence, these are names in the sense of characteristic. The Tibetan translation therefore was obliged to stick to this fourfold division of the verse in those six chapters of Mañjuśrī "names," not permitting a spillover from one line to the next of the four lines. The general rule for reading such verses, if we assign A, B, C, D, to the Tibetan lines, is C is to D as A is to B.

The strict adherence to lines in those six chapters can be illustrated by this one, Chapter VIII, verse 10:

/ñon moṅs dri ma kun las 'das/
/dus gsum dus med rtogs pa po/
/sems can kun gyi gtso bo che/
/yon tan thod can rnams kyi thod//

Translation: "Having transcended all defilement and dirt, comprehends the three times and the timeless; the great leader of all sentient beings, who is the crest of meritorious crests." One can see why Rin-chen-bzaṅ-po had to translate each of the four Sanskrit metrical feet by individual seven-syllable lines. A more subtle pattern is exhibited in VIII, verse 7:

/nam mkha'i mtha' la loṅs spyod pa/
/thams cad mkhyen pa'i ye śes mtsho/
/ma rig sgo ṅa'i sbubs 'byed pa/
/srid pa'i dra ba 'joms pa po//

Translation: "Enjoyment in (or, from) the vault of the sky, wisdom-ocean of omniscience; who bursts the egg-shell of nescience, destroys the net of phenomenal life." In this case, the first line presents a mysterious proposition with concrete imagery, the vault of the sky; the second line a more abstract explanation. Again, the third line presents another mysterious proposition with concrete imagery, the egg-shell (also curved like the sky); and the fourth line a more abstract explanation. While the text definitely has the *la*, in or at, the commentaries explain as though it were *las* (the ablative), i.e., from the vault of the sky, implying rain—the "sprinkling" (*abhiṣeka*) or ritual aspersion—the five initiations as Narendrakīrti explains; and the rain of course contributes to the "ocean"—here the "wisdom-ocean."

One of Nāro-pā's citations illustrates a further modification of the pattern. When commenting on Part I of *Hevajra*, Chapter 8 on the Yoginī-s, he cites the *Saṃgīti*, Chapter X, verse 3:

/rnam pa kun ldan rnam pa med/
/bcu drug phyed phyed thig le 'chaṅ/
/yan lag med pa rtsis las 'das/
/bsam gtan bźi pa'i rtse mo 'chaṅ/

Translation: "Having all images and lacking all, holding the *bindu* of sixteen halved twice; when without branches and beyond calculation, holding the pinnacle of the Fourth Dhyāna." Here, according to the commentator Narendrakīrti, the first line gives two senses, the conventional sense of having all images—which is the case of line two about the *bindu* of sixteen; and the absolute sense of lacking all, explicitly stated in line three "without branches ..." and placed at the summit of the Fourth Dhyāna.

It should not be necessary to present more of these verses to justify the conclusion that Rin-chen-bzaṅ-po richly deserved his title of "great translator," Lo-tsa-ba chen po, for his translation into Tibetan of this precious work and the many others of his long career.

Since Rin-chen-bzaṅ-po's talent in faithfully rendering the original Sanskrit is well recognized in Tibetan lamaist circles, I have had to wonder how a few spots of the *Saṃgīti*, Tibetan version, appear to depart from the Sanskrit text. For such considerations there is much evidence, because besides the Sanskrit text and the Tibetan translation as available, it happens that the Narendrakīrti commentary cites the text phrase by phrase followed by his comments, and there are those numerous verses cited in the Nāro-pā commentary.

My first example to illustrate what can happen is in Chapter VIII, verse 11a, the Peking blockprint and the Dharamsala text read: "*ñon moṅs kun las rnam grol ba*," "liberated from all defilement." Here, Narendrakīrti's commentary cites the line as "*lus kun las ni rnam grol ba*," "liberated from all bodies." To muddy the waters more, the Derge Kanjur version is "*lhag ma kun las rnam grol ba*," "liberated from all remainder." These varieties show that the Sanskrit text was available, especially among *Kālacakratantra* followers—and so it was available for the Peking Sanskrit-Tibetan text; and in certain places of difficulty, this text was evidently consulted to see if light could be cast by the original Sanskrit term. The original Sanskrit is *sarvopadhivinirmukto*. The word *upadhi* occurs several times in the Buddhist Sanskrit-Tibetan dictionary *Mahāvyutpatti*, always rendered by *phuṅ po*, in the sense of the personal aggregates (*skandha*), but in one place it is rendered in addition as *ñon moṅs pa* and never as *lus* ("body"). Now, *ñon moṅs* means "defilement" (*kleśa*); but *ñon moṅs pa* probably means "something defiled" and the Candrabhadrakīrti commentary on this verse states: "liberated from all defiled bodies." The other two commentators, Narendrakīrti and Smṛti, list the possibilities of bodies. We cannot say that the *ñon moṅs* and *lhag ma* readings are wrong.[2]

More striking is Chapter V, 2a, where the Peking and Dharamsala texts have "*khoṅ nas byuṅ ba skye ba med*," while the Sanskrit reads *mahāprāṇo hy anutpādo*. Nāro-pā cites this in his *Hevajratantra* commentary, "*srog chen po ni skye ba med*." Both the Derge Kanjur and the Narendrakīrti commentary agree that it begins *srog chen po ste*. As to the phrase *khoṅ nas byuṅ ba*, these words occur in Narendrakīrti's commentary as equivalent to *raṅ byuṅ*, "self-arisen," or "arising from within," and apparently in comment upon the *skye ba med*, "not a production," i.e., arising without dependence on causes and conditions; but not in comment upon the *srog chen po*, which in the context means "great inhalation." It follows that the expression *khoṅ nas byuṅ ba* is an unfortunate later replacement for the correct translation.

Quite different in nature is Chapter I, verse 15, which to my observation is the only verse in the whole work where the first and second lines of Sanskrit are reversed in the Tibetan translation (official version):

/ñon moṅs ma lus bsal ba daṅ/
/mi śes ma lus spaṅ ba'i phyir/
/sems can rnams kyi bsam pa yi/
/khyad par ji bźin rab bśad bgyi//

Nāro-pā, in commenting upon the *Hevajratantra*, Part II, Chapter 6, "Making a Painting," cites this verse, and the translators decided to render it in the order of the Sanskrit lines, which begin with *prakāśayiṣye* ("May I explain"):

/bsam pa'i khyad par ji bźin du/
/sems can rnams la rab gsal mdsod/
/ñon moṅs ma lus bsal ba daṅ/
/mi śes ma lus gźom slad du'o//

My English translation follows the official Tibetan version, "To dispel every bit of defilement, to eliminate every bit of ignorance, may I explain in accordance with the particular aspiration of sentient beings." I consider this order more felicitious in English than would be starting with the "May I explain" portion. So as to establish the official version as composed by Rin-chen-bzaṅ-po, we should notice that Chapter I, which contains this verse, is not one of the chapters where the translator is forced to render each of the four parts of the verse in the given order because they represent the "names" of Mañjuśrī. Reversing the order of the two lines is consistent with Narendrakīrti's commentary (Peking Tanjur, Ja. photo ed., Vol. 48, p. 66-2-5), starting his comment on the verse by citing "*ñon moṅs ma lus bsal ba daṅ.*" In short, Rin-chen-bzaṅ-po's version is artful. I presume that the translators of Nāro-pā's work, although usually following the official version of the *Saṃgīti* when this was quoted, decided to "play it safe" here by following the Sanskrit line (hemistich) order, but ended up with a rather wooden rendition.

May I say a few words about the Peking Sanskrit-Tibetan blockprint. The Tibetan here is independent of the Sanskrit text. No more evidence for this fact is necessary than noticing in Chapter VIII, verses 17 and 18, that the parallel Sanskrit version has erroneously interchanged the terms *mauñjī* (the Muñja-grass [cord])—transcribed into Tibetan in VIII, 17—and *mauṇḍī* (shaved-head one), an error copied in Minaeff's Sanskrit edition;[3] while the Tibetan is correct for both verses.

Besides, four or more spots in the Peking blockprint version disagree with the Dharamsala one, and in each case, by considering the Sanskrit and the commentary, I accepted the Dharamsala reading. One of these cases is of interest because it happens in Chapter VIII, verse 24, the important *ādibuddha* (primordial Buddha) verse, in particular 24b, where the Dharamsala text has "*daṅ po'i saṅs rgyas rgyu med pa,*" while the Peking blockprint has instead of *rgyu med pa* the reading *ris med pa*. The original Sanskrit has *ananvaya*, with a number of meanings. Rin-chen-bzaṅ-po's *rgyu med pa* "causeless" is feasible and therefore not wrong; the translation of the line would be "the primordial Buddha, causeless." Both the Narendrakīrti and Smṛti commentaries mention the *rgyu med pa* for this verse. But Narendrakīrti (78-4-1, 2) explains that this *rgyu* means something preceding (*sṅon du 'gro ba*), so the negation would mean something like "without preceding cause," the rendering I used in my translation. However, the *ris med pa* reading of the Peking blockprint, meaning something like "impartial," is definitely wrong. The alternate rendering in Nāro-pā's citation (13-2-8), the line given: *daṅ po'i sàns rgyas gñis gtogs med*, takes account of the usage of *anvaya* as succession or connection, hence the negation, "not pertaining to two," and this is also good.

A case where the Peking blockprint and the Dharamsala edition agree against the Derge Kanjur edition and the way a line is cited in Nāro-pā's commentary deserve discussion. This is Chapter VI, verse 19c, the line "*śes pas srid 'byuṅ skye gnas te.*" The Sanskrit for *śes pas* is *prajñā*, which has as standard translation into Tibetan the expression *śes rab*. And this normally correct rendition is found for this verse in the Derge Kanjur version of the *Saṃgīti* and also in Nāro-pā's citation of this verse, though not naming the source, in commenting on *Hevajratantra*, Part I, Chapter 4, on initiation (*abhiṣeka*). The Narendrakīrti commentary (73-5-2) gives the reason for the switch—I am certain it was done by Rin-chen-bzaṅ-po—to the *śes pas*. He says it is due to nonvisible middle term (*madhyamapada*) (*tshig dbu ma mi mṅon par byas pa ste*), usually in Sanskrit compounds, since the first member, here *prajñā*, has nonvisible inflection. If the great translator had rendered it as *śes rab* there would have been no room to enter a separate instrumental particle *kyis*. The reader, normally imagining an inflection, would probably attribute the genitive, misinterpreting the line to mean the gestation *of prajñā* (*śes rab*). The translator decided to forego the standard translation in order to make the instrumental visible (the "s" after vowels) and show the verbal intention with *śes pa*, thus "by knowing" (*śes pas*),[4] implying the way in which *prajñā* knows. This shows that the standard Tibetan equivalents for Sanskrit terms did not always work for the numerous texts translated in the new period. The commentaries, such as Narendrakīrti's, remind the reader that, after all, *śes rab* is meant, and presumably the editors of the Derge Kanjur replaced a reading *śes pas* with *śes rab*, thinking it was more important for the standard equivalent to be in evidence. Rin-chen-bzaṅ-po evidently felt it was more important for the reader to understand.

The above examples, though few in number, indicate that it is possible to determine the original text of Rin-chen-bzaṅ-po's translation, which is well preserved except for a few dubious spots. As to the role of Śoṅ, who is catalogued as reviser of the *Saṃgīti* translation by Rin-chen-bzaṅ-po, this requires some remarks about the events leading up to Rin-chen-bzaṅ-po's activity.

Our sources for the translation decrees and the conditions that required them are Bu-ston's *History of Buddhism* (which was translated by E. Obermiller) and a parallel Tibetan-Mongolian work called the *Li-śi'ī gur khaṅ* on the subject of old and new Tibetan words (employed extensively by B. Laufer in "Loan Words in Tibetan," *T'oung Pao*, 1916). The *Li-śi'i gur khaṅ*[5] says that the first translations, such as the *Buddhāvataṃsaka*, made at the time of Thu mi Sambhoṭa and King Khri-sroṅ-sde-btsan, were in accordance with the first royal decree (*daṅ po'i bkas bcad*). The text gives a fair-sized list of old words that occurred in the early translations, starting with *gag* for *gaṅ*. Bu-ston says these works contained many words unintelligible to the Tibetans; that there were no standard renditions, with translations made from Chinese, from the language of Li and Sahor. The *Li-śi'i gur khaṅ* goes on to the second royal decree due to the sovereign Khri Ral-pa-can, above all, and to the three grammarians known in the "new language" collectively as Ska, Cog, Źaṅ. These translations in the "new language" are said to be "led by a friend," meaning the Sanskrit-Tibetan dictionary *Mahāvyutpatti* in the early ninth century. Strict rules were made for the uniformity of translations, henceforth only from Sanskrit, and certain types of works were prohibited for translation (e.g., Hīnayāna, other than Sarvāstivādin, and tantric works). The year 841 ends the *sṅa dar* "former diffusion (of Buddhism in Tibet)" due to the blow to the Doctrine suffered under Laṅ-dar-ma. Then begins in A.D. 978 (according to George N. Roerich, *The Blue Annals*) the *phyi dar* "later diffusion (of Buddhism in Tibet)." The two chief personages of this time are the King Ye-śes-'od and the translator Rin-chen-bzaṅ-po. About the great translator, Giuseppe Tucci has written much; one may consult for example *Tibetan Painted Scrolls*. The *Li-śi'i gur khaṅ* speaks of the third royal decree, concerning the translations at the time of the Lha bla-ma Ye-śes-'od, starting with the activity of the great translator Rin-chen-bzaṅ-po. The text gives a lengthy list of the translator's changes of former renditions, for example, he changed *kva* into *kye*; *skyor skyor* into *yaṅ yaṅ*; *bla 'og* into *steṅ 'og*—terms that occurred frequently in the sacred texts translated pursuant to the second royal decree. However, the great translator also had a few artificialities of his own, thus wrote *bstan chos* for *bstan bcos* (the *śāstra*); and wrote numerals *gñis bcu*, *gsum bcu*, and *gsum brgya*, for *ñi śu*, *sum cu*, and *sum brgya* (respectively). Some of these numbers occur in the M-N-S, for example, VIII, verse 5, where we may suppose the translator wrote "*gsum bcu rtsa gñis mtshan 'chaṅ ba*."

Taking all the evidence together, we may conclude that the

revision by Śoṅ was restricted to such terms as these, where Rin-chen-bzaṅ-po had his own style of writing them.[6] Therefore, the substitution in Chapter V, 2a, of *khoṅ nas byuṅ ba* for *srog chen po ste* is something that happened much later.

The *Saṃgīti* is sufficiently short and overwhelmingly important for the great translator to have fussed over it to get every word as the right one and in the right place. Therefore, the Tibetan text is a precious document of Tibetan religion.

5. The Six Cycles of Praise

A PROSE SET OF PRAISES for the *Chanting the Names* (of Mañjuśrī) is found in some editions inserted between Chapter XI and XII of the M-N-S. This insertion is doubtless a later composition than the M-N-S itself. It is lacking in the Peking parallel text I utilized as well as in the Dharamsala edition I have alluded to. However, it is found in Sanskrit as edited by Minaeff and was translated by Rin-chen-bzaṅ-po, whose translation of this prose I have utilized in the Derge Kanjur edition. In order that my work on the M-N-S be complete, it seems appropriate to translate these prose sections. Since the Minaeff Sanskrit edition differs, by reason of corruptions, from the Tibetan in various spots, I have naturally consulted the Sanskrit but take the Tibetan version by Rin-chen-bzaṅ-po as my guide here. It should be pointed out that the *Vimalaprabhā* exegesis of the *Kālacakratantra* (Bu-ston, Vol. Ga, Ye-śes le'u, f. 107b-4) states that the M-N-S has 162 verses. This should be clear by the following detailing in terms of the M-N-S chapters:

Chapter	*Verses*
I	1–16
II	17–22
III	23–24
IV	25–27
V	28–41
VI	42–66
VII	67–76
VIII	77–118
IX	119–142
X	143–157
XI	158–162

Therefore, according to the *Vimalaprabhā* the M-N-S is fact ends with Chapter XI. The remainder is to be taken as appendices, namely, the six cycles of praise (*anuśaṃsā*), the mantra section, and the five epilogue verses (*upasaṃhāra*).

For annotating these prose sections, I shall utilize my own resources and just one of the M-N-S commentaries (which I do not elsewhere employ), namely Mañjuśrīmitra's *Ārya-Mañjuśrīnāmasaṃgīti-ṭikā*, translated into Tibetan by Rin-chen-bzaṅ-po, which is a prolix commentary in PTT, Vol. 74, pp. 226-312, and near its end treats these prose sections.

(1) This is the first cycle's eleven praises: "Vajrapāṇi, the *vajradhara*, this Chanting of the Names, exclusive and pure, is of Mañjuśrī the 'knowledge being' (*jñāna-sattva*),[1] who is the knowledge body of the Bhagavat, the knowledge body of all the Tathāgatas.[2] Vajrapāṇi, the *vajradhara*, it was revealed, clarified, uncovered, analyzed, opened fully, and empowered, in your stream of consciousness, by me and by the empowerment of the underlying nature (*dharmatā*) of all mantras;[3] for generating in you supreme joy, pure faith, and ecstasy; for purifying the secret Body, Speech, and Mind;[4] for completing and purifying the Stages, Perfections,[5] and Collection of Merit and Knowledge, that are still incomplete and unpurified; for the realization of the supreme goal that is still unrealized; for attaining the still unattained; and so on, up to, for protecting the rules of the Illustrious Dharma of all the Tathāgatas."

(2) This is the second cycle's fifty-two praises: "Besides, Vajrapāṇi, the *vajradhara*, this Chanting of the Names is the pure and immaculate omniscient knowledge (*sarvajñajñāna*) and the secret Body, Speech, and Mind. It is the enlightenment (*bodhi*) of the Buddha belonging

to all the Tathāgatas; and the realization belonging to the rightly completed Buddhas. It is the ultimate for all the Tathāgatas; and the comprehension of the Dharmadhātu for all the Sugatas.[6] It is the Victors' defeat of all of Māra's armies; and the power of the ten powers of all those having the ten powers. It is the omniscience of those with omniscient knowledge. It is the *āgama* (hand-down) of all (the Buddha's) doctrines (*dharma*) and the *samudāgama* (complete knowledge) of all Buddhas. It is the fulfillment of the immaculate, spotless Collection of Merit and Knowledge belonging to all the Bodhisattva great beings (*mahāsattva*). It is the procreation of all the Śrāvakas and Pratyekabuddhas; and the field for the perfection of all men and gods. It is the foundation of the Mahāyāna; and the source of Bodhisattva practice. It is the culmination of the right, Noble Path; the touchstone of those who are liberated; and the generation of the path that is the way of liberation. It is the noninterruption of the Tathāgata's lineage; and the growth of the great Bodhisattvas' family and clan. It is the rout of all the opposing disputants; the victory over all the heretics; and the defeat of the forces, armies, and divisions of the four Māras. It is the conversion (to the Dharma) of all sentient beings; and the maturation on the Noble Path on the part of all those traveling to liberation. It is the *samādhi* of those dwelling in the four sublime abodes;[7] and the meditation of those with single-pointed mind.[8] It is the application (*yoga*) of those who exercise their body, speech, and mind; and the dissociation from all bonds. It is the elimination of all defilements and secondary defilements; the pacification of all hindrances; and the release of all bonds. It is the liberation from all remaining basis (of personal aggregate). It is the stilling of all issuances (to external objects) of the mind. It is a mine of all wealth; and the overcoming of all misfortune. It seals all doors to evil destiny; and is the illustrious path to the city of liberation. It is the bringing to halt the wheel of *saṃsāra* (cyclical flow); and the setting in motion of the wheel of Dharma. It is the holding aloft of the parasol, ensign, and victory banner of the Tathāgata's Teaching; and the spiritual support (*adhiṣṭhāna*) for teaching the Illustrious Doctrine. It is the speedy success of the Bodhisattvas who engage in the practice by way of Mantra. It is the comprehension of the cultivation on the part of those applied to the Perfection of Insight; and is the penetration into voidness on the part of those applied to the cultivation of penetration into nontwo.[9] It brings about all the Perfections and Collections (of Merit and Knowledge); and fulfills all the Perfections and pure Stages. It is the penetration into the four right Noble Truths; and is the single penetration into all the natures (*dharma*) of the four stations of mindfulness.[10] This Chanting of the Names continues up to the fulfillment of all the Buddha merits."

(3) This is the third cycle's fifty-two praises: "Besides, Vajrapāṇi, the *vajradhara*, this Chanting of the Names completely lays to rest all the sinful commerce of body, speech, and mind, of all the sentient beings. It purifies all the evil destinies of all the sentient beings; and obstructs all evil destinies. It cuts off all the hindrance of karma; and avoids all birth in the births with the eight untimely conditions.[11] It lays to rest the eight great dangers.[12] It drives away all bad dreams; and drives away all bad signs. It stills all bad omens and demons; and drives far away all the enemy acts of the Māras. It makes grow all the roots of virtue and all the merits. It avoids the generation of all mental orientations that are unmethodical; and overcomes all intoxication, pride, haughtiness, and self-centeredness. It avoids all suffering and dissatisfaction; and is the heart of all the Tathāgatas. It is the secret to all Bodhisattvas; and the great secret to all the Śrāvakas and Pratyekabuddhas. It is all *mudrā* and *mantra*. It generates the mindfulness and awareness of those who bespeak all the inexpressible Dharmas. It creates the incomparable insight and prudent mind; and creates perfect health, strength, and lordliness. It promotes glory, virtue, calm, and goodness; and illumines fame, celebrity, renown, and praise. It pacifies all sickness and the great dangers. It is the utmost cleansing of all who are utmost cleansed;

and the utmost purity of those who are utmost pure. It possesses the utmost fortune of those with utmost fortune; and is the utmost good auspice of those with utmost good auspice. It is the refuge for those desiring refuge; a resting place for those without a resting place. It is a resort for those wishing a resort; a final resort for those without a final resort. It is an island for those wishing an island; the incomparable basis for those without a basis. It is the boat for those going across the ocean of phenomenal life. Because it overcomes all illnesses, it is the great Medicine Buddha (*bhaiṣajya-rāja*). Because it discriminates between the given things to be accepted and to be rejected, it is insight. Because it dispells all the darkness and blindness of bad views, it is the light of wisdom (*jñānāloka*). Because it fulfills exactly as is wished all the hopes of sentient beings, it is the wish-granting gem. Because it achieves the *jñānakāya* (knowledge body) of Mañjuśrī, it is the omniscient knowledge. Because it achieves the five eyes, it is the vision by pure wisdom. Because the giving of material things, of fearlessness and of the Dharma, is the complete abandonment, it is the fulfillment of the six Perfections.[13] Because it completes the *samādhi*-s and the Collection of Merit and Knowledge, it achieves the ten Stages.[14] Because it is free from the Dharma of two, it is the underlying nature of nontwo. Because it is lacking superimposition, it is the thusness nature and the underlying nature that is not otherwise. Because it is the pure nature of all the Tathāgatas' *jñānakāya*, it is the nature of the true end (*bhūtakoṭi*). Because it clears away all the dense thickets of bad views, it is the great voidness of all aspects. This Chanting of the Names, because in this way preserving the names and clarifying the meaning of the underlying nature of nontwo, is the inexpressibility of all dharmas."

(4) This is the fourth cycle's nineteen praises:[15] "Besides, Vajrapāṇi, the *vajradhara*, whatever son of the family or daughter of the family engages in the practice by way of Mantra, and chants the nontwo and absolute names of the *jñānakāya* of Bhagavat Mañjuśrī the 'knowledge being,' which is the *jñānakāya* of all the Tathāgatas; (names) which consummate all this 'crest-jewel' that is not deficient and not in parts; and (that son or daughter of the family) will apply three times a day to the verses, verse-feet, and words, recite and master them, orient his mind methodically to them; and clarify the meaning of the names to others at the appropriate time and exactly as they are *in extenso*, whether each one or any one of the many;—Mañjuśrī the *jñānakāya* will be revealed to him (or her); with onepointedness of mind (on it), contemplation, conviction, orienting the mind just to it, he (or she) will abide with abidings in all directions, with the best, undisturbed penetration into all dharmas, with the penetration by insight attended with faith. And to that person, all the Buddhas and Bodhisattvas who are gathered in the three times and in no time, having come and having arrived, will reveal all the dharma-gates, and will reveal their embodiment. His body, speech, and mind will be empowered in the stream of consciousness (*saṃtāna*) by the empowerment of all the Buddhas and Bodhisattvas. He will be induced to have fearlessness and eloquence toward all the dharmas. They will reveal their embodiment with loving intention toward the Noble Dharma also of all the Arhats, Śrāvakas, and Pratyekabuddhas. With their Nirmāṇakāyas that as great Fury Kings (*krodha-rāja*) and Thunderbolt Wielders (*vajradhara*) tame those hard to tame, and that in their diverse forms protect the living beings, they reveal their shining faces, powers, unassailable splendor; also (reveal) *mantras*, *mudrā*-s, realizations (*abhiṣamaya*), and *maṇḍala*-s. All the *mantravidyārājñī*-s;[16] also the removers of demons, enemies of Māra,[17] Mahāpratyaṅgirā, and Mahāparājitā,[18] at every instant of day and night will protect, guard, and shield his diverse postures.[19] Brahmā, Indra, Upendra, Rudra, Nārāyaṇa, Sanatkumāra, Maheśvara, Kārttikeya, Mahākāla, Nandikeśvara, Yama, Varuṇa, Kubera, Hārītī, and the world-protectors in the ten directions, all of them, will continually in day and night, well protect, guard, and shield

him at the time when he is walking, standing, lying down, or sitting; asleep or awake; equipoised (*samāhita*) or nonequipoised; in solitude or among many persons; living in a village, town, city, district, kingdom, or capital city; staying near the city gate (the Indrakīla) or at the porch of a house; on main street or a path; at crossroads or road fork; a distant city or a goods-store; and so on, up to, when he has proceeded to a deserted house, a mountain (cave), forest, river, cemetery, wilderness; or, when he is unclean or clean, intoxicated or delirious. Day and night they will bring him happy events. Moreover, the gods, *nāga*-s, *yakṣa*-s, *gandharva*-s, *asura*-s, *garuḍa*-s, *kiṃnāra*-s, *mahoraga*-s, humans and nonhumans; moreover, the planets, asterisms (*nakṣatra*), 'mothers' (*mātṛ*), *gaṇapati*-s, as well as the Seven Mothers,[20] *yakṣiṇī*-s, *rākṣasī*-s, and *piśācī*-s, all well disposed toward him, along with their followers and retinues, will well protect, guard, and shield him during his diverse postures, and they will instill in his body good complexion and strength; and they will arrange for him health, vitality, and lengthening of life."

(5) *This is the fifth cycle's fifty-one praises:* "Besides, Vajrapāṇi, the *vajradhara*, when one takes on this Chanting of the Names, called 'crest jewel,' without losing a day of voicing it three times,[21] whether reciting it from memory or reading it aloud from the book, and takes as meditative object the form of Bhagavat Mañjuśrī the 'knowledge being,' repeatedly giving thought to the form, and again meditating on the form; taking it to himself, on account of the candidate,[22] before long he will see that (form) by the formal body (*rūpakāya*) materializing.[23] He will also see in accompaniment all the Buddhas and Bodhisattvas stationed in the vault of the sky, their formal bodies materializing in diverse ways. No matter what the birth of that great being, he need not fear an evil destiny or a fall into a lower birth. Nor will he be born into a bad family; nor take birth in a border country. He will not have inferior faculties, or incomplete faculties. He will not be born in a family with wayward views. He will not be born in Buddha fields wherein a Buddha is not resident. He will not be born when a Buddha appears and teaches the Dharma, but it is rejected or is out of sight. He will not be born among the long-lived gods.[24] He will not be reborn in eons (*kalpa*) subject to famine, sickness, and sword. He will not be reborn at the time of the five degeneracies (*kaṣāya*).[25] He will not be reborn when there are dangers of king, robbers, and enemies; or when there are the dangers of misery and poverty. Nor is he born when there is the danger of ill-fame, reviling, censure, ill-repute, disgrace. He is born with fine birth, and perfection of family and clan. His form and color will be thoroughly attractive. To the sight of the world he will be attractive, gratifying, good for companion, and pleasing. He will shine among men, have good fortune, and his words will be accepted. In whatever places he was born, he will remember those places. Of great possessions and great retinues, he will not exhaust his possessions or exhaust his retinues. He will be endowed with aspiration and wisdom that is the best among all sentient beings. He will naturally be endowed with the merits of the six Perfections. He will abide in the four sublime abodes. Be endowed with mindfulness and awareness, with means and powers, with aspiration and wisdom. He will be fearless toward all treatises and be skilled in speaking; he will have clear words, no foolishness, and a sharp mind. He will be skilled, hard-working, satisfied, with high goals, and be free from craving. He will be an authority for all sentient beings, and have the assent of masters (*ācārya*) and gurus. He will understand clearly according to the meaning and according to the texts all the crafts, arts, (branches of) knowledge, and treatises, even though not having previously studied them. He will possess pure morality, livelihood, and performance.[26] He will go forth to the religious life in fine manner and be ordained in fine manner. He will not forget (the goal of) omniscience or the Mind of Enlightenment. Never will he descend to the certainty of the Śrāvakas, Arhats, and Pratyekabuddhas."[27]

(6) This is the sixth cycle's immeasurable praises: "Vajrapāṇi, the *vajradhara*, one cannot plumb the merits with which he (or she) is endowed, according to that (foregoing description). He will also become endowed with other merits of that sort and that one cannot plumb. Vajrapāṇi, the *vajradhara*, the bull of men who embraces this supreme Chanting of the Names will easily and in not too long a time amass the Collections of Merit and Knowledge; will quickly accomplish the Buddha merits, and become manifestly awakened to the incomparable rightly perfected enlightenment. With the rule to not pass into *nirvāṇa* for many eons, he will be a teacher of the incomparable Dharma for all sentient beings. Empowered as King of the Dharma, his drum of the Dharma (will sound) in the ten directions."

The foregoing six cycles of praise appear susceptible of association with the chapters of M-N-S. Speaking approximately, it does appear possible to correlate various M-N-S chapters by name with cycles among the six cycles of praise, in the following manner:

M-N-S chapters	*Six Cycles of Praise*
IV. Abhisambodhi Sequence of the *Net of Illusion*	1st cycle
V. The Great Maṇḍala of Vajradhātu	2nd cycle
VI. The Pure Dharmadhātu Wisdom	3rd cycle
VII. Praising the Mirrorlike Wisdom	4th cycle
VIII. Discriminative Wisdom	5th cycle
IX. Sameness Wisdom	6th cycle
X. Procedure-of-Duty Wisdom	
XI. Praise of the Five Tathāgatas	

The correlation was accomplished by noticing certain key words in the cycles of praise. For example, near the end of the third cycle were traditional equivalents to the Dharmadhātu, so this cycle goes with the Dharmadhātu wisdom. Earlier I pointed out that Chapter VII may actually begin with some of the final verses presently in Chapter VI. This is one reason the above correlation is approximate. It may be noticed that these "praises," which in fact show the benefits to be derived from reciting the M-N-S and from contemplating Mañjuśrī's formal body, cover more chapters than those devoted to the "names" of Mañjuśrī.

Texts Used for the Sanskrit-Tibetan Edition and Annotations

Sanskrit text of *Mañjuśrī-nāma-saṃgīti*: I. P. Minaeff, ed., St. Petersburg University, Historo-Philological Faculty, Vol. 16 (1885), pp. 137-159.

Parallel Sanskrit-Tibetan blockprint (Peking), Lantsa script, Sanskrit text transcribed into Tibetan letters, and Tibetan translation.

Tibetan text, in the Derge Mtshal-par Bka'-'gyur, Vol. 77.

Tibetan text, *'Phags pa 'jam dpal gyi mtshan yaṅ dag par brjod pa bklag thabs bcas* (attended with recitation method), traditional version (? Dharamsala, no date).

Narendrakīrti, *Ārya-mañjuśrī-nāma-saṃgīti-vyākhyānam*, Tibetan translation in Peking Tanjur (PTT, Vol. 48, pp. 60-4-4 to 87-5-7).

Candrabhadrakīrti, *Ārya-mañjuśrī-nāma-saṃgīti-nāmavṛtti*, Tibetan translation in Peking Tanjur (PTT, Vol. 75, 1-1-1 to 15-2-1).

Smṛtijñānakīrti ("Smṛti"), *Mañjuśrī-nāmasaṃgīti-lakṣabhāṣya*, Tibetan translation in Peking Tanjur (PTT, Vol. 75, 33-3-3 to 56-a-4).

A few annotations were also drawn from the following commentaries:

Padma-dkar-po, *Ārya-mañjuśrī-nāma-saṃgīti-ṭīkāvimalaprabhā*, Tibetan translation in Derge Tanjur, Rgyud 'grel, Vol. Pha.

Candragomin, *Ārya-mañjuśrī-nāmasaṃgīti-mahāṭīkā-nāma*, in Peking Tanjur (PTT, Vol. 75, p. 79).

(Author unknown), *Nāmasaṃgīti-vṛtti-trinaya-prakāśakaraṇa-dīpa-nāma*, Peking Tanjur (PTT, Vol. 75, p. 86).

Ḍombīheruka, *Nāmasaṃgīti-vṛtti*, Peking Tanjur (PTT, Vol. 75, p. 96).

Corrections to Minaeff's Sanskrit Text

Chapter VII. v.2, *vighnarāḍ* to *vighnarājo*. Chapter VIII. v.17, *mauṇḍī* to *mauñjī*. v.18, *mauñjī* to *mauṇḍī*. v.32, *sarasvatiḥ* to *sarasvatī*. v.36, *mahāyāna-* to *mahāyāno*. Chapter IX. v.3, *ākṣepa-* to *ākṣepaḥ*. v.4, *ākrānta-* to *ākrāntaḥ*. v.13, *-sthaḥ* to *-ṣṭhaḥ*. v.17, *opāya-* to *opāyaḥ*. v.20, *-dhṛk* to *-kṛt*. Chapter X. v.16, *jñeyo* to *jñeya-*. Chapter XI. v.1, *namas te* to *namo*. Chapter XII. *mahāvāca* to *mahāpaca*. And rearrangement of mantras.

Notes

Background of the *Mañjuśrī-nāma-saṃgīti*

1. *Āryamañjuśrīmūlakalpa*, ed. by T. Gaṇapati Śāstri (Trivandrum, 1920), Part I, p. 163.23-24: kumāraḥ sarvabhūtānāṃ mañjughoṣaḥ sadā śubhaḥ/buddhakṛtyaṃ tathā loke śāsane 'smin kariṣyati//. The word *śubha* is here translated "pure" by authority of the Tibetan translation, Peking Kanjur, Photo ed., Vol. 6, p. 210.5-8, rendering it by the Tibetan word *dag* ("pure").

2. Cf. Étienne Lamotte, "Mañjuśrī," *T'oung Pao*, 1960, pp. 1-96.

3. *Aparimitāyur-jñāna-nāma-mahāyāna-sūtram*, tr. by Max Walleser (Heidelberg, 1916).

4. Cf. Leon Hurvitz, *Scripture of the Lotus Blossom of the Fine Dharma* (New York: Columbia University Press, 1976), Index, under "Mañjuśrī."

5. *A Complete Catalogue of the Tibetan Buddhist Canons*, ed. by Hakuju Ui, et al., and *A Catalogue-Index of the Tibetan Buddhist Canons* (Sendai, Japan, 1934).

6. See E. Obermiller, "The Doctrine of Prajñāpāramitā as exposed in the Abhisamayālaṃkāra of Maitreya," reprint from *Acta Orientalia*, Vol. XI, 1932, p. 57 (under the heading of Stage No. 10), where he cites, "so that he may be called a Buddha, though not a fully accomplished Buddha."

7. Lamotte, *op. cit.*, p. 95.

8. *Aṣṭasāhasrikā Prajñāpāramitā*, tr. by Edward Conze (Calcutta, 1958), p. 93.

9. Photo ed. of Tibetan Kanjur-Tanjur (PTT), Vol. 94, p. 175-4-2, 3, with parenthesis remarks from p. 175-3-1, 2, 3. For the last sentence of my citation: de la bu lta bu ni saṅs rgyas bcom ldan 'das so/ma lta bu ni śes rab kyi pha rol tu phyin pa'o/. Vimalamitra then states that the subject is treated clearly and at length in the *Tathāgatotpattisaṃbhava-nirdeśa*, which was early (3rd century A.D.) translated into Chinese as a separate *sūtra* and is incorporated into the huge scripture *Avataṃsaka*.

10. Lamotte, *op. cit.*, p. 29.

11. Alex Wayman, "Reflections on the Theory of Barabuḍur as a Maṇḍala," in *Barabudur: History and Significance of a Buddhist Monument*, ed. by L. Gómez and H. W. Woodward, Jr. (Berkeley, 1981), p. 143.

12. Ferdinand D. Lessing and Alex Wayman, *Mkhas grub rje's Fundamentals of the Buddhist Tantras* (The Hague, 1968), p. 111. At the same place, it is taught that Mañjuśrī has another tantra called *Mañjuśrī-siddhaikavīra-tantra* with the Arapacana, five deities, both in white and saffron forms; so this popular Arapacana form is part of the Kriyātantra. Mañjuśrī also figures in the Vajra family with the angry form, and figures in other tantric works (cf. *Mkhas grub rje's*, Index).

13. Lamotte, *op. cit.*, p. 35.

14. Lamotte, *op. cit.*, p. 34.

15. R. S. Panchamukhi, *Gandharvas & Kinnaras in Indian Iconography* (Dharwar: Kannada Research Institute, 1951), p. 33. Since Mañjuśrī is frequently depicted with the sword of *prajñā*, it is of interest to note a terracotta plaque showing a Gandharva holding a sword and a noose (Panchamukhi, *op. cit.*, Pl. XIV).

16. Marcelle Lalou, *Iconographie des Étoffes paintes (paṭa)* (Paris: Paul Geuthner, 1930), p. 68.

17. Cf. Lalou, *op. cit.*, p. 25, and Ariane Macdonald, *Le Maṇḍala du Mañjuśrīmūlakalpa* (Paris: Adrien-Maisonneuve, 1962), p. 130.

18. *Mkhas grub rje's Fundamentals*, pp. 31, 33.

19. Cf. Maurice Winternitz, *A History of Indian Literature*, Vol. II, Buddhist Literature and Jaina Literature, revised English tr. (University of Calcutta, 1933), p. 365.

20. Cf. Alex Wayman and Hideko Wayman, tr. *The Lion's Roar of Queen Śrīmālā: A Buddhist Scripture on the Tathāgatagarbha Theory* (New York and London, 1974), pp. 9-11.

21. *Mkhas grub rje's Fundamentals*, p. 127.

22. Told me by a Columbia University student Douglas Rhoton, preparing a doctoral dissertation on a work by Sa-paṇ.

23. After the present work was in the hands of the intended publisher (Shambhala), there came to hand the translation by Ronald M. Davidson of the M-N-S in the volume *Tantric and Taoist Studies* (Bruxelles, 1981); I believe he is correct in arguing that the correct Sanskrit form for this name is Vilāsavajra.

24. I took notes from this commentary years ago in the Derge Tanjur available at the East Asiatic Library, University of California, Berkeley. The passages here cited are in the Derge, *Rgyud 'grel*, Vol. Pha, fol. 60b-2, ff.; 72b-6, ff.; and 88a-1, ff., for the M-N-S, VI, 18; VIII, 17; and X, 3, respectively.

25. While this is translated from Tibetan, subsequently I consulted the Sanskrit text furnished in *Kālacakra-tantra and Other Texts*, Part I, ed. by Raghu Vira and Lokesh Chandra (New Delhi: International Academy of Indian Culture, 1966), numbered lines II, 180, and found my rendition reasonably close to the Sanskrit.

26. Text in Raghu Vira and Lokesh Chandra, ed. (n. 23 above), line V, 256a.

27. Cf. Louis de la Vallée Poussin, *Vijñaptimatratāsiddhi*, Tome II (Paris, 1929), p. 552, where he gives this theory, followed by the rival theory that the first, second, and fourth truths are conventional, only the third absolute; and another rival theory that all four noble truths are conventional.

28. PTT, Vol. 75, p. 140-4-7:/'jam dpal źes bya ba/byaṅ chub kyi sems kyi mtshan ñid ma nor bar rtogs pa ni saṅs rgyas ma lus pa'i 'byuṅ gnas yin pa'i phyir/bder gśegs ma lus yul du gyur pa rgyal pa kun gyi lam gcig go/źes smos te/.

Citations of the *Mañjuśrī-nāma-saṃgīti* in Nāro-pā's Commentary

1. I have employed the Tibetan edition in the Peking Tanjur (PTT, Vol. 54, pp. 1-41 of this photographic edition).

2. One may consult D. L. Snellgrove, *The Hevajra Tantra. A Critical Study*, two vols. (London, 1959), for the structure of the *Hevajratantra* in two parts. I follow his method of calling "chapters" the sections numbered 1-11 of Part I and the sections numbered 1-12 of Part II.

3. For more information on this topic of *sahaja*, cf. Per Kvaerne, "On the Concept of Sahaja in Indian Buddhist Tantric Literature," *Temenos*, Vol. 11, 1975, pp. 88-135.

4. By comparison with the *karma*-seal, this *jñāna*-seal is evidently meant in the absolute sense, thus agreeing with the term *paramārtha* applied to the tantric path in the M-N-S, per my chapter on "Background," with n. 27.

5. Sarat Chandra Das, in his *Tibetan-English Dictionary*, reprint of 1902 edition, mentions (p. 203) one of the explanations for *ga*, "it moves and it is also motionless."

6. Cf. Kvaerne, *op. cit.*, pp. 90-102, for his exposition of "The Tantric Ritual of Initiation," but wherein he decides that the best translation of *abhiṣeka* is apparently "consecration," which goes with the literal meaning of the Sanskrit term, a "sprinkling" or "aspersion," although he acknowledges that it really is an "initiation." However, Nāro-pā's considerable stress on "birth" in his commentary on this chapter has led me to continue the translation "initiation" of my previous writings. Here "initiation" means the induction into a new group of fellow "initiates" and even the introduction to a new level of consciousness.

7. Cf. Alex Wayman, *The Buddhist Tantras; Light on Indo-Tibetan Esotericism* (New York. Samuel Weiser, 1973), p. 116.

8. For this *gandharva-sattva*, cf. Alex Wayman, *Yoga of the Guhyasamājatantra* (Delhi, 1977), pp. 200, 202-205, where this generation sequence involving the *vijñāna* is set forth with terminology drawn from the *Guhyasamājatantra* lineage and apparently compatible with Nāro-pā's description.

9. Cf. Kvaerne, *op. cit.*, pp. 109-124, for a detailed exposition of the "four Joys."

10. "Gaurī II" is Snellgrove's way (cf. n. 2, above) of differentiating this goddess from one of the same name previously mentioned in the *Hevajratantra*.

11. Apparently this striking sentence means that the day is the black of the moon (because it disintegrates) as also when the sun and moon are in

"conjunction"; and that the night is the white of the moon (because then it rules) as also when the sun and moon are in "opposition"—time of full moon.

12. Cf. the *āgama Kālacakra* Sanskrit text published by Raghu Vīra and Lokesh Candra, V, 178d: na prajñā nāpy upāyaḥ sahajatanur iyaṃ stūparūpaṃ samantāt, "This *sahaja*-body with *stūpa* form is entirely neither *prajñā* nor *upāya*."

13. Wayman, *Yoga of the Guhyasamājatantra*, pp. 299-301, translates the verses for each of the five goddesses that represent their "exhortation" to the Lord.

The Seven Maṇḍalas of the *Mañjuśrī-nāma-saṃgīti*

1. Benoytosh Bhattacharyya, *The Indian Buddhist Iconography* (Calcutta: Firma K. L. Mukhopadhyay, 1958), Chap. III, "Bodhisattva Mañjuśrī," pp. 100-123.

2. Marie-Thérèse de Mallmann, *Étude iconographique sur Mañjuśrī* (Paris: École française d'Extrême-Orient, 1964).

3. This is the reprint of Bu-ston's collected works (New Delhi: International Academy of Indian Culture, 1969), Pt. 14 (Pha), the work entitled *Chos kyi dbyiṅs gsuṅ gi dbaṅ phyug gi dkyil 'khor gyi cho ga: Mkhas pa'i dga' ston.*

4. This information is drawn from the catalog entry in *A Catalogue of the Tohoku University Collection of Tibetan Works on Buddhism* (The Seminary of Indology, Tohoku University, 1953), where the work of n. 3, above, has the no. 5147.

5. *Niṣpannayogāvalī of Mahāpaṇḍita Abhayākaragupta*, ed. by Benoytosh Bhattacharyya (Baroda: Oriental Institute, 1949).

6. Cf. Lessing and Wayman, *Mkhas grub rje's Fundamentals*, p. 21, for the "five certainties of the Sambhogakāya," including "It proclaims only Mahāyāna doctrine," and "Its retinue includes only Bodhisattvas of the tenth stage." Also, p. 27, "After completing the five Abhisaṃbodhi, he became a Manifest Complete Buddha as Mahāvairocana, the Sambhogakāya." This shows that the M-N-S saying "great void is five-syllabled" applies to the Sambhogakāya.

7. There are three standard "gates to liberation" in Mahāyāna Buddhism: the voidness, wishless, and signless (see M-N-S, V, 2, comments), to which this tradition adds a fourth "noninstigation gate" (*anabhisaṃskāramukha*). In the Mādhyamika section of the Tanjur there is a work by Vimalamitra, *Kramapraveśika-bhāvanākrama*, wherein (PTT, Vol. 102, p. 178-5-2) the fourth gate is said to be the Prātimokṣa.

8. *Mkhas grub rje's Fundamentals*, pp. 100-101.

9. The four-volume *Thob yig* of the Jaya-paṇḍita Blo-bzan-'phrin-las has been reprinted by Lokesh Chandra (New Delhi, 1981) under the title *Collected Works of* .... However, I recall seeing in the East Asiatic Library, University of California, Berkeley, a further two-volume set of sādhanas of this author in a Peking blockprint (unfortunately from damaged blocks).

10. For the full list, cf. Bhattacharyya, *Niṣpannayogāvalī*, pp. 60-66.

11. Alex Wayman, *The Buddhist Tantras*, p. 51.

12. For a number of examples of this division of *maṇḍala* into *maṇḍa* and *la*, cf. Alex Wayman, "Reflections on the Theory of Barabuḍur as a Maṇḍala," pp. 144-148.

13. *Mkhas grub rje's Fundamentals*, p. 33.

14. For a Japanese Shingon discussion of Mahāvairocana and Vairocana, see Shin'ichi Tsuda, "A Critical Tantrism," *Memoirs of the Research Department of the Toyo Bunko*, no. 36 (Tokyo, 1978), p. 198.

15. *Étude iconographique sur Mañjuśrī*, p. 66.

16. *Mkhas grub rje's Fundamentals*, p. 37.

17. *Mkhas grub rje's Fundamentals*, p. 33.

18. Edward Conze, *The Large Sutra on Perfect Wisdom, with the Divisions of the Abhisamayālaṅkara* (University of California Press, Berkeley, 1975).

19. *Mkhas grub rje's Fundamentals*, p. 222n.

20. Bhattacharyya, *The Indian Buddhist Iconography*, pp. 120-121.

21. This is a large collection of *maṇḍalas* of the Sa-skya-pa tradition, published by N. Lungtok & N. Gyaltsan, Delhi, 1971.

22. It should be noted that three of the five "Wisdoms" show illumination character. Thus besides the natural luminescence of the Dharmadhātu, Akṣobhya's family, governing the Mirrorlike Wisdom, is called in M-N-S, III, 1-2, the great family that illuminates the world—apparently like sunlight. Then, Discriminative Wisdom, M-N-S, VIII, 37, has "the heart-light

of the moon." That leaves the remaining Wisdoms, Sameness and Procedure-of-Duty, to be called possibly "hairy" and "associate hairy."

23. *Mkhas grub rje's Fundamentals*, p. 236n.

24. The expression "six-eyed" feasibly stands for three persons, because there is a Sanskrit expression *aṣaḍakṣīṇa*, "not seen by six eyes," i.e., known by two persons only.

25. This is part of a lengthy series of volumes published by Lokesh Chandra, New Delhi: International Academy of Indian Culture.

26. The *Sādhana-mālā*, ed. by Benoytosh Bhattacharya in two vols., was reprinted (Baroda: Oriental Institute, 1968).

27. This is a series of volumes of evocations (*sādhana*) published at Dehradun (U.P.), India, 1970.

28. This Sudhanakumāra is evidently the well-known youth of the *Gaṇḍavyūha*. Cf. Jan Fontein, *The Pilgrimage of Sudhana* (The Hague: Mouton, 1967); and Lokesh Chandra, *Sudhana's Way to Enlightenment* (New Delhi, 1975).

Remarks on the Tibetan text of *Mañjuśrī-nāma-saṃgīti*

1. This is the second work in a booklet, without notice of publisher, place, or date. The first work is the *Byaṅ chub lam gyi rim pa'i dmar khrid myur lam gyi sṅon 'gro'i ṅag 'don gyi rim pa khyer bde bklag chog bskal bzaṅ mgrin rgyan*. Several other popular texts follow the M-N-S. I neglected to write in the book where it was obtained, but I am confident it was at Dharamsala, H.P., and in early 1970.

2. In one case, "liberated from all defilement," is the old Arhat ideal. In the other case, "liberated from all remainder," suggests the Nirvāṇa without remainder, which is the so-called "Hīnayāna" ideal. When the *Vimalaprabhā* cites this (Bu-ston, collected works, Vol. Ka, Khams le, f.42b-2), it is with *lhag ma*. Rin-chen-bzaṅ-po's line, "liberated from all bodies," refers to ordinary bodies because he uses the Tibetan word *lus* for "body." When a Buddha body is mentioned, it is always referred to by *sku* (the honorific word for "body").

3. The Sanskrit edition of *Mañjuśrī-nāma-saṃgīti* published in Raghu Vira and Lokesh Chandra, *Kālacakra-tantra and Other Texts*, Part I (New Delhi, 1966), numbered verses (consecutive) 93 and 94, exhibits the same erroneous interchange of *mauñjī* and *mauṇḍī*.

4. The great translator's point is further shown in Smṛti's commentary on the verse, that the "*śe pas*" (Literally: "by knowing") means "by knowing the nature of all the *dharmas*"; hence, this implies the ancient Buddhist precept about knowing as they really are, often attributed to the "eye of *prajñā*."

5. I took notes from this text many years ago (in the late 1950s) from the copy in the Tibetan collection of the East Asiatic Library, University of California, Berkeley.

6. Since Rin-chen-bzaṅ-po sets the standard for the new translations, his translation could not be subject to the drastic revisions that occurred when fixing up various old translations and weeding out the obsolete forms. For this process as applied to such texts as the *Saddharmapuṇḍarīka*, see Nils Simonsson, *Indo-tibetische Studien* (Uppsala, 1957), exhibiting many examples where lines and even individual words were interchanged.

The Six Cycles of Praise

1. Mañjuśrīmitra (hereafter, Mañ), PTT, Vol. 74, p. 307-1-2: called "knowledge being" as Master of the Maṇḍala (*dkyil 'khor gyi bdag po*).

2. Mañ, p. 307-1-2: "knowledge body" (of the Bhagavat) because the nature of pure wisdom, and "of all Tathāgatas" because the nature of the Dharmakāya.

3. For "by me and by the *dharmatā* of all mantras," it appears that the writer of these words has in mind the *Vairocanābhisaṃbodhitantra*, Chapter 2, wherein is said (as to be included in a work by A. Wayman under preparation): "Master of the Secret Ones (= Vajrapāṇi), besides, the mantra-character was not made, nor arranged to be made, nor rejoiced in, by any of the Buddhas. Why so? It is like this: There is this continuum (*dharmatā*) of natures (*dharma*) whether a Tathāgata arises or does not arise. The continuum of dharmas remains immemorially. And this is the mantra-character of mantras...." The words "by me" refer to the Tathāgata.

4. Mañ, p. 307-1-6: "secret of Body" means that the body which has

proceeded into the maṇḍala of the Tathāgatas is not in common with the body of Śrāvakas, Pratyekabuddhas, Māras, and so on. "Secret of Speech" means the kind in common with the Tathāgatas and with Bodhisattvas of the Tenth Stage, but not in common with others. "Secret of Mind" means the "body made of mind" (Skt. *manomaya-kāya*; Tib. here: *yid kyi raṅ bźin gyi lus*), which operates by acts of the Mind of all Tathāgatas.

5. Mañ, p. 307-2-2: "Stages, Perfections": the ten Stages and their ten Perfections.

6. Mañ, p. 307-3-5: "Sugata" means those who have gone without turning back (T. *slar mi ldog par gśegs pa rnams*).

7. Mañ, p. 307-5-8: "sublime abodes" are love (*maitrī*), compassion (*karuṇā*), sympathetic joy (*anumodanā*), equanimity (*upekṣā*); their samādhi(s), the Śūraṅgama, etc.

8. Mañ, p. 308-1-1: "single-pointed mind" means all four Dhyāna (i.e., in the "realm of form," *rūpa-dhātu*).

9. Mañ, p. 308-3-3: "penetration into nontwo" means the omniscient knowledge (*sarvajñajñāna*).

10. Mañ, p. 308-3-6: "single penetration" means the comprehension of all dharmas in a single instant by a state-of-mind (*citta*) that is of single "taste" (S. *ekarasa*). (As to the "stations of mindfulness," the four are the well known ones, on bodies, feelings, states of mind, and dharmas.)

11. See *Nāgārjuna's Letter to King Gautamīputra*, tr. by Lozang Jamspal, et. al. (Delhi, 1978), p. 38 (v. 63-64): "Whoever is born as a heretic animal, hungry ghost, hell being, barbarian, fool, long-lived deity or where there is no teaching from a Buddha is declared to be born in the eight faulty and unfavorable (states). Having gotten the opportunity to be free from them, then strive to put an end to birth."

12. There are various lists of "eight great dangers"; see M-N-S, VIII, 16, for Smṛti's list.

13. Mañ, p. 309-5-3: (of the six Perfections) "giving of material things" fulfills the perfection of giving (*dāna-pāramitā*); "giving of fearlessness" fulfills the perfections of morality and forbearance (*śīla-p.* and *kṣānti-p.*); "giving of the Dharma" fulfills the perfections of meditation and insight (*dhyāna-p.* and *prajñā-p.*); and the perfection of striving (*vīrya-p.*) goes with all three.

14. Mañ, p. 309-5-6: "Collection of Merit" is prevalent on the first five Bodhisattva Stages going with the first five Perfections, here called "*samādhi*-s"; and "Collection of Knowledge" is prevalent on the last five Bodhisattva Stages going with the last five Perfections, also called "*samādhi*-s." (For the list of the ten Perfections, see M-N-S, VI, 2.)

15. This fourth cycle has the most differences between the extant Sanskrit text and the Tibetan translation, especially in the arrangement of certain long phrases. As was mentioned, I follow Rin-chen-bzaṅ-po's rendition and also employ the Sanskrit text.

16. Mañ, p. 311-1-5: *mantravidyārājñī-s* ("queens of the *mantra*-s and *vidyā*-s") are supramundane goddesses such as Buddhalocanā.

17. Mañ, p. 311-1-6: "enemies of Māra" are Uṣṇīṣa-Sitātapatrā and so on. (There is a color representation of this goddess as the Frontispiece to George Roerich, *Tibetan Paintings*, Paris, 1925, and discussed on pp. 66-68.) Mañ here evidently includes Mahāpratyaṅgirā among the enemies of Māra.

18. Mañ, p. 311-1-7: Mahāparājitā is among the supramundane goddesses who cannot be overcome by other Fury deities.

19. "Diverse postures" means the four—walking, standing, lying down, or sitting and probably the extended list that follows.

20. The only sprightly comment I have so far noticed in Vimalamitra's commentary on the M-N-S (PTT, Vol. 67), at p. 250-4-4, is to explain the "Seven Mothers" as four widows—Brāhmī, Vaiṣṇavī, Aindrī, Kaumārī; and three wives of Mahādeva (= Śiva)—Raudrī, Vārāhī, and for the third, Rgan-byad-mo (she with an old countenance) apparently Cāmuṇḍā.

21. Mañ, p. 311-2-3: "three times" means the three *saṃdhi*. These are sunrise, moon, and sunset.

22. The Tibetan correctly renders the presumed Sanskrit by *gdul bya'i dbaṅ ñe bar bzuṅ nas*, going with the Sanskrit *vineyavaśād upādāya*. Minaeff theorized a reading *dharmavinayam upādāya* from the MS corruption, which included *vaśād*. Tibetan *gdul bya* (subject to training) means the "candidate"; and here "according to the candidate" means that candidates see in different ways. Mañ, p. 311-2-6, helped for the solution by its *'dul ba'i dbaṅ gis phyir*, where *dbaṅ gis phyir* equals *vaśād*.

23. Mañ, p. 311-2-5: The beginner will see it as the Nirmāṇakāya; when his roots of virtue (*kuśalamūla*) are matured he will see the formal body

(*rūpakāya*) as the Sambhogakāya.

24. Birth among the Bṛhatphala deities (in the "realm of form") is considered unfortunate (see La Vallée Poussin, *L'Abhidharmakośa*, Chapter II, pp. 199-200).

25. Mañ, p. 311-3-2, gives the traditional list in this order: view (*dṛṣṭi*), defilement (*kleśa*), sentient being (*sattva*), eon (*kalpa*), and longevity (*āyus*).

26. Mañ, p. 311-5-4: He stays away from practices that are faults of body, speech, or mind.

27. Mañ, p. 311-5-7: He has no attraction to their vehicles, because he is skilled in the rule of a single vehicle.

PART TWO

TRANSLATION OF THE

MAÑJUŚRĪ-NĀMA-SAṂGĪTI

WITH SANSKRIT & TIBETAN TEXTS & ANNOTATIONS

CHAPTER I. Asking for Instruction

Homage to Mañjuśrīkumārabhūta

[1] atha vajradharaḥ śrīmān durdāntadamakaḥ
parah/
trilokavijayī vīro guhyarāṭ kuliśeśvaraḥ//

/de nas dpal ldan rdo rje 'chaṅ/
/gdul dka' 'dul ba rnams kyi mchog/
/dpa' po 'jig rten gsum las rgyal/
/rdo rje dbaṅ phyug gsaṅ ba'i rgyal//

Now Vajradhara, *śrīmat*, supreme tamer of those hard to tame, the hero, victorious over the three worlds, lord of secrets, the adamantine lord;

"Now" (*atha*): Smṛti (33-5), *de la thag pa* (probably, Skt. *sadhyas*, "at once"). [There is an implication that the term *atha* requires a previous setting, such as the initial sentence of Buddhist scriptures.] "Vajradhara": Smṛti (33-3), Vajradhara is a name of Vajrapāṇi, the compiler (*saṃgrāhaka*) of the Tantra called *Mañjuśrī-nāma-saṃgīti*; *vajra* ("diamond") means "unbreakable"; *dhara* ("holding") means "not separate from." Narendrakīrti (60-5), there are two kinds of "compiling"—of time and of given things; here it is a case of "compiling of time" [or, temporal compiling; hence what will soon be called "good in the beginning, middle, and end"]. "Vajrapāṇi": Smṛti (34-2), as to the name Vajrapāṇi ("having a *vajra* in hand"), *vajra* here means, in the absolute sense, profound voidness; in the conventional sense, the broad seven *maṇḍalas*. "*Śrīmat*": Smṛti (33-4), it is claimed that he is called *śrīmat* (possessed of *śrī*, glory) because it is the source of all excellent merits. "Those hard to tame": Narendrakīrti (60-5), those to tame (*vineya*, the tantric candidate) are of two kinds, to be tamed by stilling (*źi ba*) or to be tamed by being made to experience pain; and here it is a case of the latter. "Hero, victorious over the three worlds": Smṛti (33-4), the three worlds are the realm beneath, ruled by Camuṇḍī; the realm upon, called Madhukāra ("honey making," the bee); the realm above, called Sarvārthasādhaka ("accomplishing all aims"). "Lord of secrets": Narendrakīrti (61-2), because he possesses the exclusive knowledge. "Adamantine lord": Narendrakīrti (61-1 and -2), "adamantine" means the character of right knowledge of all the Tathāgatas; "lord" means he wields power over all *dharmas* (natures). [Notice that the fundamental Tantra of the Yogatantra class, called *Tattvasaṃgraha* has four divisions called Diamond Realm (*vajradhātu*), Victory over the Three Worlds (*trilokyavijaya*); Training the Living Beings (*jagad-vinaya*), and Achieving the Objective (*siddhārtha*); and that these names all appear implicated in the words of *gāthā* no. 1.]

[2] vibuddhapuṇḍarīkākṣaḥ
protphullakamalānanaḥ/
prollālayan vajravaraṃ svakareṇa muhur
muhuḥ//

/pa dma dkar po rgyas 'dra'i spyan/
/pa dma rgyas 'dra'i źal mṅa' ba/
/raṅ gi lag gis rdo rje mchog/
/yaṅ daṅ yaṅ du gsor byed pa//

his eye like an opening white lotus; his face like a wide-open lotus; with his hand again and again brandishing the excellent thunderbolt

"Eye like an opening white lotus": Candrabhadrakīrti (3-3-3), eye-*mudrā* shows Amitābha nature. "Face like a wide-open lotus": Candrabhadrakīrti (3-3-4), face-*mudrā* shows Amoghasiddhi nature. "Hand brandishing the *vajra*": Candrabhadrakīrti (3-3-4), shows Vairocana nature. [Previously, on *gāthā* no. 1,] Candrabhadrakīrti, 3-3-2, explains "hero" as nature of Akṣobhya; and 3-3-3, "lord of secrets" as the nature of Ratnasambhava, by holding the marks of initiation (*abhiṣeka*).

[3] bhṛkuṭītaraṅgapramukhair anantair
vajrapāṇibhiḥ /
durdāntadamakair vīrair
vīravībhatsarūpibhiḥ //

/ khro gñer rim par ldan la sogs /
/ lag na rdo rje mtha' yas pa /
/ dpa' bo gdul dka' 'dul ba po /
/ 'jigs su ruṅ daṅ dpa' byad can //

[4] ullālayadbhiḥ svakaraiḥ
prasphuradvajrakoṭibhiḥ /
prajñopāyamahākaruṇājagadarthakaraiḥ
paraiḥ //

/ rdo rje rtse mo rab 'phro ba /
/ raṅ gi lag gis gsor byed pa /
/ sñiṅ rje che daṅ śes rab daṅ /
/ thabs kyis 'gro don byed pa'i mchog //

[5] hṛṣṭatuṣṭāśayair muditaiḥ
krodhavigraharūpibhiḥ /
buddhakṛtyakarair nāthaiḥ sārdhaṃ
praṇatavigrahaiḥ //

/ dga' mgu raṅs pa'i bsam pa can /
/ khro bo'i lus kyi gzugs ldan pa /
/ saṅs rgyas 'phrin las byed pa'i mgon /
/ lus btuṅ rnams daṅ lhan cig tu //

was along with (retinue) lords having ripples of furried brow, and so on, their thunderbolt-holding hands limitless; heroes who tame those hard to tame, their appearances heroic and fearful; whose hands brandish *vajras* with tips of intense radiation; uppermost in serving the aim of living beings through insight and through compassion as the means; with thrilled and satisfied expectations, and with sympathetic joy; and have fierce corporeal forms while performing the deeds of the Buddha, who were bowing their bodies.

"Retinue": Smṛti (33-5), according to the *Vajrapāṇyabhiṣeka-tantra*, Vajrapāṇi's retinue amounts to five hundred, and each of the five hundred has its own large retinue. "Appearance fearful": Narendrakīrti (61-2), they bare fangs (*mche ba gtsigs*), have compressed furried brows (*khro gñer bsdus pa*), round eyes (*spyan zlum pa*), ornaments of the burning ground (*dur khrod kyi rgyan*), and so on; and (61-3), cites the *Vajraśekhara-tantra* for what they carry in their hands: bejewelled *vajra* (*rdo rje phra mo*), wheel (*cakra*), sword (*ral gri*), and so on. "Thrilled expectations": Narendrakīrti (61-3 to -4), goes with compassion. "Satisfied expectations": Narendrakīrti (61-3 to -4), goes with insight. "Sympathetic joy": Narendrakīrti (61-3 to -4), engages the aims of living beings. "Deeds of the Buddha": Smṛti (34-1), deeds of the Saṃbhogakāya and of the Nirmāṇakāya.

[6] praṇamya nāthaṃ saṃbuddhaṃ bhagavan-
taṃ tathāgataṃ /
kṛtāñjalipuṭo bhūtvā idam āha sthito
'grataḥ //

/ mgon po bcom ldan de bźin gśegs /
/ rdsogs saṅs rgyas la phyag 'tshal te /
/ thal mo sbyar ba byas gyur nas /
/ spyan sṅar 'dug ste 'di skad gsol //

Bowing to the *nātha*, the Sambuddha, the Bhagavat, the Tathāgata; and having folded his hands in homage, and having seated himself in front, he (Vajrapāṇi) spoke as follows:

"Tathāgata": Smṛti (34-1, -2), this means one who has well engaged in "going," "comprehension," and "speech," to wit: going successively higher in stages (*bhūmi*) and path is the perfection of "going" and is the perfection of "elimination" (*spaṅs pa phun sum tshogs*). Knowing all the knowables of phenomenon (*ji sñed pa*) and noumenon (*ji lta ba*) is the perfection of "comprehension" (*rtogs pa phun sum tshogs*). Besides, teaching to others the goal that was comprehended (i.e. engaging in "speech") is the perfection of others' aim. "Bhagavan": Smṛti (34–2) has destroyed (*bhaga*) the four Māras, also has (*vān*) perfect merits.

[7] maddhitāya mamārthāya me 'nukampāya
he vibho/
māyājālābhisaṃbodher yathā lābhī bha-
vāmy ahaṃ//

/khyab bdag bdag la sman pa daṅ/
/bdag don bdag la thugs brtse'i phyir/
/sgyu 'phrul dra bas mṅon rdsogs pa'i/
/byaṅ chub ci nas bdag thob mdsod//

Pervading Lord! For my benefit, for my sake, for compassion to me—(pray tell) how I may obtain the manifest awakening from the net of illusion.

"Net of illusion": Smṛti (34-4 and -5), there are three kinds of "net of illusion"—causal, path, and fruitional. (1) The causal kind is an illusion of diverse appearance for what is actually nontwo knowledge. It is the hindrance by adventitious dirt. The net amounts to bonds and lacks sides (*pakṣa*). (2) The path kind is an illusion not free from some side (*pakṣa*). The net is the circle of fifty-three views. [However, "Brahmā's net," according to the Buddhist scripture *Brahmajāla*, has sixty-two subjects.] (3) The fruitional kind is an illusion not free from the mere appearance of five Bodies, five Wisdoms, five Buddhas, and so on.

[8] ajñānapaṅkamagnānāṃ
kleśavyākulacetasāṃ/
hitāya sarvasattvānām
anuttaraphalāptaye//

/ñon moṅs pas ni sems dkrugs śiṅ/
/mi śes 'dam du byiṅ ba yi/
/sems can kun la sman pa daṅ/
/bla med 'bras bu thob ya'i phyir//

So that all the sentient beings sunk in the bog of ignorance, their minds disturbed by defiled things, may obtain benefit and the incomparable fruit—

"Minds disturbed by defiled things": Smṛti (34-5), "defiled things" means the basic six *kleśa* [Cf. *Vijñaptimātratāsiddhi*, La Vallée Poussin, I, p. 256, citing *Abhidharmakośa* for these: lust (*rāga*), hostility (*pratigha*), pride (*māna*), nescience (*avidyā*), (false) views (*dṛṣṭi*), doubt (*vimati*).] They disturb the mind that is innate (*gñug ma*), not artificial (*ma bcos pa*). "Bog": Smṛti (34-5), of ignorance (*mi śes*) and nescience (*ma rig pa*).

[9] prakāśayatu saṃbuddho bhagavāṃ śāstā
jagadguruḥ/
mahāsamayatattvajña indriyāśayavit
paraḥ//

/rdsogs pa'i saṅs rgyas bcom ldan 'das/
/'gro ba'i bla ma ston pa po/
/dam tshig chen po de ñid mkhyen/
/dbaṅ po bsam pa mkhyen mchog gi//

May the Sambuddha, the Bhagavat, Teacher, Guru of the world, who best knows the great pledge and the reality, who best knows the faculty and the aspiration, tell it!

"Pledge": Smṛti (35-1), the *bodhicittavajra* (Diamond of the Mind of Enlightenment). "Knows reality": Smṛti (35-1), knows the Diamond of Voidness (*śūnyatāvajra*) or knows the diverse true natures (*dharmatā*) in diverse *dharma*-holders (*dharmin*). "Faculty": Smṛti (35-1), of candidates, whether superior, middling, or inferior.

[10] bhagavaṃ jñānakāyasya mahoṣṇīṣasya
gīṣpateḥ /
mañjuśrījñānasattvasya jñānamūrteḥ
svayaṃbhuvaḥ //

/ bcom ldan 'das kyi ye śes sku /
/ gtsug tor chen po tshig gi bdag /
/ ye śes sku ste raṅ byuṅ ba /
/ 'jam dpal ye śes sems dpa' yi //

O Bhagavat, you have self-originated the gnosis-body, the great *uṣṇīṣa*, the master of speech, the gnosis-embodiment of Mañju-śrī the knowldge being.

"Mañjuśrī": Smṛti (33-3), *mañju* ("smooth"), because free from the hard, rough afflictions of defilement; *śrī* ("glory"), because of the arising of all the excellent merits. [Hence the name stands for the double process which is the life of the Buddhist path, of rejecting the bad and accepting good; almost equivalent to the title Bhagavān, cf. above, under *gāthā* no. 6.] There are three kinds of Mañjuśrī: (1) Mañjuśrī of the self-existence cause, attended with all bonds; (2) Mañjuśrī of the cultivation-path, not free from some side (*pakṣa*); (3) Mañjuśrī of the final result, free from extremes. Smṛti (35-2), according to "śrāvaka theory-systems" Mañjuśrī is a youth, aged eight or sixteen, in the family of the āryas; according to general Mahāyāna, he is a *bodhisattva* of the Tenth Stage; according to the special theory of this Mahāyāna tradition, he has represented Buddhahood for uncountable ages. "Great uṣṇīṣa": Smṛti (35-3), the *uṣṇīṣa* of the Tathāgata, because it is Ratnasambhava, head ornament of the five [Progenitor] families. "Self-originated": Smṛti (35-3), in the Dharmadhātu, free from all defiled *dharmas* of *saṃsāra*, as only a Buddha can. "Gnosis-body": Smṛti (35-3), which functions for the aim of others. "Knowledge-being": Smṛti (35-3), in the absolute sense, the heart (*citta*) of all the Tathāgatas that is the unborn gnosis; in the conventional sense, the knowledge beings that are the masters in the seven *maṇḍalas* and have means of ARAPACANA, etc.

[11] gambhīrārthām udārārthāṃ mahārthām
asamāṃ śivāṃ /
ādimadhyāntakalyāṇīṃ nāmasaṃgītim
uttamāṃ //

/ mtshan ni yaṅ dag brjod pa'i mchog /
/ doṇ zab don ni rgya che źin /
/ don chen mtshuṅs med rab źi ba /
/ thog ma bar daṅ mthar dge ba //

(Pray tell) the supreme rehearsal of names (*nāmasaṃgīti*) which has profound meaning and broad meaning, the incomparable great meaning, which is benevolent; which is good in the beginning, the middle, and the end;

"Profound": Smṛti (35-3 to -4), by voidness or by being incomparable; and which is good in the beginning, etc. "Broad": Smṛti (35-3 to -4), by way of seven *maṇḍalas* in a *samvṛti* sense, and which causes the stilling of defilement. "Good": Smṛti (35-4), good in the beginning, is enthusiastic with hearing; good in the middle, is happy with pondering; good in the end, has obtained the cathartic (*praśrabdhi*) with cultivation. [Hence, these are Mañjuśrī's three kinds of insight, *prajñā*, those consisting of hearing, of pondering, and of cultivation.]

[12] yātītair bhāṣitā buddhair bhāṣiṣyante hy
anāgatāḥ /
pratyutpannāś ca saṃbuddhā yāṃ bhā-
ṣante punaḥ punaḥ //

/ 'das pa'i saṅs rgyas rnams kyis gsuṅs /
/ ma 'oṅs rnams kyaṅ gsuṅ 'gyur la /
/ da ltar byuṅ ba'i rdsogs saṅs rgyas /
/ yaṅ daṅ yaṅ du gsuṅ ba gaṅ //

which was told by the former Buddhas, will be told by the future Buddhas, and which is told again and again by present Buddhas;

"Told": Smṛti (35-4), by former Buddhas, like Dīpaṃkara; will be told by future Buddhas, like Maitreya; and told repeatedly by present Buddhas, i.e., Śākyamuni, and by the Buddhas of Sukhāvatī and Padmāvatī.

[13] māyājālamahātantre yā cāsmiṃ saṃpragīyate / mahāvajradharaiḥ hṛṣṭair ameyair mantradhāribhiḥ //	/ rgyud chen sgyu 'phrul dra ba las / / rdo rje 'chaṅ chen gsaṅ sṅags 'chaṅ / / dpag med rnams kyis dgyes pa yis / / rab gsuṅs gaṅ lags bśad du gsol //	which is proclaimed in the *Māyājālamahātantra* by the uncountable ecstatic *mahāvajradharas*, retainers of the *mantras*.

"*Māyājālamahātantra*": Narendrakīrti (62-1-7) refers to the *Gīti* Chapter (*glu'i le'u*) of the *Māyājāla*. [The *Māyājālatantra* has two commentaries in the Yogatantra section of the Tanjur, one of them by Ānandagarbha. The basic tantra, translated by Rin-chen bzaṅ-po, is, however, included in the Anuttarayogatantra section of the Kanjur at the end of Vajrapāṇi tantras of this class; and *The Tibetan Tripitaka, Peking Edition*, Catalogue & Index (Tokyo, 1962), pp. 17-18, details the chapters of this Tantra with no inclusion of a "*Gīti* Chapter." Narendrakīrti's text, here given as *glu'i* could be read *klu'i* (*Nāga*); however, the *Nāma-saṃgīti* commentary by Avadhūtī-pa (that immediately follows the Candrabhadrakīrti *vṛtti*), mentions at p. 15-2-4, "*sgyu 'phrul glu yi le'u 'dis*" (by this *Gīti* chapter of the *Māyājāla*), which suggests that the *Mañjuśrī-nāma-saṃgīti* was itself regarded in some quarters as the *Gīti* chapter.]

(14) ahaṃ caināṃ dhārayiṣyāmy āniryāṇād dṛdhāśayaḥ / yathā bhavāmy ahaṃ nātha sarvasaṃbuddhaguhyadhṛk //	/ mgon po rdsogs saṅs rgyas kun gyi / / gsaṅ 'dsin ci nas bdag 'gyur phyir / / ṅes par 'byuṅ gi bar du 'di / / bdag gis bsam pa brtan pos gzuṅ //	O *nātha*, so that I may be a retainer of the secrets of all the Sambuddhas, may I retain this (= *Saṃgīti*) with steadfast aspiration up to (my) release.

"Retainer": Candrabhadrakīrti (4-1-5), because he seeks to explain it to the sentient beings.

(15) prakāśayiṣye sattvānāṃ yathāśayaviśeṣataḥ / aśeṣakleśanāśāya aśeṣājñānahānaye //	/ ñon moṅs ma lus bsal ba daṅ / / mi śes ma lus spaṅ ba'i phyir / / sems can rnams kyi bsam pa yi / / khyad par ji bźin rab bśad bgyi //	To dispel every bit of defilement, to eliminate every bit of ignorance, may I explain in accordance with the particular aspiration of sentient beings.

"Particular aspiration": Candrabhadrakīrti (4-1-6), to some the Pāramitā-Vehicle and to others the Outer, Inner, or Secret Vehicles.

(16) evam adhyeṣya guhyendro vajrapāṇis tathāgataṃ/ kṛtāñjalipuṭo bhūtvā prahvakāyasthito 'grataḥ//	/gsaṅ dbaṅ lag na rdo rje yis/ /de bźin gśegs la de skad du/ /gsol btab thal mo sbyar byas te/ /lus btud nas ni spyan sṅar 'dug//	Thus Guhyendra Vajrapāṇi expressed to the Tathāgata, while joining his palms in homage, bowing his body and staying in front.

"Bowing his body and staying in front": Candrabhadrakīrti (4-1-8), this shows he will get a response.

//adhyeṣaṇāgāthāḥ ṣoḍaśa//	/gsol ba 'debs pa'i tshigs su bcad pa bcu drug go/	Sixteen *gāthā* on Asking for Instruction.

CHAPTER II. THE REPLY

[1] atha śākyamunir bhagavāṃ saṃbuddho dvipadottamaḥ/ nirṇamayāyatāṃ sphītāṃ svajihvāṃ svamukhāc chubhāṃ//	/de nas bcom ldan śākya thub/ /rdsogs pa'i saṅs rgyas rkaṅ gñis mchog/ /ñid kyi źal nas ljags bzaṅ ba/ /riṅ źiṅ yaṅs pa brkyaṅ mdsad de//	Now Śākyamuni, Bhagavat, Sambuddha, best of the two-footed, extended from his mouth a fine tongue that was long and wide,

"Tongue that was long and wide": Candrabhadrakīrti (4-2-2), filling the three worlds, of desire, form, and formless.

[2] smitaṃ saṃdarśya lokānām apāyatrayaśodhanaṃ/ trailokyābhāsakaraṇaṃ caturmārāriśāsanaṃ//	/'jig rten gsum po snaṅ byed ciṅ/ /bdud bźi dgra rnams 'dul byed pa/ /sems can rnams kyi ṅan soṅ gsum/ /sbyoṅ bar byed pa'i 'dsum bstan nas//	Showing a smiling purification of the three bad destinies of worldlings and an illumination of the three realms that tames the four enemy Māras,

"Purification of the three bad destinies": [this is the topic of an Explanatory Tantra of the Yogatantra *Tattvasaṃgraha* called *Sarvadurgatipariśodhana*]. "Illumination of the three realms that tames": [this is the topic of an Explanatory Tantra of the *Tattvasaṃgraha*, 2d Section, called *Trailokyavijaya*].

[3] trilokam āpūrayantyā brahmyā madhurayā girā/ pratyabhāṣata guhyendraṃ vajrapāṇiṃ mahābalaṃ//	/tshaṅs pa'i gsuṅ ni snaṅ ba yis/ /'jig rten gsum po kun bkaṅ ste/ /lag na rdo rje stobs po che/ /gsaṅ dbaṅ la ni slar gsuṅs pa//	With sweet *brahmā* sounds filling the three realms, replied to Guhyendra Vajrapāṇi, of great strength.

"*Brahmā* sounds": [the commentaries agree that this means the sixty speech elegancies of the Buddha's voice].

[4] sādhu vajradhara śrīmāṃ sādhu te vajrapāṇaye / yas tvaṃ jagaddhitārthāya mahākaruṇayānvitaḥ // [5] mahārthaṃ nāmasaṃgītiṃ pavitrām aghanāśanīṃ / mañjuśrījñānakāyasya mataḥ śrotuṃ samudyataḥ //	/ sñiṅ rje che daṅ ldan gyur pas / / 'gro la phan pa'i don du khyod / / ye śes lus can 'jam dpal gyi / / miṅ brjod pa ni don che ba // / dag par byed ciṅ sdig sel ba / / ṅa las mñan par brtson pa ni / / legs so dpal ldan rdo rje 'chaṅ / / lag na rdo rje khyod legs so //	"Very well, śrīmat Vajradhara; to you, Vajrapāṇi, very well! Since you are possessed of great compassion for the sake of the world, attend to hearing from me the name-rehearsal of Mañjuśrī the knowledge-body; which is of great purpose, that purifying, eliminates sin.

"Name rehearsal": Narendrakīrti (67-3-4), will be taught by way of the sacredness (or, solemnity) of the names (*miṅ dam tshig gi sgo nas bstan par bya ste*). "Of great purpose": Narendrakīrti (67-3-5), teaches the knowledge body by way of the sacredness of the names (*miṅ dam tshig gi sgo nas ye śes kyi sku ston par byed pa ste*). "Purifying, eliminates sin": Smṛti (36-3), it purifies the obscuration of defilement (*kleśa*) by the broad way (*rgya che ba'i sgo*) of contemplating the *maṇḍala* of the gods and eliminates the obscuration of the knowable (*jñeya*) by the profound (*zab pa*).

[6] tat sādhu deśayāmy eṣa ahaṃ te guhyakādhipaḥ / śṛṇu tvam ekāgramanās tat sādhu bhagavann iti //	/ gsaṅ ba'i bdag po de phyir ṅas / / khyod la legs par bstan par bya / / khyod ni rtse gcig yid kyis ñon / / bcom ldan de ni legs śes gsol //	Therefore, I shall well reveal it to you, Guhyakādhipa. Listen with one-pointed mind!" "That is fine, Bhagavat," [he responded].

"You": Narendrakīrti (67-4-3), the compiler (*sdud pa po*).

// prativacanagāthāḥ ṣaṭ //	/ lan gyi gsuṅ tshigs su bcad pa drug go /	Six *gāthā* on The Reply.

CHAPTER III. SURVEYING THE SIX FAMILIES

[1] atha śākyamunir bhagavāṃ sakalaṃ mantrakulaṃ mahat/
mantravidyādharakulaṃ vyavalokya kulatrayaṃ//
[2] lokalokottarakulaṃ lokālokakulaṃ mahat/
mahāmudrākulaṃ cāyaṃ mahoṣṇīṣakulaṃ mahat//

/de nas bcom ldan śākya thub/
/gsaṅ sṅags rigs chen thams cad daṅ/
/gsaṅ sṅags rig sṅags 'chaṅ ba'i rigs/
/rigs gsum la ni rnam par gzigs//
/'jig rten 'jig rten 'das pa'i rigs/
/'jig rten snaṅ byed rigs chen daṅ/
/phyag rgya chen po'i rigs mchog daṅ/
/rigs chen gtsug tor cher gzigs nas//

Now Śākyamuni, the Bhagavat, surveyed the entire great family of Mantra: (1) the family that retains the *mantra* and *vidyā*, (2) the triple family, (3) the mundane and the supramundane family, (4) the great family that illuminates the world, (5) the great *mahāmudrā* family, and (6) the great family of the *mahauṣṇīṣa*.

"The entire great family of Mantra": Candrabhadrakīrti (4-3), it means all six, namely, (1) the family that retains the *mantra* and *vidyā* is the Vajrasattva-family, (2) the triple family is the Vairocana family (Body, Speech, and Mind), (3) the mundane and the supramundane family is the Amitābha family, (4) the great family that illuminates the world is the Akṣobhya family, (5) the great *mahāmudrā* family is the Amoghasiddhi family, and (6) the great family of the *mahauṣṇīṣa* is the Ratnasambhava family. Smṛti (36-3), following Līlavajra, namely, (1) Karma Family, (2) Tathāgata Family, (3) Padma Family, (4) Vajra Family, (5) Bodhicittavajra Family, (6) Ratna Family. [In fact, these names agree with Candrabhadrakīrti's identifications.]

//ṣaṭkulāvalokanagāthe dve//

/rigs drug la gzigs pa'i tshigs su bcad pa gñis so//

Two *gāthā* on Surveying the Six Families.

CHAPTER IV. ABHISAMBODHI SEQUENCE OF THE *NET OF ILLUSION*

[1] imāṃ ṣaḍmantrarājanasaṃyuktām
advayodayāṃ/
anutpādadharminīṃ gāthāṃ bhāṣate sma
girāṃ pateḥ//

/tshig gi bdag pos tshigs su bcad/
/gsaṅ sṅags rgyal po drug ldan źiṅ/
/gñis su med par 'byuṅ ba daṅ/
/mi skye chos can 'di gsuṅs pa//

And proclaimed the *gāthā* whose nature is nonproduction and occurs nontwo, accompanied by the six Mantra Kings, belonging to the Master of Speech.

"Six Mantra Kings": Smṛti (37-2), the six named in *gāthā* (3), Vajratīkṣṇa to Arapacana. Candrabhadrakīrti (15-1), these knowledge beings (*jñānasattva*) are the six *ādibuddhas*.

[2] A Ā I Ī U Ū E AI O AU AṂ AḤ: sthito hṛdi/
jñānamūrtir ahaṃ buddho buddhānāṃ
tryadhvavartināṃ//

/A Ā I Ī U Ū E AI O AU AṂ AḤ:
sñiṅ la gnas/
/ye śes sku bdag saṅs rgyas te/
/saṅs rgyas dus gsum bźugs rnams kyi'o//

A Ā I Ī U Ū E AI O AU AṂ AḤ: Stationed in the heart of the Buddhas abiding in the three times, am I (*aham*) the Buddha, gnosis embodiment.

The twelve vowels: Smṛti (37-2 and -3), defends the theory of the ācārya Līlavajra that the twelve stand for the twelve *bhūmis*, ten of the Bodhisattva and two more that are Buddha and Complete Buddha stages. For this purpose, the Bodhisattva's Adhimukticaryā is counted as the first stage; then comes the standard ten, Pramuditā to Dharmameghā, with a stage called Samantaprabhā as the number twelve. Smṛti (37-2-8 to 37-3-1), gives a number of synonyms of the twelfth stage, all having a word "light" (*prabhā*) as last member of compound. [Supporting this is the *Niṣpannayogāvalī*—Abhayākaragupta's text of *maṇḍalas*—which in the Dharmadhātu-Vāgīśvara-maṇḍala (No. 21 in the text) has the list of twelve *bhūmis*, but also has a list of twelve *pāramitā*-s, twelve *vaśitā*-s, and twelve *dhāriṇī*-s. Each of these is a list of twelve goddesses, that can feasibly go with the twelve vowels. The twelve-stage interpretation agrees with the temporal triad, "good in the beginning, the middle, and the end."] "Stationed in the heart": Smṛti (38–1), the six knowledge beings are each stationed in the heart of their respective family progenitor.

[3] OṂ vajratīkṣṇaduḥkhacchedaprajñājñāna-
mūrtaye/
jñānakāyavāgīśvara arapacanāya te
namaḥ//

/OṂ rdo rje rnon po sdug bsṅal gcod/
/śes rab ye śes sku can te/
/ye śes sku can gsuṅ dbaṅ phyug//
/'gro ba smin byed khyod la 'dud//

OṂ. Homage to Thee, Vajratīkṣṇa (Diamond Sharp), Duḥkhaccheda (Cutting Off of Suffering), Prajñājñānamūrti (Embodiment of Insight-Wisdom), Jñānakāya (Knowledge Body), Vāgīśvara (Lord of Speech), Arapacana (Five-syllabled Mañjuśr

"Homage to Thee": Smṛti (38-1), Vajratīkṣṇa in the Padma Family in the heart of Amitābha; Duḥkhaccheda in the Vajra Family in the heart of Akṣobhya; Prajñājñānamūrti belongs to the Tathāgata Family; Jñānakāya belongs to the Karma Family; Vāgīśvara belongs to the Ratna Family; Arapacana belongs to the Bodhicittavajra Family.

Not necessarily consistent with the above, but worthy of citing here is a passage from the Tibetan work by 'Jam-mgon Kong-sprul Blo-gros-mtha'-yas, entitled *Rgyud thams cad kyi bdag po 'jam dpal mtshan brjod rigs bsdus kyi sgrub thabs ye śes 'bar ba'i ral gri*, in *Rgyud sde kun btus*, Vol. X (Delhi, 1971), Arabic no. 456 of folio side (f. 11b-3), among the six spokes, on the eastern spoke, OṂ. Homage to Thee Duḥkhaccheda, blue (*sṅon po*). On the southern spoke, OṂ. Homage to Thee Vāgīśvara, yellow (*ser po*). On the western spoke, OṂ. Homage to Thee Vajratīkṣṇa, red (*dmar po*). On the northern spoke, OṂ. Homage to Thee Jñānakāya, green (*ljaṅ gu*). On the eastern "upper" (*stod*) spoke, OṂ. Homage to Thee Prajñājñānamūrti, white (*dkar po*). On the eastern "lower" (*smad*) spoke, OṂ. Homage to Thee Arapacana, white (*dkar po*). [By "upper" and "lower" I understand two by the eastern spoke, one more toward the North ("upper") and one more toward the South ("lower").]

//māyājālābhisaṃbodhikramagāthās tisraḥ//

/sgyu 'phrul dra bas mṅon par rdsogs par byed par byaṅ chub pa'i rim pa tshigs bcad gsum mo/

Three *gāthā* on the *Abhisaṃbodhi* sequence of the *Net of Illusion*.

CHAPTER V. THE GREAT MAṆḌALA OF VAJRADHĀTU

[1] tad yathā bhagavāṃ buddhaḥ saṃbuddho
'kārasaṃbhavaḥ/
akāraḥ sarvavarṇāgryo mahārthaḥ
paramākṣaraḥ//

/'di ltar saṅs rgyas bcom ldan 'das/
/rdsogs pa'i saṅs rgyas a las byuṅ/
/a ni yig 'bru kun gyi mchog/
/don chen yi ge dam pa yin//

Accordingly, is the Buddha, Bhagavat, the Sambuddha arisen from A. A is the best of letters, of great purpose, the supreme syllable.

"Arisen from A": [in Chapter IV, A is the first of the twelve stages. "Accordingly," all those in higher stages and in the Buddha stage can be said to have "arisen from A."] "A is the best of letters": Smṛti (38-3), it is the inner life of all the vowels and consonants. "Of great purpose": Smṛti (38-3), understood in a lesser way, one is a disciple (*śrāvaka*); in a middling way, one is a Bodhisattva; in the great way, one is a Buddha.

[2] mahāprāṇo hy anutpādo
vāgudāhāravarjitaḥ/
sarvābhilāpahetvagryaḥ
sarvavāksuprabhāsvaraḥ//

/srog chen po ste skye ba med/
/tshig tu brjod pa spaṅs pa ste/
/brjod pa kun gyi rgyu yi mchog/
/tshig kun rab tu gsal bar byed//

The great inhalation is not a production, free from utterance by speech, chief cause of all speech, the clarification of all words.

"The great inhalation is not a production": Narendrakīrti (69-1-1), "not a production" because occurring without dependence on causes and conditions. [Now deities of the Vajradhātu-maṇḍala]: I. Not a Production (*anutpāda*): Smṛti (38-4), "Mañjuśrī, you are Not a Production," the goddess Sattvavajrī, the letter A, the cause of the mirrorlike wisdom (*ādarśa-jñāna*), voidness gate (*śūnyatā-[vimokṣa]-mukha*). II. Free from Utterance by Speech (*vāgudāhāravarjita*): Smṛti (38-4), "Mañjuśrī, you are Free from Utterance by Speech," the goddess Ratnavajrī, the letter Ā, the comprehension of the sameness wisdom (*samatā-jñāna*), signless gate (*ānimitta-[vimokṣa]-mukha*). III. Chief Cause of All Speech (*sarvābhilāpahetvadhya*): Smṛti (38-4), "Mañjuśrī, you are the Chief Cause of All Speech," the goddess Dharmavajrī, the letter AṂ, the condition for expressing the discriminative wisdom (*pratyavekṣaṇā-jñāna*), wishless gate (*apraṇihita-[vimokṣa]-mukha*). IV. Clarification of All Words (*sarvavāksuprabhāsvara*): Smṛti (38-4 and -5), "Mañjuśrī, you are the Clarification of All Words," the goddess Karmavajrī, the letter AḤ, clarifying the procedure-of-duty wisdom (*kṛtyānuṣṭhāna-jñāna*), noninstigation gate (*anabhisaṃskāra-[vimokṣa]-mukha*) (among four gates to liberation). [In the following, the commentarial "Mañjuśrī, you are ..." is omitted, but should be understood in each case.]

[3] mahāmahamahārāgaḥ
sarvasattvaratiṃkāraḥ/
mahāmahamahādveṣaḥ
sarvakleśamahāripuḥ//

/mchod pa chen po 'dod chags che/
/sems can thams dga' bar byed/
/mchod pa chen po źe sdaṅ che/
/ñon moṅs kun gyi dgra che ba//

Great offering, great love, gratifying all sentient beings. Great offering, great hatred, great enemy of all defilement.

V. Great Offering (*mahā-āmaha*), Great Love (*mahārāga*): Smṛti (39-4), Great Love is the Buddha Amitābha; Great Offering as Mañjuśrī is the offering of Amitābha's discriminative wisdom. VI. Great Offering, Great Hatred (*mahādveṣa*): Smṛti (39-5), Great Hatred is the Buddha Akṣobhya; Great Offering is the offering of Akṣobhya's mirrorlike wisdom.

[4] mahāmahamahāmoho mūḍhadhīmohasūdanaḥ/ mahāmahamahākrodho mahākrodharipur mahān//	/mchod pa chen po gti mug che/ /gti mug blo ste gti mug sel/ /mchod pa chen po khro ba che/ /khro ba chen po dgra che ba//	Great offering, great delusion, driving away the delusion of deluded minds. Great offering, great fury, great enemy of great fury.

VII. Great Delusion (*mahāmoha*): Smṛti (39-5), the Buddha Vairocana; Great Offering is the offering of Vairocana's Dharmadhātu wisdom (the topic of Chapter VI). VIII. Great Fury (*mahākrodha*): Smṛti (39-5), the Buddha Amoghasiddhi; Great Offering is the offering of Amoghasiddhi's procedure-of-duty wisdom.

[5] mahāmahamahālobhaḥ sarvalobhanisūdanaḥ/ mahākāmo mahāsaukhyo mahāmodo mahāratiḥ//	/mchod pa chen po chags pa che/ /chags pa thams cad sel bar byed/ /'dod pa chen po bde ba che/ /dga' ba chen po mgu ba che//	Great offering, great clinging, driving away all clinging. Great desire, great pleasure, great delight, great joy.

IX. Great Clinging (*mahālobha*): Smṛti (59-5), the Buddha Ratnasambhava; Great Offering is the offering of Ratnasambhava's sameness wisdom. X. Great Desire (*mahākāma*): Smṛti (40-2), Vajrasattva (Diamond Being), inner void (*adhyātma-śūnyatā*), because Vajrasattva is the comprehension of voidness, for generating the mind of enlightenment (*bodhicitta*) with Great Desire, i.e., longing, for the characteristics of a Buddha, and to serve the aim of others. XI. Great Pleasure (*mahāsaukhya*): Smṛti (40-3), Vajrarāja (Diamond King), outer void (*bahirdhā-ś.*), because he does not release his "hook" while there is Great Pleasure that is nonfluxional (*anāsrava*). XII. Great Delight (*mahāmoda*): Smṛti (40-3), Vajrarāga (Diamond Passion), inner and outer void (*adhyātmabahirdhā-ś.*), because of repeatedly considering the preceding (two). XIII. Great Joy (*mahārati*): Smṛti (40-3), Vajrasādhu (Diamond Excellence), great void (*mahā-ś.*), while experiencing the result, like the snap of fingers. So the four *sattvas* in Akṣobhya's family in the East.

[6] mahārūpo mahākāyo mahāvarṇo mahāvapuḥ/ mahānāmā mahodāro mahāvipulamaṇḍalaḥ//	/gzugs che lus kyaṅ che ba ste/ /kha dog che źiṅ lus boṅs che/ /miṅ yaṅ che źiṅ rgya che ba/ /dkyil 'khor chen po yaṅs pa yin//	Great form, great body. Great color, great complexion. Great and far-extended name. Great and wide *maṇḍala*.

XIV. Great Form, Great Body (*mahārūpa, mahākāya*): Smṛti (40-3), Vajraratna (Diamond Jewel), voidness of voidness (*śūnyatā-ś.*), because it shines in all the Buddha fields, and because it multiplies out of jewels. XV. Great Color, Great Complexion (*mahāvarṇa, mahāvapus*): Smṛti (40-4), Vajratejas (Diamond Shining), absolute void (*paramārtha-ś.*), because the own-presence (*svabhāva*) of the six colors of sunlight and because an insight (*prajñā*) body. XVI. Great and Far-extended Name (*mahānāman, mahodāra*): Smṛti (40-4), Vajraketu (Diamond Banner), voidness of the constructed (*saṃskṛta-ś.*), because of great fame in all the directions and because coming from an ultimate gift. XVII. Great and Wide Maṇḍala (*mahāvipulamaṇḍala*): Smṛti (40-4), Vajrahāsa (Diamond Laughter), voidness of the unconstructed (*asaṃskṛta-ś.*), because it embraces (*-la*) an inner content (*maṇḍa-*), and because it pervades the whole world. So the four *sattvas* in Ratnasambhava's family in the South.

[7] mahāprajñāyudhadharo mahākleśāṅkuśo 'graṇīḥ/ mahāyaśā mahākīrtir mahājyotir mahādyutiḥ//	/śes rab mtshon chen 'chaṅ ba ste/ /ñon moṅs lcags kyu che ba'i mchog/ /grags chen sñan grags chen po ste/ /snaṅ ba chen po gsal ba che//	Wielding the great sword of insight. The foremost great hook of defilement. Great renown, great fame. Great light, great shining.

XVIII. Wielding the Great Sword of Insight (*mahāprajñāyudhadhara*): Smṛti (40-5), Vajradharma (Diamond Nature), transcendent voidness (*atyanta-ś.*), because holding the sword of insight is discriminative wisdom and because thunderbolt-holding makes understood the true nature (*dharmatā*). XIX. Foremost Great Hook of Defilement (*mahākleśāṅkuśa, agraṇī*): Smṛti (40-5), Vajratīkṣṇa (Diamond Sharp), voidness of what is without beginning or end (*an-avarāgra-ś.*), is here the hook of (i.e., belonging to) insight-wisdom (*prajñā-jñāna*) which knows the true nature of defilement through change of place, elimination, and cognition (of it), so it is what knows the place. XX. Great Renown, Great Fame (*mahāyaśas, mahākīrti*): Smṛti (40-5), Vajracakra (Diamond Wheel) [in other lists, Vajrahetu, Diamond Motive], voidness of the undeniable (*an-avakāra-ś.*), because it is the Wheel of the Dharma which does not reverse itself from maturing the sentient beings and because it is all-pervasive by turning the wheel(s) of the seven kinds of *maṇḍala*. XXI. Great Light, Great Shining (*mahājyotis, mahādyuti*): Smṛti (41-1), Vajrabhāṣa (Diamond Speech), voidness of ultimate substance (*prakṛti-ś.*), because having the Dharmadhātu's light that pervades the three realms and illuminates the streams of consciousness of sentient beings and because free from "dark" speech such as double-talk and incoherent words. So the four *sattvas* in Amitābha's family in the West.

[8] mahāmāyādharo vidvān mahāmāyārthasādhakaḥ/ mahāmāyāratirato mahāmāyendrajālikaḥ//	/mkhas pa sgyu 'phrul chen po 'chaṅ/ /sgyu 'phrul chen po'i don sgrub pa/ /sgyu 'phrul chen po dga' bas dga'/ /sgyu 'phrul chen po mig 'phrul can//	Wise one, holding the great illusion. Performing the aim of great illusion. Pleased with the pleasure of great illusion. Using the hallucination of great illusion.

XXII. Wise One, Holding the Great Illusion (*mahāmāyādhara, vidvan*): Smṛti (41-2), Vajrakarma (Diamond Action), voidness of inherent character (*svalakṣaṇa-ś.*), because wise in the diamond action, the wondrous Buddha offering that generates the merits of sentient beings, and because (Mañjuśrī) holds the illusion of magical manifestations (*nirmita*). XXIII. Performing the Aim of Great Illusion (*mahāmāyārthasādhaka*): Smṛti (41-2), Vajrarakṣa (Diamond Protection), voidness of all *dharmas* (*sarvadharma-ś.*), because he protects while performing offerings and protects with the mirror of the yoga-path, and because he performs the aim of others by the "net of illusion." XXIV. Pleased with the Pleasure of Great Illusion (*mahāmāyāratirata*): Smṛti (41-2), Vajrayakṣa (Diamond Harm-bringer), voidness of absence (*abhāva-ś.*); since the Vajrayakṣa is the secret enemy (Tib. read: *dgra gab*) Mañjuśrī is pleased to pacify the hindering demons by way of an illusion, because he himself has the wondrous action of protection. XXV. Using the Hallucination of Great Illusion (*mahāmāyendrajālika*): Smṛti (41-2), Vajrasandhi (Diamond Fist), voidness of absent self-existence (*abhāvasvabhāva-ś.*), since Mañjuśrī can compress everything into a single taste, as a diamond fist, thus creating the hallucination of something persisting. So the four *sattvas* in Amoghasiddhi's family in the North.

[9] mahādānapatiḥ śreṣṭho mahāśīladharo 'graṇīḥ/ mahākṣāntidharo dhīro mahāvīryaparākramaḥ//	/sbyin bdag chen po gtso bo ste/ /tshul khrims chen po 'chaṅ ba'i mchog/ /bzod chen 'chaṅ ba brtan pa po/ /brtson 'grus chen po brtul ba yin//	Best as a great patron. Foremost bearer of great morality. Steadfast as a bearer of great forbearance. Enterprise of great striving.

XXVI. Best as a Great Patron (*mahādānapati, śreṣṭha*): Smṛti (41-4), Lāsyā (She, the Female Dance), who donates to the Buddha with faith and donates to the sentient beings with generosity (*thugs rje*). XXVII. Foremost Bearer of Great Morality (*mahāśīladhara, agraṇī*): Smṛti (41-4), Mālā (She, the Garland), of the three kinds of morality, keeps the vows of body, speech, and mind. XXVIII. Steadfast as a Bearer of Great Forbearance (*mahākṣāntidhara, dhīra*): Smṛti (41-5), Gītā (She, the Song), of the three kinds of forbearance, forbears, bears up with the profound meaning. XXIX. Enterprise of Great Striving (*mahāvīryaparākrama*): Smṛti (41-5), Nṛtyā (She, the Actress), enthusiastically promoting the root of supramundane virtue. So the four secret goddesses (= the first four *pāramitā*, i.e., *dāna*, *śīla*, *kṣānti*, *vīrya*).

[10] mahādhyānasamādhistho mahāprajñāśarīradhṛk/ mahābalo mahopāyaḥ praṇidhijñānasāgaraḥ//	/bsam gtan chen po tiṅ 'dsin gnas/ /śes rab chen po lus 'chaṅ ba/ /stobs po che la thabs che ba/ /smon lam ye śes rgya mtsho ste//	Dwelling in a *samādhi* of great meditation. Bearing the body of great insight. Great power, great means. Aspiration and knowledge ocean.

XXX. Dwelling in a Samādhi of Great Meditation (*mahādhyānasamādhistha*): Smṛti (42-1), Vajrapuṣpā (She, the Diamond Flower), dwells in the supramundane meditation without any straying. XXXI. Bearing the Body of Great Insight (*mahāprajñāśarīradhṛk*): Smṛti (42-1), Vajradhūpā (She, the Diamond Incense), bearing the body of all the *dharmas* supernally analyzed by insight. XXXII. Great Power, Great Means (*mahābala, mahopāya*): Smṛti (42-1), Vajrālokā (She, the Diamond Lamp), because her means are not weak, and because she has all the necessary means for fulfilling the expectations of sentient beings. XXXIII. Aspiration and Knowledge Ocean (*praṇidhijñānasāgara*): Smṛti (42-1), Vajragandhā (She, the Diamond Perfumed Water), because opposing all bad wishes by her right aspiration [comment only on "aspiration"]. Candrabhadrakīrti (6-1-5), Vajragandhā stands for "aspiration perfection" and "knowledge perfection." So the four offering goddesses (= the last six *pāramitā*, i.e., *dhyāna*, *prajñā*, *bala*, *upāya*, *praṇidhāna*, and *jñāna*).

[Note that of the thirty-seven deities of the Vajradhātu-maṇḍala, the *Mañjuśrī-nāma-saṃgīti* has no verse for the four gatekeepers, which are Vajrāṅkuśa (Diamond Hook), Vajrapāśa (Diamond Noose), Vajrasphoṭa (Diamond Chain), and Vajrāveśa (Diamond Bell), with the implication that Mañjuśrī is not identified with these. The *Saṃgīti* goes on to the 16 Bodhisattvas. The list of 16 upon which Smṛti and Candrabhadrakīrti agree is exactly that found in the *Mañjuvajra-maṇḍala*, No. 20, *Niṣpannayogāvalī*, as well as in the *Māyājāla-mahātantrarāja* (*Sde-dge Mtshal par Bka'-'gyur*, Vol. 83, Ja, 97b-3, 4, 5), but which differs from the list in *Vajradhātu-maṇḍala*, No. 19, *Niṣpannayogāvalī*, which mentions are the Tantra *Vajrapañjarā* as the source. The preceding thirty-three identifications plus the subsequent 16 amount to 49, which Candrabhadrakīrti (at 5-2-5) calls Supreme Horse Maṇḍala (*paramāśva-maṇḍala*).]

[11] mahāmaitrīmayo 'meyo mahākāruṇiko
'gradhīḥ/
mahāprajño mahādhīmāṃ mahopāyo
mahākṛtiḥ//

/byams chen raṅ bźin dpag tu med/
/sñiṅ rje chen po blo yi mchog/
/śes rab chen po blo chen ldan/
/mkhas pa chen po thabs che ba//

Made of intense love immeasurable. Best mind of great compassion. Of great insight and lofty intellect. Great means, great deed.

XXXIV. Made of Intense Love Immeasurable (*mahāmaitrīmaya, ameya*): Smṛti (42-3), Maitreya, who treats all sentient beings as though he were their mother, and no matter how numerous those beings he treats them as though they were an only child. XXXV. Best Mind of Great Compassion (*mahākāruṇika, agradhī*): Smṛti (42-3), Mañjuśrī, performing the aim of sentient beings with great compassion impartially, with best mind that is nontwo. XXXVI. Of Great Insight and Lofty Intellect (*mahāprajña, mahādhīmant*): Smṛti (42-3 to -4), Gandhahasti (Perfume Elephant), whose insight supernally analyzes all the *dharmas*. Candrabhadrakīrti (6-1-6,7), whose lofty intellect shows compassion. XXXVII. Great Means, Great Deed (*mahopāya, mahākṛti*): Candrabhadrakīrti (6-1-7), Jñānaketu, whose great means is perfect knowledge, whose great deed is wise. Smṛti (42-4-1), wise in the means of taming the beings according to whether their faculty is superior, middling, or inferior. So the four Bodhisattvas associated with Akṣobhya in the East.

[12] mahā-ṛddhibalopeto mahāvego
mahājavaḥ/
maharddhiko maheśākhyo
mahābalaparākramaḥ//

/rdsu 'phrul chen po stobs daṅ ldan/
/śugs chen mgyogs pa chen po ste/
/rdsu 'phrul chen po cher grags pa/
/stobs chen pha rol gnon pa po//

Empowered with great magical ability. Great impetus, great speed. Majestically powerful, renowned. Forward thrust with great power.

XXXVIII. Empowered with Great Magical Ability (*mahā-ṛddhibalopeta*): Smṛti (42-4), Bhadrapāla (Good Protection), using magical ability of bodily parts, such as with the nail of the big toe dominating Brahmā's battleground. XXXIX. Great Impetus, Great Speed (*mahāvega, mahājava*): Candrabhadrakīrti (6-1-8 to -2-1), Sāgaramati (Oceanic Mind). Smṛti (42-4), "great impetus," because of the fierce impetus of wisdom (*jñāna*); "great speed," because passing through the many world-realms as a Buddha-offering. XL. Majestically Powerful, Renowned (*maharddhika, maheśākhya*): Smṛti (42-4), Akṣayamati (Inexhaustible Mind), "majestically powerful" because fulfilling the collections of merit and knowledge of worldlings, disciples, and self-enlightened ones; "renowned" because fulfilling the collections of merit and knowledge of the Buddha. XLI. Forward Thrust with Great Power (*mahābalaparākrama*): Smṛti (42-4), Pratibhānakūṭa (Heaped-up Eloquence), because the ten powers, i.e., "knowing the possible and the impossible," and the rest, domineer the disciples. So the four Bodhisattvas associated with Ratnasambhava in the South.

[13] mahābhavādrisaṃbhettā mahāvajradharo
ghanaḥ/
mahākrūro mahāraudro
mahābhayabhayaṃkaraḥ//

/srid pa'i ri bo chen po 'joms/
/mkhregs śiṅ rdo rje chen po 'chaṅ/
/drag po chen po drag śul che/
/'jigs chen 'jigs par byed pa po//

Shattering the great mountain of phenomenal life. Stoutly holding the great thunderbolt. Highly wrathful, very formidable. Frightful to the great fear.

XLII. Shattering the Great Mountain of Phenomenal Life (*mahābhavādrisaṃbhettṛ*): Smṛti (42-4), Mahāsthāmaprāpta (Who is Mature in Great Power), since the great mountain consists of the impervious five grasping aggregates (*skandha*), and Mañjuśrī, mature in right knowledge, shatters it. XLIII. Stoutly Holding the Great Thunderbolt (*mahāvajradhara, ghana*): Smṛti (42-5), Sarvāpāyañjaha (Banishment of All Misfortune), because misfortune is itself stout and for its banishment one needs Mañjuśrī's stout thunderbolt of entirely good (*samantabhadra*) wisdom which cannot be broken into two as apprehension and apprehended. XLIV. Highly Wrathful, Very Formidable (*mahākrūra, mahāraudra*): Smṛti (42-5), Sarvaśokatamonirghātamati (Mind That Has Removed All Sorrow and Darkness), "highly wrathful" because of a fierce manifestation to candidates difficult to tame; "very formidable" because taming by a sham wrath. XLV. Frightful to the Great Fear (*mahābhayabhayaṃkara*): Smṛti (42-5), Jālinīprabha (Ensnaring Light), because of being frightful to the three gods who are great fears, namely, the realm above is frightened by Brahmā; the realm upon, by Mahādeva (= Śiva); the realm beneath, by Viṣṇu. So the four Bodhisattvas associated with Amitābha in the West.

[14] mahāvidyottamo nātho mahāmantrottamo guruḥ/ mahāyānanayārūḍho mahāyānanayottamaḥ//	/mgon po rig mchog chen po ste/ /bla ma gsaṅ sṅags che ba'i mchog/ /theg pa chen po'i tshul la gnas/ /theg pa chen po'i tshul gyi mchog//	Lord with great *vidyā* and supreme. Guru with great *mantra* and supreme. Resorting to the method of great vehicle. Supreme method of great vehicle.

XLVI. Lord with Great Vidyā and Supreme (*mahāvidyottama*): Smṛti (42-5), the youth Candraprabha (Moonlight), because "great *vidyā*" (the female type of incantation) protects the sentient beings; and "supreme" means the Diamond Vehicle (*vajrayāna*). XLVII. Guru with Great Mantra and Supreme (*mahāmantrottama, guru*): Smṛti (42-5), Amitaprabha (Immeasurable Light), because "great *mantra*" (the male type of incantation) demonstrates on the basis of knowing the diverse faculties of sentient beings as well as the makeup of their defilements; and "supreme" means the Diamond Vehicle. XLVIII. Resorting to the Method of Great Vehicle (*mahāyānanayārūḍha*): Smṛti (42-5 to 43-1), Gaganagañja (Treasury of the Sky), because this is the Mahāyāna route to the goal. XLIX. Supreme Method of Great Vehicle (*mahāyānanayottama*): Smṛti (43-1), Sarvanivaraṇaviṣkambhi (Dispelling All the Obscurations), because this is the Diamond Vehicle kind of Mahāyāna. And Mañjuśrī, you are Sarvanivaraṇaviṣkambhi (as you are the other Bodhisattvas). Candrabhadrakīrti (6-2-8 to -3-1), so the four Bodhisattvas associated with Amoghasiddhi in the North.

//vajradhātumahāmaṇḍalagāthāś caturdaśa//	/rdo rje dbyiṅs kyi dkyil 'khor chen po'i tshigs su bcad pa bcu bźi'o/	Fourteen *gāthā* on the Great Maṇḍala of Vajradhātu.

CHAPTER VI. PURE DHARMADHĀTU WISDOM

[1] mahāvairocano buddho mahāmaunī
mahāmuniḥ/
mahāmantranayodbhūto
mahāmantranayātmakaḥ//

/saṅs rgyas rnam par snaṅ mdsad che/
/thub pa chen po thub chen ldan/
/gsaṅ sṅags tshul chen las byuṅ ba/
/gsaṅ sṅags tshul chen bdag ñid can//

Buddha Mahāvairocana, possessed of great silence, the Mahāmuni, arisen from the great *mantra* method, identical with the great *mantra* method.

"Buddha, Mahāvairocana": Smṛti (43-3), Buddha is the Sambhogakāya in the Akaniṣṭha (Heaven). Mahāvairocana is the Dharmakāya, a "knowing of all" (*sarvavid*) sentient beings, the three Tathāgatagarbha, without beginning or end. [By "three Tathāgatagarbha" Smṛti apparently intends the three of the *Śrīmālādevīsiṃhanāda-sūtra*: (1) the illustrious Dharmadhātu womb, (2) the Dharmakāya embryo, (3) the essential of supramundane *dharma* and the essential of the intrinsically pure *dharma*, cf. A. Wayman, "The Title and Textual Affiliation of the Guhyagarbhatantra," *Dajiō Bukkyō kara Mikkyō e* (Tokyo: Shunjūsha, 1981), p. 1331 = p. (4).] "Possessed of great silence, the Mahāmuni": Smṛti (43-3), Mahāmuni is the Nirmāṇakāya. "Arisen from the great *mantra* method": Smṛti (43-3), arisen from the path of the Diamond Vehicle (*vajrayāna*). "Identical with the great *mantra* method": Smṛti (43-3), since Mañjuśrī has reached the fruit of the Diamond Vehicle, he is identical with it.

[2] daśapāramitāprāpto daśapāramitāśrayaḥ/
daśapāramitāśuddhir daśapāramitānayaḥ//

/pha rol phyin bcu thob pa ste/
/pha rol phyin pa bcu la gnas/
/pha rol phyin bcu dag pa ste/
/pha rol phyin pa bcu yi tshul//

Who has attained the ten perfections (*pāramitā*), whose site is the ten perfections, who is the purity of the ten perfections, who is the principle of the ten perfections.

"Ten perfections": Narendrakīrti (71-2-7), giving (*dāna*), morality (*śīla*), forbearance (*kṣānti*), striving (*vīrya*), meditation (*dhyāna*), insight (*prajñā*), means (*upāya*), power (*bala*), aspiration (*praṇidhāna*), and knowledge (*jñāna*).

[3] daśabhūmīśvaro nātho
daśabhūmipratiṣṭhitaḥ/
daśajñānaviśuddhātmā
daśajñānaviśuddhadhṛk//

/mgon po sa bcu'i dbaṅ phyug ste/
/sa bcu la ni gnas pa po/
/śes bcu rnam dag bdag ñid can/
/śes bcu rnam dag 'chaṅ ba po//

Nātha, who is lord of the ten stages, whose site is the ten stages, whose nature is the purity of ten knowledges, bearer of the purity of ten knowledges.

"Ten stages": Smṛti (43-5), the standard ten, Pramuditā to Dharmameghā. "Ten knowledges": Smṛti (44-1), presumably from the *Abhidharmakośa*, Chapter VII: (1) knowing Dharma, (2) knowing in agreement, (3) knowing other minds, (4) knowing convention (*saṃvṛti*), (5-8) knowing suffering, its source, its cessation, and the path to its cessation, (9) knowing termination (*kṣaya*), and (10) knowing nonproduction (*anutpāda*).

[4] daśākāro daśārthārtho munīndro daśabalo
vibhuḥ/
aśeṣaviśvārthakaro daśākāravaśī mahān//

/rnam pa bcu po don bcu'i don/
/thub dbaṅ stobs bcu khyab pa'i bdag/
/kun gyi don ni ma lus byed/
/rnam bcu dbaṅ ldan che ba po//

Having ten mental images (*ākāra*), having the aim of ten goals, Munīndra, the pervading lord with ten powers, who performs the diverse aims without remainder, great one who controls the ten features (*ākāra*).

"Having ten mental images": Smṛti (44-1), presumably from *Madhyāntavibhāga*, Vasubandhu's commentary on III, 15-16, positing (1) singleness, (2) causality, (3) experience, (4) agency, (5) independence (*svatantra*), (6) dominance, (7) permanence, (8) the defiled and purification, (9) yogi-state, (10) state of being unliberated or liberated. [The *Madhyāntavibhāga* says these are "self"-views, operating by way of the personal aggregates (*skandha*), etc.] "Having the aim of ten goals": Smṛti (44-1), the ten realities (*tattva*) of the *Madhyāntavibhāga*, Chapter III, basic reality, of characteristic, against waywardness, consisting of cause and effect, either gross or fine, accepted reality, reality of purification scope, of inclusion, of differentiation, reality of skill. "Munīndra": Narendrakirti (71-5-4), the Buddha Bhagavat. "Ten powers": Smṛti (44-2) and Narendrakīrti (71-5) agree that these are the standard ten that begin with power to know the possible and the impossible (*sthānāsthāna-jñāna-bala*). "Who controls the ten features": Smṛti (44-2-3), the ten controls (*vaśitā*), apparently ten arising on the Eighth Bodhisattva Stage, per *Daśabhūmika-sūtra*; cf. J. Rahder, ed. (Paris, 1926), p. 70, sect. O, *āyur-vaśitā*, etc.

[5] anādir niṣprapañcātmā śuddhātmā
tathatātmakaḥ//
bhūtavādī yathāvādī tathākārī ananyavāk//

/thog ma med pa spros med bdag/
/de bźin ñid bdag dag pa'i bdag/
/bden par smra źiṅ tshig mi 'gyur/
/ji skad smras pa de bźin byed//

Beginningless, devoid of elaboration, pure natured and self likewise; speaks truly, as he says so he does, does not speak (anything else).

"Beginningless. . . .": Narendrakīrti (71-1-4), the pure Dharmadhātu and other wisdoms (*chos kyi dbyiṅs rnam par dag pa la sogs pa ye śes rnams*). "Beginningless": Candrabhadrakīrti (6-5-8), mirrorlike wisdom. "Devoid of elaboration": Candrabhadrakīrti (7-1-1), sameness wisdom. Narendrakīrti (72-1), his beginning is the Thought of Enlightenment (*bodhicitta*). "Speaks truly": Candrabhadrakīrti (7-1-2), discriminative wisdom. "Does not speak (anything else)": ibid., sameness wisdom. "As he says so he does": ibid., mirrorlike wisdom.

[6] advayo 'dvayavādī ca
bhūtakoṭivyavasthitaḥ/
nairātmyasiṃhaninādī
kutīrthyamṛgabhīkaraḥ//

/gñis med gñis su med par ston/
/yaṅ dag mtha' la rnam par gnas/
/bdag med seṅ ge'i sgra daṅ ldan/
/mu stegs ri dvags ṅan 'jigs byed//

Not the two, preaching there is not two; situated in the ultimate limit, having the lion's roar of nonself that frightens the deer of bad heretics.

"Not the two": Smṛti (44-3-1), not apprehendable (*grāhya*) or apprehender (*grāhaka*). "Preaching there is not two": Smṛti (44-3-2), conventionally teaching others that there is not the two. "Nonself": Narendrakīrti (72-2-2), nonself of person (*pudgala*) or nature (*dharma*).

[7] sarvatrago 'moghagatis
tathāgatamanojavaḥ/
jino jitārir vijayī cakravartī mahābalaḥ//

/kun tu 'gro ba'i don yod stobs/
/de bźin gśegs pa'i yid ltar mgyogs/
/rgyal ba rnam rgyal dgra las rgyal/
/'khor la sgyur ba stobs po che//

Goes everywhere, going without fail,
speeding like the mind of the Tathāgata;
Jina and Vijayi who has conquered the
enemy, wheel-turner of great power.

"Goes everywhere": Smṛti (44-3-6), with sense contact (*sparśa*) and feelings (*vedanā*). "Going without fail": Smṛti (44-3-7), without hindrance. "Speeding like the mind of the Tathāgata": Smṛti (44-3-7), speeding to unequalled (*atulya*) worlds in a single instant. "Jina": Smṛti (44-3-8), victorious over defilement (*kleśa*). "Vijayi": Smṛti (44-3-8), victorious by way of all the knowable (*jñeya*). "Conquered the enemy": Smṛti (44-4-1), you (Mañjuśrī) are the sole victor over those two enemies. "Wheel-turner": Smṛti (44-4-1), the six wheel turners (Cakravartin) of the six families, Vajrasattva, etc. The wheel is made of a compound of gold, silver, copper, zinc (cf. Das, *Tibetan-English Dictionary*, p. 1090) and with this he conquers the four continents. "Of great power": Smṛti (44-4-3), having defeated the four Māras and their troops.

[8] gaṇamukhyo gaṇācāryo gaṇesó gaṇapatir
vaśī/
mahānubhāvo dhaureyo 'nanyaneyo
mahānayaḥ//

/tshogs kyi slob dpon tshogs kyi mchog/
/tshogs rje tshogs bdag dbaṅ daṅ ldan/
/mthu chen gces par 'dsin pa ste/
/tshul chen gźan gyi driṅ mi 'jog//

Instructor of the troop and head of the
troop; lord of the troop and master of the
troop, magically subduing; highly
resourceful, carrying the burden; whose
way is great, not needing another way.

"Troop": Smṛti (44-4-3), when the troop is *śrāvakas* he is their instructor (*ācārya*); when the troop is *pratyekabuddhas* he is at their head; when the troop is *bodhisattvas* he is their lord; when the troop is the Buddhas he is their master. [The Hindu deity Ganeṣa was adopted by the Buddhist pantheon. In Tibet he was referred to as Tshogs bdag (Gaṇapati) and represented, as expected, with elephant head.] "Magically subduing": [translation due to entry '*vaśin*' in the Monier-Williams *Sanskrit-English Dictionary*]. "Highly resourceful": [translation due to entry '*mthu*' in Das, *Tibetan-English Dictionary*]. "The burden": Narendrakīrti (72-3-2), the pure scripture collection (*dag pa sde snod*). "Whose way is great": Narendrakīrti (72-3-3): the Diamond Vehicle (*vajrayāna*). "Not needing another way": Narendrakīrti (72-3-4), not needing the incalculable eons of the Pāramitā Vehicle.

[9] vāgīśo vākpatir vāgmī vācaspatir
anantagīḥ/
satyavāk satyavādī ca
catuḥsatyopadeśakaḥ//

/tshig rje tshig bdag smra mkhas pa/
/tshig la dbaṅ ba tshig mtha' yas/
/tshig bden bden par smra ba ste/
/bden pa bźi ni ston pa po//

Lord of speech, master of speech, skillful in
speech, master over words, of limitless
words; true speech, speaking the truth,
preceptor of the four truths.

"Lord of speech": Smṛti (44-4-7), among the four "special knowledges" (*pratisaṃvid*), this is of meaning (*artha*). "Master of speech": ibid., this is of languages (*nirukti*). "Skillful in speech": ibid., this is of natures (*dharma*). "Master over words": Smṛti (44-4-8), this is of eloquence (*pratibhāna*). "Of limitless words": Smṛti (44-4-8), Buddha knows the languages of all sentient beings. "True speech, speaking the truth": Smṛti (44-4-8), when the Buddha teaches the Dharma, he takes right recourse to two truths, conventional and absolute. "Preceptor of the four truths": Smṛti (44-5-4), Source is the cause, and Suffering the result, thus the cause and result of *saṃsāra*; Path is the cause and Cessation the result, thus the cause and result of *nirvāṇa*; he is the preceptor of these, the four Noble Truths.

[10] avaivartiko hy anāgāmī khaḍgaḥ
pratyekanāyakaḥ/
nānāniryāṇaniryāto
mahābhūtaikakāraṇaḥ//

/phyir mi ldog pa phyir mi 'oṅ/
/'dren pa raṅ rgyal bse ru'i tshul/
/ṅes 'byuṅ sna tshogs ṅes 'byuṅ ba/
/'byuṅ ba chen po rgyu gcig pa//

Irreversible, not returning, rhinoceros, solitary guide, liberated by diverse ways of deliverance; a single cause amidst the great elements.

"Irreversible": Smṛti (44-5-6), the *bodhisattva* of the Eighth Stage does not fall back to be a *śrāvaka* or *pratyekabuddha*. "Not returning": Smṛti (44-5-6), does not return to *saṃsāra* since he has eliminated the various fractions of defilement. Narendrakīrti (72-3-8), the *arhat*-fruit. "Rhinoceros, solitary guide": Narendrakīrti (72-4-1), the *pratyekabuddha*. "Liberated by diverse ways of deliverance": Narendrakīrti (74-4-2), by the three vehicles. "A single cause amidst the great elements": Narendrakīrti (72-4-3), the pure Thought of Enlightenment amidst the four elements.

[11] arhan kṣīṇāsravo bhikṣur vītarāgo
jitendriyaḥ/
kṣemaprāpto 'bhayaprāptaḥ śītībhūto hy
anāvilaḥ//

/dge sloṅ dgra bcom zag pa zad/
/'dod chags bral ba dbaṅ po thul/
/bde ba rñed pa 'jigs med thob/
/bsil par gyur pa rñog pa med//

Bhikṣu, *arhat*, who has destroyed the fluxes, devoid of passion, his senses controlled; peace-attained, fearlessness-attained, "cooled," without turbulence.

"Bhikṣu": Narendrakīrti (72-4-4), among four kinds of *bhikṣu*—by name, avowed, begging, and in the highest sense—he is the *bhikṣu* in the highest sense because completely pure. "Arhat": Narendrakīrti (72-4-5), "who has destroyed the enemy," where the enemy is defilement. "Fluxes": Narendrakīrti (72-4-5), the imagination based on sense objects and sense organs (*yul daṅ dbaṅ po la brten pa'i rtog pa*). "Passion": Narendrakīrti (72-4-7), the attraction and clinging to sense objects. "Turbulence": Narendrakīrti (72-5-2), the waves of imagination (*rtog pa'i rlabs*). "Peace-attained": Narendrakīrti (72-4-7 to -5-1), attained by depending on the "five strands of desire" (*pañcakāmaguṇa*), i.e., the five sense objects. "Fearlessness-attained": Narendrakīrti (72-5-1), attained when engaging any object.

[12] vidyācaraṇasaṃpannaḥ sugato
lokavitparaḥ/
nirmamo nirahaṃkāraḥ satyadvayanaye
sthitaḥ//

/rig pa daṅ ni rkaṅ bar ldan/
/bde gśegs 'jig rten rig pa mchog/
/bdag gir mi 'dsin ṅar mi 'dsin/
/bden pa gñis kyi tshul la gnas//

Endowed with clear vision and good walking; Sugata, supreme knower of the world; without "mine," without "I"; abiding in the manner of two truths.

"Clear vision": Narendrakīrti (72-5-3), according to precepts of the *guru*, *vidyā* should be understood as like an eye; *caraṇa* should be traveled as like the feet. Smṛti (45-1-6), *vidyā* is like the eye of *adhiprajñā*, the right view of the layout of entities (*dṅos po'i gnas lugs kyi yaṅ dag pa'i lta ba*); *caraṇa* is the walking of the path with *adhiśīla* and *adhisamādhi*. "In the manner of two truths": [taking the comments of Narendrakīrti (72-5-6), and Smṛti (45-2-3) together, it appears that the absolute manner (*paramārthatas*) is with the clear vision, and that the conventional manner (*saṃvṛtitas*) is with the good walking].

[13] saṃsāraparakoṭiṣṭhaḥ kṛtakṛtyaḥ sthale sthitaḥ/
kaivalyajñānaniṣṭhyūtaḥ prajñāśastro vidāraṇaḥ//

/'khor ba'i pha rol mthar son pa/
/bya ba byas pa skam sar gnas/
/śes pa 'ba' źig ṅes gsal ba/
/śes rab mtshon chas rnam 'joms pa//

Gone to the bank beyond *saṃsāra*, duty-done, standing on the dry land; whose sword of insight has disclosed the unique knowledge and has cut out (defilement).

"Dry land": Smṛti (45-2-7), a term for Nirvāṇa.

[14] saddharmo dharmarāḍ bhāsvāṃ lokālokakaraḥ paraḥ/
dharmeśvaro dharmarājā śreyomārgopadeśakaḥ//

/dam chos chos rgyal gsal bar ldan/
/'jig rten snaṅ bar byed pa'i mchog/
/chos kyi dbaṅ phyug chos kyi rgyal/
/legs pa'i lam ni ston pa po//

Shining King of the Dharma, whose Dharma is illustrious; supreme illuminator of the world; Lord of the Dharma and Ruler of the Dharma; preceptor of the best path.

"Whose Dharma is illustrious": Narendrakīrti (73-1-3), the twelve branches of scripture. "Supreme illuminator": Narendrakīrti (73-1-5), sets into motion the Wheel of the Dharma.

[15] siddhārthaḥ siddhasaṃkalpaḥ sarvasaṃkalpavarjitaḥ/
nirvikalpo 'kṣayo dhātur dharmadhātuḥ paro 'vyayaḥ//

/don grub bsam pa grub pa ste/
/kun tu rtog pa thams cad spaṅs/
/rnam par mi rtog dbyiṅs mi zad/
/chos dbyiṅs dam pa zad mi śes//

Aim accomplished, purpose accomplished; avoiding all imagination; whose incessant realm is without constructive thought; the unchanging supreme *dharmadhātu*.

"Aim accomplished, purpose accomplished": Ḍombīheruka (96-1-2), accomplished the *paramārtha* Mahāmudrā in the manner of nondiscursive thought. "Avoiding all imagination": Ḍombīheruka (96-1-3), namely, as to mundane places, bodies, and possessions. "Incessant realm": Ḍombīheruka (96-1-3,4), of immeasurable knowledge.

[16] puṇyavān puṇyasaṃbhāro jñānaṃ jñānākaro mahat/
jñānavān sadasajjñāni saṃbhāradvayasaṃbhṛtaḥ//

/bsod nams ldan pa bsod nams tshogs/
/ye śes ye śes 'byuṅ gnas che/
/ye śes ldan pa yod med śes/
/tshogs gñis tshogs ni bsags pa po//

Having merit, whose collection of merit is great; having knowledge, whose mine of knowledge is the great knowledge; knowing what is and what is not; collected the two collections.

"Having merit": Narendrakīrti (73-2-6), having former merit that has suddenly become great. "Great knowledge": Narendrakīrti (72-2-7,8), the Dharmadhātu wisdom, the mine for the other four wisdoms, mirrorlike, etc. "Knowing what is": Narendrakīrti (72-2-8), having that knowledge, he has direct perception (*pratyakṣa*) of what is; and when it is not there, beyond the senses (*parokṣa*), he also knows it. "Collected the two collections": Narendrakīrti (73-3-1), from which manifests the Buddha bodies and the wisdoms.

[17] śāsvato viśvarāḍ yogī dhyānaṃ dhyeyo dhiyāṃpatiḥ /
pratyātmavedyo hy acalaḥ paramādyas trikāyadhṛk //

/ rtag pa kun rgyal rnal 'byor can /
/ bsam gtan bsam bya blo ldan bdag /
/ so so raṅ rig mi g'yo ba /
/ mchog gi daṅ po sku gsum 'chaṅ //

Yogin ruling all, the eternal; master of the intelligent ones, being contemplated, the meditation; the nonswerving one to be introspected; supreme primeval bearing the three bodies.

"Yogin ...": Ḍombīheruka (96-2-1), the *yogin*, master of the intelligent ones, is the accomplisher; ruling all, the meditation, is the method of accomplishing; the eternal, being contemplated, is to be realized. "Nonswerving one ...": Ḍombīheruka (96-2-2), the nonswerving one, supreme primeval, is the pure Dharmakāya free from all elaboration, the single lineage which is the seed of all the Buddhas, to be introspected as the single lineage for one's own aim; who bears the three bodies, namely Vairocana, Amitābha, and Akṣobhya, who are the Body, the Speech, and the Mind for the aim of others.

[18] pañcakāyātmako buddho pañcajñānātmako vibhuḥ /
pañcabuddhātmamakuṭaḥ pañcacakṣur asaṅgadhṛk //

/ saṅs rgyas sku lṅa'i bdag ñid can /
/ khyab bdag ye śes lṅa yi bdag /
/ saṅs rgyas lṅa bdag cod pan can /
/ spyan lṅa chags pa med pa 'chaṅ //

Buddha with five-body nature; pervading lord with five-wisdom nature; crowned with five Buddhas; bearing unhindered the five eyes.

"Buddha": Smṛti (46-2), Mañjuśrī, with the fivefold nature: [notice that with five families, Amoghasiddhi heads the Karma family, while previously (Chapter III) when there are six families, Vajrasattva heads the Karma family while Amoghasiddhi has the Bodhicittavajra one].

Buddha	*Family*	*Body*	*Wisdom*	*Eye*
Vairocana	Tathāgata	Dharma	Dharmadhātu	*dharma*
Akṣobhya	Vajra	Svābhāvika	Ādarśa	*buddha*
Amitābha	Padma	Sambhoga	Pratyavekṣaṇa	*prajñā*
Ratnasambhava	Ratna	Vipāka	Samatā	*divya*
Amoghasiddhi	Karma	Nirmāṇa	Kṛtyānuṣṭhāna	*māṃsa*

[19] janakaḥ sarvabuddhānāṃ buddhaputraḥ paro varaḥ/ prajñābhavodbhavo yonir dharmayonir bhavāntakṛt//	/saṅs rgyas thams cad skyed pa po/ /saṅs rgyas sras po dam pa mchog/ /śes pas srid 'byuṅ skye gnas te/ /chos las byuṅ ba srid pa sel//	Progenitor of all the Buddhas; most excellent son of the Buddhas; womb-source for the gestation by insight; *dharma*-womb making an end to phenomenal life.

"Progenitor ...": Smṛti (46-3-1), progenitor (*yab*) of all the Buddhas, but since he appears as a Bodhisattva he is also their son (*sras*); the *śrāvakas* are the son of the Body and the *pratyekabuddhas* the son of Speech, but he is the son of the Mind and so "most excellent." "Womb-source": Smṛti (46-3-3), by knowing the nature of all the *dharmas*. "*Dharma*-womb": Smṛti (46-3-3), because devoid of personal-self or dharma-self, makes an end to phenomenal life. [Notice the three kinds of Tathāgatagarbha set forth above under VI, no. 1, so "progenitor" is the Dharmadhātu womb; "son" is the Dharmakāya embryo; and "womb-source" as well as "*dharma*-womb" amount to the third kind, with two qualifications of *dharma*.]

[20] ghanaikasāro vajrātmā sadyojāto jagatpatiḥ/ gaganodbhavaḥ svayaṃbhūḥ prajñājñānānalo mahān//	/gcig pu sra mkhregs rdo rje'i bdag/ /skyes ma thag pa 'gro ba'i bdag/ /nam mkha' las byuṅ raṅ byuṅ ba/ /śes rab ye śes me bo che//	Whose diamond nature has solid single essence; no sooner born, the master of living beings; born from the sky, self-born; great fire of insight-knowledge.

"Diamond nature": Smṛti (46-3-4), Mañjuśrī's diamond body. "No sooner born": Smṛti (46-3-4), no sooner do the beings see him, than he is their master. "Born from the sky": Narendrakīrti (73-5-8), sky is here a term for the Dharmadhātu, which has features in common with the sky. "Self-born": Narendrakīrti (73-5-8), the knowledge-body is called "self-born." "Great fire": Smṛti (46-3-6), a bonfire with fuel consisting of defilements (*kleśa*) along with habit-energy (*vāsanā*).

[21] vairocano mahādīptir jñānajyotir virocanaḥ/ jagatpradīpo jñānolko mahātejāḥ prabhāsvaraḥ//	/'od chen rnam par snaṅ bar byed/ /ye śes snaṅ ba lam me ba/ /'gro ba'i mar me ye śes sgron/ /gzi brjid chen po 'od gsal ba//	Vairocana the great light is the light of knowledge, shining upon, the torch of knowledge that is the lamp for the world, the great brilliance, the clear light.

"Vairocana ...": Smṛti (46-3-8 to -4-2), identifies with the five wisdoms, as follows: "light of knowledge" (*jñāna-jyotis*), sameness wisdom; "shining upon" (*virocana*), mirrorlike wisdom; "lamp for the world" (*jagatpradīpa*), discriminative wisdom; "great brilliance" (*mahātejas*), procedure-of-duty wisdom; and "clear light" (*prabhāsvara*), Dharmadhātu wisdom.

[22] vidyārājo 'gramantresó mantrarājā mahārthakṛt / mahoṣṇīṣodbhūtoṣṇīṣo viśvadarśī viyatpatiḥ //	/ sṅags mchog mṅa' bdag rig pa'i rgyal / / gsaṅ sṅags rgyal po don chen byed / / gtsug tor chen po rmad byuṅ gtsug / / nam mkha'i bdag po sna tshogs ston //	King of magic charms and sovereign over the best incantations; king of the *mantras* that work a great purpose; great *uṣṇīṣa* and wondrous *uṣṇīṣa*; lord of the sky, revealing the multitudinous.

"King of *mantras* . . .": [notice that in Chapter III, above, the family that retains the *mantra* and *vidyā* is the Vajrasattva family. It is standard in the Tantras that the *vidyā* is a female *mantra*, and in contrast the *mantra* is taken as male *mantra*, while the word *mantra* can be used in generality to cover these two subtypes]. "Uṣṇīṣa": Smṛti (46-4-5), on the head of the king of the three realms and decorated by a head crest with the Tathāgatas. "Wondrous uṣṇīṣa": Smṛti (46-4-5), endowed with lightrays. "Lord of the sky": Smṛti (46-4-5,6), the sky is voidness (*śūnyatā*), the lord is Mañjuśrī. "Revealing the multitudinous": Smṛti (46-4-6), reveals the forms of the world and beyond and reveals a host of *samādhis*.

[23] sarvabuddhātmabhāvāgryo jagadānandalocanaḥ / viśvarūpī vidhātā ca pūjyo mānyo mahā-ṛṣiḥ //	/ saṅs rgyas kun bdag sku yi mchog / / 'gro kun dga' ba'i mig daṅ ldan / / sna tshogs gzugs can skyed pa po / / mchod 'os rjed 'os draṅ sroṅ che //	Best embodiment of all the Buddhas, with eye that is the joy of all the world, the disposer with diverse bodies, great seer worthy of offerings and worthy of esteem.

"All the Buddhas": Narendrakīrti (74-2-3), in the three times. "With eye": Smṛti (46-5-7), eye of insight (*prajñā*) that knows what to accept and what to reject (*blaṅ dor*). "Diverse bodies": Smṛti (46-4-7), diverse manifestations (*nirmita*). "Great *ṛṣi*": Dombīheruka (96-4-7), possessed of magical power (*ṛddhi*) and supernormal cognition (*abhijñā*).

[24] kulatrayadharo mantrī mahāsamayamantradhṛk / ratnatrayadharaḥ śreṣṭhas triyānottamadeśakaḥ //	/ rigs gsum 'chaṅ ba gsaṅ sṅags ldan / / dam tshig chen po gsaṅ sṅags 'dsin / / gtso bo dkon mchog gsum 'dsin pa / / theg pa mchog gsum ston pa po //	Mantrin who bears the three families, maintaining the *mantra* that is great and a pledge; chief one bearing the three jewels; teacher of the three that are best and vehicles.

"Three families": Smṛti (46-4-8), of Body, Speech, and Mind. "Great": Smṛti (46-5-1), because in no case to be transgressed. "Three jewels": Smṛti (46-5-4), there are three jewels in terms of scripture (*gźuṅ*), in terms of path (*lam*), and in terms of fruit (*'bras bu*). In terms of scripture, there is the speaker, the Buddha; the motive of speaking, the Dharma, and because he speaks, the Saṅgha. In terms of path, by way of the stage of generation (*utpattikrama*), the Buddha has the nature of five families or three families of deities and of five bodies; the Dharma is the *mantras* of the *prajñā*-circle; the Saṅgha is the *upāya*-Bodhisattvas. And by way of the stage of completion (*sampannakrama*), the Buddha is the not-two; the Saṅgha is that comprehension; the Dharma is the repeated practice. In terms of fruit, the Buddha is comprised of five dharmas; the Dharma is the *mantras*; and the Saṅgha is Samantabhadra and other celestial Bodhisattvas. "Vehicles": Smrti (46-5-7), of *śrāvakas*, *pratyekabuddhas*, and *bodhisattvas*.

[25] amoghapāśo vijayī vajrapāśo mahāgrahaḥ/ vajrāṅkuśo mahāpāśo . . .

/don yod źags pa rnam par rgyal/ /'dsin pa chen po rdo rje źags/ /rdo rje lcags kyu źags pa che//

Victorious one with unfailing noose; great seizer with diamond noose; diamond hook with great noose.

"Victorious one": Smṛti (46-5-8), Vajra Family. "Great seizer": Smṛti (47-1-1), Padma Family. "Diamond hook": Smṛti (47-1-2), Akṣobhya of the Vajra Family.

//suviśuddhadharmadhātujñānagāthāḥ pañcaviṃśatiḥ//

/śin tu rnam par dag pa choś dbyiṅs ye ses kyi tshigs bcad rkaṅ bas dman pa ñi śu rtsa lṅa'o/

Twenty-five *gāthā* on Pure Dharmadhātu Wisdom.

CHAPTER VII. PRAISING THE MIRRORLIKE WISDOM

(VI. 25d) .... vajrabhairavabhīkaraḥ//

.../rdo rje 'jigs byed 'jigs par byed/

.... Vajrabhairava who creates fear.

"... Vajrabhairava": Smṛti (47-1-5), cites the *Vajrabhairavatantra*, that this is the fierce form of Mañjuśrī. Candrabhadrakīrti (8-2-8), Vajrahūṃkāra.

[1] krodharāṭ ṣaṇmukho bhīmaḥ ṣaḍnetraḥ
ṣaḍbhujo balī/
daṃṣṭrākarālakaṅkālo halāhalaśatānanaḥ//

/khro bo'i rgyal po gdoṅ drug 'jigs/
/mig drug lag drug stobs daṅ ldan/
/keṅ rus mche ba gtsigs pa po/
/ha lā ha la gdoṅ brgya pa//

Six-faced, fearful Ruler of the Furies; six-eyed, six-armed powerful one; skeleton with terrible tusks; the hundred faces of Halāhala.

"Six-faced ...": Candrabhadrakīrti (8-3-2), this is Ratnahūṃkāra. "Skeleton": Candrabhadrakīrti (8-3-4), this is Padmahūṃkāra. "Halāhala": Candrabhadrakīrti (8-3-4), a black poison, making the neck blue. "Hundred faces": Candrabhadrakīrti (8-3-5), a red snake with a hundred hoods; Smṛti (47-2-8), the Krodha deity Amoghapāśa. [Notice that his deity is a form of Avalokiteśvara, who is in the Padma Family.]

[2] yamāntako vighnarājo vajravego
bhayaṃkaraḥ/
vighuṣṭavajro hṛdvajro māyāvajro
mahodaraḥ//

/gśin rje gśed po bgegs kyi rgyal/
/rdo rje śugs can 'jigs byed pa/
/rdo rje drag po rdo rje'i sñiṅ/
/sgyu 'phrul rdo rje gsus po che//

Yamāntaka the king of the hindering demons; the thunderbolt gust that arouses fear; big bellied one with dreadful thunderbolt, heart thunderbolt, illusion thunderbolt.

"Yamāntaka": Candrabhadrakīrti (8-3-5), this is Karmahūṃkāra. "Thunderbolt gust": Candrabhadrakīrti (8-3-6), his four kinds of rites leading to *siddhis* (occult powers) arouses fear. "Dreadful thunderbolt ...": Candrabhadrakīrti (8-3-7), this is the voidness [gate to liberation]; "heart thunderbolt": this is the signless one; "illusion thunderbolt": this is the wishless one.

[3] kuliśeśo vajrayonir vajramaṇḍo
nabhopamaḥ/
acalaikajaṭāṭopo gajacarmapaṭārdradhṛk//

/rdo rje las skyes rdo rje'i bdag/
/rdo rje'i sñiṅ po mkha' 'dra ba/
/mi g'yo ral pa gcig gis bsgyiṅs/
/glaṅ chen ko rlon gos su gyon//

Adamantine lord born from the *vajra*, whose diamond precincts are like space, unswerved and hair bound in a single tuft, also wearing clothes of elephant hide.

"Adamantine lord": Candrabhadrakīrti (8-3-8), the retinue of Ratnahūṃkāra. "Unswerved": Smṛti (47-3-6), according to the *Māyājāla*, because he is not swerved by the Māras.

[4] hāhākāro mahāghoro hīhīkāro bhayānakaḥ/ aṭṭāhāso mahāhāso vajrahāso mahāravaḥ//	/drag chen hā hā źes sgrogs pa/ /hī hī źes sgrogs 'jigs par byed/ /gad mo chen mo gad rgyaṅs can/ /rdo rje gad mo cher sgrogs pa//	Fierce one shouting "HĀ, HĀ"; fearful one shouting "HĪ, HĪ"; with long laughter, great laughter, diamond laughter, great roar.

"Fierce one": Candrabhadrakīrti (8-4-3), the retinue of Karmahūṃkāra. "Shouting HĀ, HĀ": Candrabhadrakīrti (8-4-3), striving (*vīrya*) of praxis. "Shouting HĪ, HĪ": Candrabhadrakīrti (8-4-3), armored striving that gives fear. "Long laughter, great laughter": Candrabhadrakīrti (8-4-4), discriminative striving. "Diamond laughter, great roar": Candrabhadrakīrti (8-4-4), striving of assiduous application.

[5] **vajrasattvo mahāsattvo vajrarājo mahāsukhaḥ/ vajracaṇḍo mahāmodo vajrahūṃkāra hūṃkṛtiḥ//**	/rdo rje sems dpa' sems dpa' che/ /rdo rje rgyal po bde ba che/ /rdo rje drag po dga' ba che/ /rdo rje hūṃ ste hūṃ źes sgrogs//	Vajrasattva the great being, diamond king, with great bliss, diamond heat, great joy; Vajrahūṃkāra muttering HŪṂ.

"Vajrasattva": Candrabhadrakīrti (8-4-5), retinue of Vajrahūṃkāra. "Great being": Smṛti (47-4-4), according to the *Guhyasamājatantra* because he holds the great pledge (*mahāsamaya*) or because he holds the equality (*samatā*).

[6] vajrabāṇāyudhadharo vajrakhaḍgo nikṛntanaḥ/ viśvavajradharo vajrī ekavajrī raṇaṃjahaḥ//	/mtshon du rdo rje'i mda' thogs pa/ /rdo rje ral gris ma lus gcod/ /rdo rje kun 'chan rdo rje can/ /rdo rje gcig pu g'yul sel ba//	Holding a diamond arrow as weapon, with diamond sword severing, wielding all of *vajra* as *vajrin*, defeating the (opposing) warriors as *ekavajrin*.

"Holding a diamond arrow as weapon": Candrabhadrakīrti (8-4-6), retinue of Dharmahūṃkāra. "Wielding all of *vajra*": Candrabhadrakīrti (8-4-7), emanating all magical ability (*ṛddhi*). "Defeating the warriors": Smṛti (47-5-1), deeds of the Victor over the Three Worlds, because defeating defilement.

[7] vajrajvālākarālākṣo vajrajvālāśiroruhaḥ/ vajrāveśo mahāveśaḥ śatākṣo vajralocanaḥ//	/rdo rje 'bar ba mig mi bzaṅ/ /skra yaṅ rdo rje 'bar ba ste/ /rdo rje 'bebs pa 'bebs pa che/ /mig brgya pa ste rdo rje'i mig//	Dreadful eye of blazing *vajra*, hair of blazing *vajra*, diamond chain and great chain, hundred-eyed and diamond-eyed.

"Diamond chain and great chain": Narendrakīrti (75-3-2), from all the pores emanates a lightning-type radiance called "diamond chain" and as those chains amass without hindrance they are called "great chain." "Hundred-eyed and diamond-eyed": Candrabhadrakīrti (8-5-1), "hundred-eyed" for the (many) *samādhis* and "diamond-eyed" for the six supernormal faculties (*abhijñā*).

[8] vajraromāṅkuratanur
vajraromaikavigrahaḥ/
vajrakoṭinakhārambho
vajrasāraghanacchaviḥ//

/lus ni rdo rje'i ba spu can/
/rdo rje'i spu ni gcig pu'i lus/
/sen mo skyes pa rdo rje'i rtse/
/rdo rje sñiṅ po pags pa mkhregs//

Whose body has diamond hair shoots, body solitary with diamond hairs, nails diamond-tipped, skin thick with diamond essence.

"Diamond hair shoots": Candrabhadrakīrti (8-5-2), [perfection of] giving (dāna). "Solitary with diamond hairs": Candrabhadrakīrti (8-5-2), [perfection of] morality (śīla). "Nails diamond-tipped': Candrabhadrakīrti (8-5-3), [perfection of] forbearance (*kṣānti*). "Skin thick": Candrabhadrakīrti (8-5-3), [perfection of] striving (*vīrya*).

[9] vajramālādharaḥ śrīmāṃ
vajrābharaṇabhūṣitaḥ/
hāhāṭṭahāso nirghoṣo vajraghoṣaḥ
saḍakṣaraḥ//

/rdo rje'i 'phreṅ thogs dpal daṅ ldan/
/rdo rje'i rgyan gyis brgyan pa ste/
/gad rgyaṅs hā hā ṅes par sgrags/
/yi ge drug pa rdo rje'i sgra//

Holding a diamond garland and possessed of *śrī*, decorated with a diamond ornament, sounding a long laughter of HĀ HĀ, whose diamond sound has six syllables.

"Holding a diamond garland and possessed of *śrī*": Candrabhadrakīrti (8-5-3), the meditation (*dhyāna*) with calming (*śamatha*) [of the mind]. "Decorated with a diamond ornament": Candrabhadrakīrti (8-5-4), decorated with just discerning (*vipaśyanā*) [= perfection of insight]. "Sounding a long laughter of HĀ HĀ": Narendrakīrti (75-4-1), showing a mind without timidity, and the sound frightening others. "Six syllables": Candrabhadrakīrti (8-5-5) and Narendrakīrti (75-4-2), OṂ VĀGĪŚVARA MUṂ; Narendrakīrti, however, saying it is what some claim; that others claim the six syllables are the mantra of the six Cakravartins, but that he takes the six as the bell sound of six faces, whether quickly pronouncing six HŪṂ-s, or saying A-LA-LA LA-LA-LA. Smṛti (45-5-7) says the six are A-RA-PA-CA-NĀ-YA, thus "[homage] to Arapacana."

[10] mañjughoṣo mahānādas trailokyaikaravo
mahān/
ākāśadhātuparyanto ghoṣo ghoṣavatāṃ
varaḥ//

/'jam dbyaṅs chen po sgra che ba/
/'jig rten gsum na sgra gcig pa/
/nam mkha'i mtha' klas sgra sgrogs pa/
/sgra daṅ ldan pa rnams kyi mchog//

Mañjughoṣa with great sounding, whose single great sound in the three worlds is great, sounding throughout the sky expanse, best of those who are sounding.

"Mañjughoṣa with great sounding": Candrabhadrakīrti (8-5-5), this indicates the eastern direction. "Single great sound in the three worlds": Candrabhadrakīrti (8-5-6), this indicates the southern direction. "Sounding throughout the sky expanse": Candrabhadrakīrti (8-5-7), this indicates the northern direction. "Best of those who are sounding": Candrabhadrakīrti (8-5-8), this indicates the western direction.

//ādarśajñānastutigāthā daśa//

/me loṅ ye śes kyi tshigs bcad rkaṅ pa daṅ bcas pa bcu'o/

Ten *gāthās* Praising the Mirrorlike Wisdom.

CHAPTER VIII. DISCRIMINATIVE WISDOM

[1] tathatābhūtanairātmyaṃ bhūtakoṭir
anakṣaraḥ/
śūnyatāvādī vṛṣabho
gambhīrodāragarjanaḥ//

/yaṅ dag pa bdag med de bźin ñid/
/yaṅ dag mtha' ste yi ge med/
/stoṅ ñid smra ba'i khyu mchog ste/
/zab ciṅ rgya che'i sgra sgrogs pa//

True nonself that is thusness, true limit, and without syllables; leader of bulls who tells voidness, whose roaring is deep and far-spread.

"True" (*bhūta*): Narendrakīrti (75-4-7), not mistaken (*ma nor ba*), not deceptive (*mi slu ba*). "Nonself": Narendrakīrti (75-5-1), free of *dharma* and *pudgala* self, defined as "thusness," "true limit," inconceivable realm (*acintya-dhātu*), *dharmatā*, and so on. "Without syllables": Narendrakīrti (75-5-2), not in the range of logicians. "Leader of bulls who tells voidness": Narendrakīrti (75-5-4), who tells the "thusness" and so on (as in the first line of the verse). "Deep": Smṛti (48-2-1), voidness. "Far-spread": Narendrakīrti (75-5), by way of many means (*upāya*) and the great means.

[2] dharmaśaṅkho mahāśabdo dharmagaṇḍī
mahāraṇaḥ/
apratiṣṭhitanirvāṇo
daśadigdharmadundubhiḥ//

/chos kyi duṅ ste sgra chen ldan/
/chos kyi gaṇḍī sgra bo che/
/mi gnas mya ṅan 'das pa po/
/phyogs bcu'i chos kyi rṅa bo che//

Whose conch shell of Dharma has a loud sound, whose gong of Dharma rings, who is in the *nirvāṇa* of no fixed abode, whose large drum of the Dharma (is heard) in the ten directions.

"Conch shell of Dharma": Smṛti (48-2-3), the acts of the Buddha, starting with the three gazes (*gzigs pa gsum*) in the Tuṣita (heaven), and descent into the womb of Queen Māyā. "Gong of Dharma": Smṛti (48-2-5), after the Buddha had defeated the four Māras and attained enlightenment, but was reluctant to teach, Brahmā offered him a golden wheel with a thousand spokes, Indra offered him a divine umbrella; and upon the Buddha's proceeding to Varaṇāsi, Brahmā rang the gong of the Dharma to assemble the first retinue (= the fortunate band of five). "*Nirvāṇa* of no fixed abode": Narendrakīrti (75-5-6), not staying in either *saṃsāra* or *nirvāṇa*, i.e., with the body of knowledge (*jñānadeha*).

[3] arūpo rūpavān agryo nānārūpo
manomayaḥ/
sarvarūpāvabhāsaśrīr
aśeṣapratibimbadhṛk//

/gzugs med gzugs bzaṅ dam pa ste/
/sna tshogs gzugs can yid las skyes/
/gzugs rnams thams cad snaṅ ba'i dpal/
/gzugs brñan ma lus 'chaṅ ba po//

Formless, of lovely form, and foremost; multiform and made of mind, glorious appearance of all forms, bearing no end of reflected images.

"Formless": Smṛti (48-2-8), the Dharmakāya. "Lovely form": Smṛti (48-2-8), the Sambhogakāya. "Foremost": Smṛti (48-2-8), Svābhāvikakāya. "Multiform": Smṛti (48-3-1), the Nirmāṇakāya. "Made of mind": Smṛti (48-3-1), the Vipākakāya. "Glorious appearance of all forms": Smṛti (48-3-2), appearances in the four sections (of the basic Tantra, the *Tattvasaṃgraha*). "Reflected images": Narendrakīrti (76-1-4), nonsubstantial, like reflected images in the water. "All forms": Narendrakīrti (76-1-5), forms are of three kinds, like rainbows, like lotuses, like those arising from maturation.

[4] apradhṛṣyo maheśākhyas
tridhātukamaheśvaraḥ/
samucchritāryamārgastho dharmaketur
mahodayaḥ//

/tshugs pa med ciṅ che bar grags/
/khams gsum dbaṅ phyug chen po ste/
/'phags lam śin tu mtho la gnas/
/dar ba chen po chos kyi tog//

Not susceptible of harm and celebrated for greatness, great lord of the three realms, abiding in the elevated path of nobles, the Dharma banner spread far.

"Not susceptible of harm": Narendrakīrti (76-1-6), i.e., by the four elements, since he has a rainbowlike consciousness. "Celebrated for greatness": Smṛti (48-3-4), i.e., for greatness of merit collection. "Path": Smṛti (48-3-5), the eightfold path. "Nobles": Smṛti (48-3-5), who teach and see all the path.

[5] trailokyaikakumārāṅgaḥ sthaviro vṛddhaḥ
prajāpatiḥ/
dvātriṃśallakṣaṇadharaḥ kāntas
trailokyasundaraḥ//

/'jig rten gsum na gźon lus gcig/
/gnas brtan rgan po skye rgu'i bdag/
/sum cu rtsa gñis mtshan 'chaṅ ba/
/sdug gu 'jig rten gsum na mdses//

Whose body of youth is unique in the three worlds; elder, old man, lord of creatures; bearing the thirty-two characteristics; handsome and (most) lovely in the three worlds.

"Three worlds": Narendrakīrti (76-2-2), of desire, form, and formless. "Body of youth unique": Narendrakīrti (76-2-2), while performing the aim of beings dwelling in those (three worlds) is unsullied by their faults. Narendrakīrti (76-2-3), or in the profound sense, the three worlds are joy (*ānanda*), super-joy (*paramānanda*), absent-joy (*viramānanda*); and body of youth unique is together-born joy (*sahajānanda*). [This explanation in terms of the *ānanda*-s brings in Anuttarayoga-tantra vocabulary.] "Elder, old man": Narendrakīrti (76-2-4), because from time immemorial he is self-created. "Lord of creatures": Narendrakīrti (76-2-4), performs the aim of all that is born. "Thirty-two characteristics": Narendrakīrti (76-2-5), and the eighty minor marks of the Buddha.

[6] lokajñānaguṇācāryo lokācāryo viśāradaḥ/
nāthas trātā trilokāptaḥ śaraṇaṃ tāyī
nīruttaraḥ//

/'jig rten śes legs slob dpon te/
/'jig rten slob dpon 'jigs pa med/
/mgon skyabs 'jig rten yid gcugs pa/
/skyabs daṅ skyob pa bla na med//

Excellent instructor of wisdom to the world, confident instructor to the world; *nātha*, savior, adept of the three worlds; the refuge and protector without superior.

"The refuge and protector without superior": Narendrakīrti (76-3-5), i.e., is the nature of the Three Jewels [the Buddha, Dharma, and Saṅgha, in which the Buddhists take refuge.]

[7] gaganābhogasaṃbhogaḥ
sarvajñajñānasāgaraḥ /
avidyāṇḍakośasaṃbhettā
bhavapañjaradāraṇaḥ //

/ nam mkha'i mtha' la loṅs spyod pa /
/ thams cad mkhyen pa'i ye śes mtsho /
/ ma rig sgo ṅa'i sbubs 'byed pa /
/ srid pa'i dra ba 'joms pa po //

Enjoyment from the curve of the sky, wisdom-ocean of omniscience; who bursts the eggshell of nescience, destroys the net of phenomenal life.

"Enjoyment": Narendrakīrti (76-4-5), assistance to the sentient beings by the two formal bodies [i.e., Sambhogakāya and Nirmāṇakāya]. "Sky": Narendrakīrti (76-4-5), the Dharmakāya. "Wisdom-ocean of omniscience": Narendrakīrti (76-4-5,6), "ocean" is a source of jewels, likewise omniscience is derived from the *guru*; "wisdom of omniscience" is the three bodies; "ocean" also stands for Ratnasambhava, since he is in charge of "initiation" (or, sprinkling, *abhiṣeka*). "Bursts the eggshell": Narendrakīrti (76-4-7 to -5-3), the personal aggregates (*skandha*), realms (*dhātu*), and sense-bases (*āyatana*) are within an "eggshell" in that nescience (*avidyā*) hides or encloses the five wisdoms (*jñāna*); the five wisdom (*vidyā*) initiations in the Tantras are a means (*upāya*) of empowering (*adhiṣṭhāna*) the personal aggregates, etc., while the three higher initiations (*dbaṅ gsum*) are a means of breaking the "eggshell." "Net of phenomenal life": Narendrakīrti (76-5-3), *saṃsāra* along with its defilement (*kleśa*).

[8] śamitāśeṣasaṃkleśaḥ
saṃsārārṇavapāragaḥ /
jñānābhiṣekamakuṭaḥ
samyaksaṃbuddhabhūṣaṇaḥ /

/ ñon moṅs ma lus źi byed pa /
/ 'khor ba'i rgya mtsho'i pha rol son /
/ ye śes dbaṅ bskur cod pan can /
/ rdsogs pa'i saṅs rgyas rgyan du thogs //

Laid to rest every bit of defilement, gone to the other side of the ocean of *saṃsāra*, on the crown the gnosis initiation and decorated with the complete Buddhas.

"Gnosis initiation": Narendrakīrti (76-5-6), initiated with the substances of the five (Buddha) families that are the nature of the five wisdoms. "On the crown": Narendrakīrti (76-5-7), sealed with the five families, i.e., decorated with the Buddhas.

[9] triduḥkhaduḥkhaśamanas tryanto 'nantas
trimuktigaḥ /
sarvāvaraṇanirmukta ākāśasamatāṃ gataḥ /

/ sdug bsṅal gsum gyi sdug bsṅal źi /
/ sum sel mtha' yas grol gsum thob /
/ sgrib pa kun las ṅes par grol /
/ mkha' ltar mñam pa ñid la gnas //

Laid to rest the suffering of three miseries, ended the three and has reached the endless triple liberation, liberated from all hindrances has attained the sameness like the sky.

"Laid to rest ...": Candrabhadrakīrti (9-2-4), laid to rest the suffering of motivational misery (*saṃskāra-duḥkhatā*), change misery (*pariṇāma-duḥkhatā*), and pain misery (*duḥkha-duḥkhatā*), ended the obscuration of the three realms, has reached the liberations of three vehicles (*yāna*), as [the Bodhisattva] Maitreya, who holds the tree of golden bark (*nāga-vṛkṣa*). And as [the Bodhisattva] Mañjuśrī holds the sword that liberates from all hindrances and holds the book (*poti*) of sameness like the sky.

[10] sarvakleśamalātītas tryadhvānadhvaga-
tiṃ gataḥ/
sarvasattvamahānāgo
guṇaśekharaśekharaḥ//

/ñon moṅs dri ma kun las 'das/
/dus gsum dus med rtogs pa po/
/sems can kun gyi gtso bo che/
/yon tan thod can rnams kyi thod//

Having transcended all defilement and dirt, comprehends the three times and the timeless; the great leader of all sentient beings who is the crest of meritorious crests.

"Having transcended ...": Candrabhadrakīrti (9-2-6), as [the Bodhisattva] Gandhahasti, holds the conch that has transcended all the hindrance of defilement and holds the water that comprehends the conventional three times and the absolute timeless. And as [the Bodhisattva] Jñānaketu, holds a crest along with flower garland among meritorious crests as leader in wisdom among sentient beings.

[11] sarvopadhivinirmukto vyomavartmani
susthitaḥ/
mahācintāmaṇidharaḥ sarvaratnottamo
vibhuḥ//

/lus kun las ni rnam grol ba/
/nam mkha' lam la rab gnas pa/
/yid bźin nor bu chen po 'chaṅ/
/khyab bdag rin chen kun gyi mchog//

Liberated from all bodies dwells in the sky-path, the pervading lord who bears the great wish-granting gem, having the best of all jewels.

"Liberated from ...": Candrabhadrakīrti (9-2-8), liberated from all defiled bodies, as [the Bodhisattva] Bhadrapāla, holds in hand the treasure chest that dwells in the sky-path. And, bearing the wish-granting gem, as [the Bodhisattva] Sāgaramati, bestows a chest of jewels by pervading all sentient beings. "All bodies": Smṛti (49-2-5), there is the body of *dharma*, i.e., divine body produced from the ten virtues; the precious body like wealth, i.e., body of man produced from giving; the body of desire, i.e., animal; fearful body, i.e., hungry ghost (*preta*) as well as hell-being. Narendrakīrti (77-2-4), there are three, body of *karma*, body of maturation (*vipāka*), body of habit-energy (*vāsanā*). Working them over by the three initiations (*dbaṅ gsum*), one gains the "body of knowledge" and dwells in the sky-path.

[12] mahākalpataruḥ sphīto
mahābhadraghaṭottamaḥ/
sarvasattvārthakṛtkarttā hitaiṣī
sattvavatsalaḥ//

/dpag bsam śiṅ chen rgyas pa ste/
/bum pa bzaṅ po che ba'i mchog/
/byed po sems can kun don byed/
/phan 'dod sems can mñes gśin pa//

Great flowering wish-granting tree, best of great auspicious flasks (*bhadrakalaśa*), agent of performing the aim of all sentient beings, with parental affection for sentient beings when seeking their benefit.

"Great ...": Candrabhadrakīrti (9-3-1), as [the Bodhisattva] Akṣayamati, holds a wish-granting tree and an auspicious flask. And, as [the Bodhisattva] Pratibhānakūṭa, is a spiritual guide (*kalyāṇamitra*) to the sentient beings, and uses discrimination [for the purpose], holding the lotus of performing the benefit of all sentient beings and holding the book that is beneficial.

[13] śubhāśubhajñaḥ kālajñaḥ samayajñaḥ
samayī vibhuḥ /
sattvendriyajño velajño
vimuktitrayakovidaḥ //

/ bzaṅ ṅan śes śiṅ dus śes pa /
/ khyab bdag dam śes dam tshig ldan /
/ dus śes sems can dbaṅ po śes /
/ rnam grol gsum la mkhas pa po //

Knowing good and evil, knowing the time, knowing the pledge, pervading lord with the pledge; knowing the faculties of sentient beings, knowing the occasion, skilled in the three liberations.

"Knowing ...": Candrabhadrakīrti (9-3-2), as [the Bodhisattva] Mahasthāmaprāpta, knowing good and evil in the cause and result of *karma*, knowing the right time for taming the sentient beings, knowing the pledge to not turn back, [accordingly] holds in hand the sword (*ral gri*), with the pledge. And, as [the Bodhisattva] Sarvāpāyañjaha, knowing the three times ("the occasion"), recognizing the superior and inferior faculties of sentient beings to be tamed, skilled in the liberations by way of three vehicles, holds a banner.

[14] guṇī guṇajño dharmajñaḥ praśasto
maṅgalodayaḥ /
sarvamaṅgalamāṅgalyaḥ kīrtilakṣmīr
yaśaḥ śubhaḥ //

/ yon tan ldan źiṅ yon tan śes /
/ chos śes bkra śis bkra śis 'byuṅ /
/ bkra śis kun gyi bkra śis pa /
/ grags pa'i bkra śis sñan grags dge //

Having merit one knows merit and knows the value; now esteemed source of the auspicious; auspicious bringer of all the auspicious, whose good fortune of renown is celebrated and good.

"Having merit ...": Candrabhadrakīrti (9-3-4), as [the Bodhisattva] Sarvaśokatamonirghatamati, himself having merit, knowing the merit of others, and knowing the value of freedom from sorrow, holds in hand a *śrīvatsa*, the source of the auspicious. And, as [the Bodhisattva] Jāliniprabha, holds in hand a palace (*g'yuṅ druṅ 'khyil pa*), auspicious bringer of all the auspicious, the auspiciousness of the two complete collections [of merit and knowledge] renowned for benefit to the sentient beings, celebrated and good for elimination of the two hindrances [of defilement and the knowable].

[15] mahotsavo mahāśvāso mahānando
mahāratiḥ /
satkāraḥ satkṛtir bhūtiḥ pramodaḥ śrīr
yaśaspatiḥ //

/ dbugs 'byin chen po dga' ston che /
/ dga' chen rol mo chen po ste /
/ bkur sti rim gro phun sum tshogs /
/ mchog tu dga' ba grags bdag dpal //

Having great confidence, reveals joy; the great joy and great revelry; plenitude as honor and devotion; glory as delight and the lord of fame.

"Having great ...": Candrabhadrakīrti (9-3-6), as [the Bodhisattva] Candraprabha, having great confidence because not retreating, reveals joy because gladdening the sentient beings; has the great revelry of an umbrella marked with a moon. And, as [the Bodhisattva] Amitaprabha, having the fierce light of honor and devotion to discrimination, stands on the delightful lotus, holding the sword of glory as lord of fame.

[16] vareṇyo varadaḥ śreṣṭhaḥ śaraṇyaḥ
śaraṇottamaḥ/
mahābhayāriḥ pravaro
niḥśeṣabhayanāśanaḥ//

/mchog ldan mchog sbyin gtso bo ste/
/skyabs kyi dam pa skyabs su 'os/
/'jigs chen dgra ste rab kyi mchog/
/'jigs pa ma lus sel ba po//

Having the best, one gives the best and is the chief; now the best refuge worthy of refuge; excels as enemy of the great dangers, remover of every last danger.

"Having the best ...": Candrabhadrakīrti (9-3-8), as [the Bodhisattva] Gaganagañja, the chief one and best of refuges, holds in hand an excellent jewel chest having the best treasure of the sky. And, as [the Bodhisattva] Sarvanivaraṇaviṣkambhi, holds in hand a superb *viśva-vajra*, which protects as the enemy of the eight great dangers, as well as a sword, which removes every last danger. Narendrakīrti (77-5-4), the great dangers are the four streams, the four Māras, the three bad destinies (*gati*), the imagination that posits duality; and every last danger is the eight dangers. Smṛti (49-5-4), apparently agreeing with Narendrakīrti about "every last danger" gives eight: lions, elephants, fire, snakes, thieves (*rkun*), robbers (*chom pa*), weapons, falling weights (*lci 'bab pa*); and for "great dangers," illness, death, etc.

[17] śikhī śikhaṇḍī jaṭilo jaṭī mauñjī kirīṭimān/
pañcānanaḥ pañcaśikhaḥ
pañcacīrakaśekharaḥ//

/gtsug phud phud pu lcaṅ lo can/
/ral pa mu-ñja cod pan thogs/
/gdoṅ lṅa gtsug phud lṅa daṅ ldan/
/zur phud lṅa pa me tog thod//

Whose braided hair has a hair-cord along with matted hair; who has curly hair, the Muñja-grass cord, along with a diadem; who has five faces, five braids, and flowers on five knotted locks.

"Whose braided hair ...": Narendrakīrti (77-5-6), at the time of meditative equipoise contemplates himself as having the adornment, apparel, and appearance of Heruka. "Who has five faces": Narendrakīrti (78-1-3), each of the five faces has five braids and flowers on five knotted locks.

[18] mahāvratadharo mauṇḍī brahmacārī
vratottamaḥ/
mahātapās taponiṣṭhaḥ snātako gautamo
'graṇīḥ//

/mgo zlum brtul źugs chen po ste/
/tshaṅs par spyod pa brtul źugs mchog/
/dka' thub mthar phyin dka' thub che/
/gtsaṅ gnas dam pa gau-ta-ma//

The shaved-head one displaying great austerity, in the pure life as best of ascetics; with great mortification at the culmination of mortification, Gautama, foremost *snātaka*.

"The shaved-head one": Smṛti (50-1-1), this is Śākyamuni, who had practiced the pure life (*brahmacarya*) for eons; "great austerity" refers to twelve years of pure life while in his parental home; "great mortification" refers to the six years next to the river [after leaving home]; "foremost *snātaka*" means superior to those who merely perform ablutions, i.e., bathe, at the conclusion of the student career.

[19] brahmavid brāhmaṇo brahmā brahmanirvāṇam āptavān /
muktimokṣo vimokṣāṅgo vimuktiḥ śāntatā śivaḥ //

/bram ze tshaṅs pa tshaṅs pa śes/
/mya ṅan 'das pa tshaṅs pa thob/
/grol ba thar pa rnam grol lus/
/rnam grol źi ba źi ba ñid//

Knowing Brahmā, one is a Brahmin and Brahmā, has attained the Brahmanirvāṇa; whose body of liberation has deliverance and release; the deliverance which is calm and the *śāntatā*.

"Brahmā": Smṛti (50-3-4), a god of the first *dhyāna* (*bsam gtan daṅ po'i lha*) [of course, the first *dhyāna* heaven of the *rūpa-loka*, when described in terms of its deity inhabitants]. "Brahmanirvāṇa": Candrabhadrakīrti (9-4-6), has attained the mirrorlike (wisdom) of the path of learning (*śaikṣa-mārga*) (*slob pa'i lam me loṅ lta bu thob pa*). "Deliverance and release": Narendrakīrti (78-2-1), "deliverance" from imagination (*rtog pa*); "release" from bondage (*bciṅs pa*). "Deliverance which is calm": Narendrakīrti (78-2-2), the *śrāvaka*'s body free of clinging; also, not abiding in *saṃsāra*. "The *śāntatā*": Narendrakīrti (78-2-2), Vajradhara's body attended with clinging; also, not abiding in *nirvāṇa*.

[20] nirvāṇaṃ nirvṛtiḥ śāntiḥ śreyo niryāṇam antakaḥ/
sukhaduḥkhāntakṛnniṣṭhā vairāgyam upadhikṣayaḥ//

/mya ṅan 'das źi mya ṅan 'das/
/legs par mya ṅan 'das daṅ ñe/
/bde sdug sel ba mthar gyur pa/
/chags bral lus las 'das pa po//

There is the *nirvāṇa* as extinction and peace; better is the nearness to escape; there is the culmination of pleasure, pain, and of dispelling; nonattachment is the termination of body.

"Better is the nearness to escape": Narendrakīrti (78-2-3), the *nirvāṇa* of no fixed abode (*apratiṣṭhitanirvāṇa*). "Pleasure, pain, and dispelling": Narendrakīrti (78-2-4), "pleasure" is joy (ānanda) and super-joy (*paramānanda*) because these are pleasure; "pain" is absent-joy (*viramānanda*) because in desire [world]; "dispelling' is of wayward reflection (*log pa rtogs pa sel ba*); "culmination" is together-born joy (*sahajānanda*) because this is said to be the best culmination. "Nonattachment": Narendrakīrti (78-2-6), the *śrāvaka*'s *nirvāṇa* [i.e., as extinction and peace], which transcends "absent-joy" (*viramānanda*) [i.e., as termination of body].

[21] ajayo 'nupamo 'vyakto nirābhāso nirañjanaḥ/
niṣkalaḥ sarvago vyāpī sūkṣmo 'bījam anāsravaḥ//

/thub pa med pa dpe med pa/
/mi mṅon mi snaṅ gsal byed min/
/mi 'gyur kun 'gro khyab pa po/
/phra źiṅ zag med sa bon bral//

Unsubdued, unexampled, unmanifest, not an appearance, without "consonants"; unchanging, going everywhere, the pervader; subtle, not a seed, fluxless.

"Unsubdued": Narendrakīrti (78-2-7 to 78-3-4), "Unsubdued" by the three joys; "unexampled", e.g., saying "like the stars, like the moon"; "unmanifest" to sense organs; "not an appearance" because not an object; "without consonants" because not dependent on other consonants; "unchanging" i.e., eternal, for, if impermanent, it would not be the Buddha's wisdom (*jñāna*); "going everywhere" because without directional parts; "the pervader" because incorporeal like space; "subtle" means difficult to comprehend; "fluxless" means it is neither object nor nonobject because it does not circle about in phenomenal life; "not a seed" means free from fluxional seeds because it has no difference of cause and effect.

[22] arajo virajo vimalo vāntadoṣo nirāmayaḥ/
suprabuddho vibuddhātmā sarvajñaḥ
sarvavitparaḥ//

/rdul med rdul bral dri ma med/
/ñes pa spaṅs pa skyon med pa/
/śin tu sad pa sad pa'i bdag/
/kun śes kun rig dam pa'o//

Without impurity, one lacks impurity and is immaculate; having ended faults, is without shortcoming; wide awake, has fully awakened nature; omniscient, is best at all-knowing.

"Without impurity": Narendrakīrti (78-3-4), "one lacks the impurity" of the three joys; and "is immaculate"—together-born (*sahaja*); "is without shortcoming" of the together-born; when "wide awake" as though awakening from sleep, one has "fully awakened nature," is a Buddha; "all-knowing" means knows all of *saṃsāra* and *nirvāṇa* in nontwo manner.

[23] vijñānadharmatātīto jñānam
advayarūpadhṛk/
nirvikalpo nirābhogas
tryadhvasaṃbuddhakāryakṛt//

/rnam par śes pa'i chos ñid 'das/
/ye śes gñis med tshul 'chaṅ ba/
/rnam par rtog med lhun gyis grub/
/dus gsum saṅs rgyas las byed pa//

Having transcended the nature of perception, knowledge maintains a nontwo nature; without constructive thought and without effort, performs the Buddha deeds in the three times.

"Having transcended ...": Narendrakīrti (78-3-6), "nature of perception" is to take perception and perceivable as two; transcending this, knowledge (or, wisdom) takes those two as not-two. Smṛti (51-1-4), Mañjuśrī performs all the Buddha deeds of the Buddhas of the three times, Dīpaṃkara, etc.

[24] anādinidhano buddha ādibuddho
niranvayaḥ/
jñānaikacakṣur amalo jñānamūrtis
tathāgataḥ//

/saṅs rgyas thog ma tha ma med/
/daṅ po'i saṅs rgyas rgyu med pa/
/ye śes mig gcig dri ma med/
/ye śes lus can de bźin gśegs//

Buddha without beginning or end, the primordial Buddha without preceding cause; the unstained single eye of knowledge; Tathāgata embodiment of knowledge.

"Single eye of knowledge": Narendrakīrti (78-4-5), "knowledge" means insight-wisdom (*prajñā-jñāna*); the expression "unstained single eye" is used because it is like an eye.

[25] vāgīśvaro mahāvādī vādirāḍ
vādipuṃgavaḥ/
vadatāṃ varo variṣṭho vādisiṃho
'parājitaḥ//

/tshig gi dbaṅ phyug smra ba che/
/smra ba'i skyes mchog smra ba'i rgyal/
/smra ba'i dam pa mchog gi gnas/
/smra ba'i seṅ ge tshugs pa med//

The great speaker as Lord of Speech, exemplary person of speech as king of speech; excellent and outstanding among speakers, the invincible lion of speech.

"Lord of Speech": Narendrakīrti (78-4-8), Amitābha.

[26] samantadarśī prāmodyas tejomālī sudarśanaḥ / śrīvatsaḥ suprabho dīptir bhābhāsvarakaradyutiḥ //	/ kun tu lta ba mchog tu dga' / / gzi brjid phreṅ ba lta na sdug / / 'od bzaṅ 'bar ba dpal gyi be'u / / lag na 'od 'bar snaṅ ba po //	The *prāmodya* seeing all around; the *sudarśana* with a fiery garland; the blaze that is *śrīvatsa* with goodly light; the hand shining with a blazing light.

"The *prāmodya* ...": [My paper, "The Mathurā Set of *Aṣṭamaṅgala* in Early and Later Times," scheduled to appear in the Mathura Seminar Proceedings, has discussed this verse, showing it to have Vaiṣṇava-coloring, hence troubling to Buddhist commentators. The intention appears to be an identification of Mañjuśrī with Viṣṇu in the meaning of the "unconquerable preserver," holding the Sudarśana wheel, and having the *śrīvatsa* symbol in the heart (as mentioned especially in Smṛti's commentary, 51-2-4).]

[27] mahābhiṣagvaraḥ śreṣṭhaḥ śalyahartā niruttaraḥ / aśeṣabhaiṣajyataruḥ kleśavyādhimahāripuḥ //	/ sman pa che mchog gtso bo ste / / zug rṅu 'byin pa bla na med / / sman rnams ma lus ljon pa'i śiṅ / / ñon moṅs nad kyi dgra che ba //	Leader as best of great healers, supreme extracter of thorns; paradise tree with every single medicinal herb, great enemy of defilement-sickness.

"Leader as best ...": Smṛti (51-2-7), the stage of generation (*utpattikrama*) extracts the thorn of defilement; the stage of completion (*sampannakrama*) extracts the thorn of the knowable.

[28] trailokyatilakaḥ kāntaḥ śrīmāṃ nakṣatramaṇḍalaḥ / daśadigvyomaparyanto dharmadhvajamahocchrayaḥ //	/ sdug gu 'jig rten gsum gyi mchog / / dpal ldan rgyu skar dkyil 'khor can / / phyogs bcu nam mkha'i mthar thug par / / chos kyi rgyal mtshan legs par 'dsugs //	Lovely preeminent mark of the three worlds, whose circle of asterisms is glorious, whose Dharma-banner is well raised throughout the ten directions of space.

"Lovely preeminent mark ...": Smṛti (51-3-1), commenting on "glorious circle of asterisms" mentions the terms *āyur-jñāna* (*tshe daṅ ye śes*). [This implicates the Buddha Amitāyus; notice that the Bodhisattva Mañjuśrī is the interlocutor in the *Aparimitāyurjñāna-Mahāyāna-sūtram* (cf. edition by Max Walleser, Heidelberg, 1916).] Narendrakīrti (79-1-6), "preeminent mark" (*tilaka*) stands for the means that makes understood nontwo. "Dharma-banner" stands for knowledge (*ye śes*), and the ten directions, for the sense objects and sense organs.

[29] jagacchatraikavipulo maitrī karuṇāmaṇḍalaḥ / padmanarteśvaraḥ śrīmāṃ ratnacchatro mahāvibhuḥ //	/ 'gro na gdugs gcig yaṅs pa ste / / byams daṅ sñiṅ rje'i dkyil 'khor can / / dpal ldan padma gar gyi bdag / / khyab bdag chen po rin chen gdugs //	The sole great umbrella in the world, having the circle of love and compassion; glorious lotus lord of dance, great pervading lord with jewel umbrella.

"Sole great umbrella": Narendrakīrti (79-2-1), protects against the hot sun [i.e., ascetic's umbrella]. "Jewel umbrella": Smṛti (51-3-5), is a pledge to protect everyone (*dam tshig tu gyur pa thams cad skyob pa*) [i.e., royal umbrella]. "Glorious lotus lord of dance": [this is a form of Avalokiteśvara according to B. Bhattacharyya, *The Indian Buddhist Iconography* (1958 edition, pp. 133f.), but here it means Amitābha-Mañjuśrī].

[30] sarvabuddhamahārājā	/saṅs rgyas kun gyi rgyal po che/	Great king of all Buddhas, maintaining the
sarvabuddhātmabhāvadhṛk/	/saṅs rgyas kun gyi sku 'chaṅ ba/	embodiment of all Buddhas; great *yoga* of
sarvabuddhamahāyogaḥ	/saṅs rgyas kun gyi rnal 'byor che/	all Buddhas, the sole instruction of all
sarvabuddhaikaśāsanaḥ//	/saṅs rgyas kun gyi bstan pa gcig/	Buddhas.

"Maintaining the embodiment of all Buddhas": Smṛti (51-3-6), the voidness (*śūnyatā*) of all dharmas. "The sole instruction of all Buddhas": Smṛti (51-3-8), while three vehicles are taught, the sole instruction is the nontwo great vehicle.

[31] vajraratnābhiṣekaśrīḥ	/rdo rje rin chen dbaṅ bskur dpal/	The glory of the diamond-jewel initation,
sarvaratnādhipeśvaraḥ/	/rin chen kun bdag dbaṅ phyug ste/	lord of all jewel masters; the master of all
sarvalokeśvarapatiḥ	/'jig rten dbaṅ phyug kun gyi bdag/	the world-lords, master of all *vajradhara*-s.
sarvavajradharādhipaḥ//	/rdo rje 'chaṅ ba kun gyi rje//	

"Diamond-jewel initiation": Narendrakīrti (79-3-1), indicates that these are initiations of the flask (*bum pa*), usually five in number: the water initiation, diadem initiation diamond initiation, bell initiation, and name initiation. Smṛti (51-4-1), "the diamond-jewel ..." refers to Akṣobhya; "lord of all jewel masters," Ratnasambhava; "master of all world-lords," Amitābha; "master of all *vajradhara*-s," Amoghasiddhi.

[32] sarvabuddhamahācittaḥ	/saṅs rgyas kun gyi thugs che ba/	Who has the great mind of all Buddhas,
sarvabuddhamanogatiḥ/	/saṅs rgyas kun gyi thugs la gnas/	dwelling in the heart-mind of all Buddhas;
sarvabuddhamahākāyaḥ	/saṅs rgyas kun gyi sku che ba/	who has the great Body of all Buddhas and
sarvabuddhasarasvatī//	/saṅs rgyas kun gyi gsuṅ yaṅ yin//	has the divine Speech of all Buddhas.

"Who has ...": Narendrakīrti (79-3-8), who has the three secrets—of Body, Speech, and Mind—of all the Buddhas.

[33] vajrasūryo mahāloko vajrenduvimala-	/rdo rje ñi ma snaṅ ba che/	The diamond sun with great light; the
prabhaḥ	/rdo rje zla ba dri med 'od/	diamond moon with pure light; the great
virāgādimahārāgo viśvavarṇo	/chags bral daṅ po chags pa che/	passion beginning with dispassion; the
jvalaprabhaḥ//	/kha dog sna tshogs 'bar ba'i 'od//	blazing light with variegated color.

"Diamond sun," "diamond moon": Narendrakīrti (79-4-4), affiliated natures to "diamond sun" are red color, arousal of pain, blood which is hot to the touch; affiliated natures to "diamond moon" are white color, arousal of pleasure, the *bodhicitta* which is cool. "The great passion beginning with dispassion": Candrabhadrakīrti (10-3-1), "dispassion" in *nirvāṇa*, "great passion" in *saṃsāra*; [Mañjuśrī] does not stay in either one. "The blazing light with variegated color": Smṛti (51-5-2), refers to the body of Vajrasattva, which displays a blazing five-colored light.

[34] saṃbuddhavajraparyaṅko
buddhasaṃgītidharmadhṛk/
buddhapadmodbhavaḥ śrīmāṃ
sarvajñājñānakośadhṛk//

/rdo rje'i skyil kruṅ rdsogs saṅs rgyas/
/saṅs rgyas brjod pa'i chos 'dsin pa/
/dpal ldan saṅs rgyas padma skyes/
/kun mkhyen ye śes mdsod 'dsin pa//

Having diamond leg posture of complete Buddha, maintaining the rehearsal Dharma of the Buddhas; glorious arising of the lotuslike Buddha, maintaining the treasury of omniscient knowledge.

"Diamond leg posture": Smṛti (51-5-3), showing the Māras cannot harm the complete Buddha. "Rehearsal Dharma": Smṛti (51-5-4), these names [of Mañjuśrī]. "Lotuslike Buddha": Smṛti (51-5-4), born like the lotus, i.e., free of [environmental] faults.

[35] viśvamāyādharo rājā buddhavidyādharo
mahān/
vajratīkṣṇo mahākhaḍgo viśuddhaḥ
paramākṣaraḥ//

/rgyal po sgyu 'phrul sna tshogs 'chaṅ/
/che ba saṅs rgyas rig sṅags 'chaṅ/
/rdo rje rnon po ral gri che/
/yi ge mchog ste rnam par dag//

The King wearing the diverse illusion, the great one wearing the Buddha's magic charm; has a great sword sharp as a diamond, the pure supreme syllable.

"The King": Narendrakīrti (80-1-3), Vajradhara. "Wearing the diverse illusion": Candrabhadrakīrti (10-3-4), adopts all forms [necessary] for taming the living beings. "Magic charm": Smṛti (51-5-6), a *dhāraṇī* [in fact, a *vidyā* is the female kind of *mantra*]. "Great sword": Smṛti (51-5-7), a symbol for cutting out the defilement. "Pure supreme syllable": Narendrakīrti (80-2-2), A is the supreme syllable.

[36] duḥkhacchedamahāyān[o]
vajradharmamahāyudhaḥ/
jinajig vajragāmbhīryo vajrabuddhir
yathārthavit//

/theg pa chen po sdug bsṅal gcod/
/mtshon cha chen po rdo rje chos/
/rdo rje zab mo rgyal bas rgyal/
/rdo rje blo gros don bźin rig//

Whose great vehicle destroys suffering, with the adamantine Dharma as the great weapon; Jinajik with profundity of *vajra*, diamond intellect knowing according to the meaning.

"Adamantine Dharma": Narendrakīrti (80-2-4), "Dharma" is the enjoyment-wheel (*loṅs spyod kyi 'khor lo*). "Jinajik": [Tibetan takes it as "conquers by the conqueror" (*rgyal bas rgyal*). Narendrakīrti (80-2-5), seizes by the conqueror; the conqueror is great bliss (*mahāsukha*) (*rgyal ba 'dsin pa ste/rgyal ba ni bde ba chen po'o*). "With profundity of *vajra*": Smṛti (52-1-2), with nontwo wisdom (*gñis med kyi ye śes te*). [The word "seizes" (*'dsin pa*) seems to mean "overpowers" in this context.]

[37] sarvapāramitāpūrī sarvabhūmivibhūṣaṇaḥ/ viśuddhadharmanairātmyaṃ samyagjñānenduhṛtprabhaḥ//	/pha rol phyin pa kun rdsogs pa/ /sa rnams kun gyi rgyan daṅ ldan/ /rnam par dag pa bdag med chos/ /yaṅ dag ye śes zla 'od bzaṅ//	Fulfilled all the perfections, adorned with all the stages; the nonself of pure *dharmas*, right knowledge and the heart-light of the moon.

"Adorned": Narendrakīrti (80-2-8), his own body is adorned with the stages. "Pure *dharmas*": Smṛti (52-1-5), as though not appearing (*mi snaṅ ba daṅ 'dra ba*). "Heart-light of the moon": Smṛti (52-1-5), moon in the heart of the knowledge-being (*jñāna-sattva*). "Right knowledge and the heart-light of the moon": Narendrakīrti (80-3-2), "right knowledge" is the supreme (*paramārtha*) *bodhicitta*; moonlight is the conventional (*saṃvṛti*) *bodhicitta*.

[38] māyājālamahodyogaḥ sarvatantrādhipaḥparaḥ/ aśeṣavajraparyaṅko niḥśeṣajñānakāyadhṛk//	/brtson chen sgyu 'phrul dra ba ste/ /rgyud kun gyi ni bdag po mchog/ /rdo rje'i gdan ni ma lus ldan/ /ye śes sku rnams ma lus 'chaṅ//	Energetically applied in the illusion net, the supreme master of all the Tantras; has the complete diamond seat, maintains every gnosis body.

"Energetically applied ..." Smṛti (52-1-6), materializing by way of procedure-of-duty wisdom is the meaning of "illusion net." "All the Tantras": Smṛti (52-1-6), the four, Kriyā, Caryā, Yoga, and Anuttarayoga. "Complete diamond seat": Narendrakīrti (80-3-6), means every place of the Tathāgatas, i.e., the supreme and the conventional as not-two. "Every gnosis body": Narendrakīrti (80-3-6), "every" of all Tathāgatas, i.e., their gnosis body is not-two.

[39] samantabhadraḥ sumatiḥ kṣitigarbho jagaddhṛtiḥ/ sarvabuddhamahāgarbho viśvanirmāṇacakradhṛk//	/kun tu bzaṅ po blo gros bzaṅ/ /sa yi sñiṅ po 'gro ba 'dsin/ /saṅs rgyas kun gyi sñiṅ po che/ /sprul ba'i 'khor lo sna tshogs 'chaṅ//	Samantabhadra the good mind, Kṣitigarbha supporting the living beings; great embryo of all the Buddhas, maintaining the variegated manifestation circle.

"Great embryo": Smṛti (52-2-5), generated by all the Buddhas. "Variegated manifestation circle": Smṛti (52-2-5), manifesting the variegated supramundane *maṇḍala*.

[40] sarvabhāvasvabhāvāgryaḥ sarvabhāvasvabhāvadhṛk/ anutpādadharmaviśvārthaḥ sarvadharmasvabhāvadhṛk//	/dṅos po kun gyi raṅ bźin mchog/ /dṅos po kun gyi raṅ bźin 'dsin/ /skye med chos de sna tshogs don/ /chos kun ṅo bo ñid 'chaṅ ba//	Best self-presence of all presences, maintaing the self-presence of all presences; having the diverse aims of the nonproduction *dharma, maintains the self-presence of all dharmas*.

"Having the diverse aims": Smṛti (52-2-6), conventionally he performs the aims of others in diverse ways, while in the absolute sense the *dharmas* are a nonproduction.

[41] ekakṣaṇamahāprājñaḥ
sarvadharmāvabodhadhṛk/
sarvadharmābhisamayo bhūtāntamunir
agradhīḥ//

/śes rab chen pos skad cig la/
/chos kun khoṅ du chud pa 'chaṅ/
/chos kun mṅon par rtogs pa ste/
/thub pa blo mchog yaṅ dag mtha'//

Who has the great insight that in a single moment holds the understanding of all natures (*dharma*); who has the realization of all natures, the ultimate Muni, the best intelligence.

"Ultimate Muni": Narendrakīrti (80-5-1), also called Buddha, Bhagavat, Sugata, and Jina.

[42] stimitaḥ suprasannātmā
samyaksaṃbuddhabodhidhṛk/
pratyakṣaḥ sarvabuddhānāṃ jñānārciḥ
suprabhāsvaraḥ//

/mi g'yo rab tu daṅ ba'i bdag/
/rdsogs pa'i saṅs rgyas byaṅ chub 'chaṅ/
/saṅs rgyas kun gyi mṅon sum pa/
/ye śes me lce 'od rab gsal//

Who is unswayed with a very serene nature, holding the enlightenment of the right complete Buddha; with direct perception of all the Buddhas; his flame of wisdom and (then) the exceedingly Clear Light.

"Unswayed": Smṛti (52-3-1), unswayed by fading (of a thought) or excitement. "Flame of wisdom": Narendrakīrti (80-5-4, 5), which burns up all the defilement. "Clear Light": Smṛti (52-3-3), emits light that illuminates the three worlds.

//pratyavekṣaṇājñānagāthā dvācatvāriṃśat//

/so sor gzigs pa'i ye śes kyi tshigs su bcad pa bźi bcu rtsa gñis so/

Forty-two *gāthā* on Discriminative Wisdom.

CHAPTER IX. Sameness Wisdom

[1] iṣṭārthasādhakaḥ paraḥ
sarvāpāyaviśodhakaḥ/
sarvasattvottamo nāthaḥ
sarvasattvapramocakaḥ//

/'dod pa'i don sgrub dam pa ste/
/ṅan soṅ thams cad rnam sbyoṅ ba/
/mgon po sems can kun gyi mchog/
/sems can thams cad rab grol byed//

Best evoker of the desired aim who purifies all the evil destiny; the *nātha* best of all beings who liberates all sentient beings.

"Desired aim": Narendrakīrti (80-5-6), two—purification of evil destiny and getting liberated.

[2] kleśasaṃgrāmaśūraikaḥ
ajñānaripudarpahā/
dhīḥ śṛṅgāradharaḥ śrīmāṃ
vīrabībhatsarūpadhṛk//

/ñon moṅs g'yul du gcig dpa' ba/
/mi śes dgra yi dregs pa 'joms/
/blo ldan sgeg 'chaṅ dpal daṅ ldan/
/dpa' bo mi sdug gzugs 'chaṅ ba//

Unique hero for destruction of defilement, who destroys the pride of the ignorance-enemy, his intelligence the glorious wearing of the "erotic," who maintains a body "heroic" and "disgusting."

"Erotic ...": [the "erotic," "heroic," and "disgusting" are the first three of the standard list of nine sentiments of dramatic art, and so the remaining ones are implied: the "furious," "humorous," "frightful," "compassionate," "wonderful," and "tranquil"; for two Anuttarayogatantra-type comments on each of the eleven, cf. A. Wayman, *Yoga of the Guhyasamājatantra*, p. 328; since the "erotic" intends a combination of male and female, it is of interest that the verse associates this with the intelligence (*dhī*) and so it is a subjective combination].

[3] bāhudaṇḍaśatākṣepa(ḥ)
padanikṣepanartanaḥ/
śrīmac chatabhujābhogo
gaganābhoganartanaḥ//

/lag pa'i dbyug pa brgya bskyod ciṅ/
/gom pa'i stabs kyis gar byed pa/
/dpal ldan lag pa brgyas gaṅ la
/nam mkha' khyab par gar byed pa//

Brandishing the hundred clubs of his arms, he dances with a thudding step; glorious one bending his hundred arms, dances through the curve of the sky.

"Dances ...": [according to information in A. Wayman, *Yoga of the Guhyasamājatantra*, p. 326, this is Vajrasattva dancing; and this identification is implied in *gāthā* no. 1, above, with the words "best of all beings" (*sarvasattvottama*); and the title "*nātha*" shows that this is the Vajrasattva who heads the Karma family per Chapter III, above]. "Hundred": Narendrakīrti (81-1-7), the hundred arms [with clubs] goes with the dancing to indicate the hundred types of dance (*gar gyi rigs brgya*); and (81-2-2), the hundred arms (that he bends) indicate that the dance fills up or pervades the sky.

[4] ekapādatalākrānta(ḥ) mahīmaṇḍatale sthitaḥ /
brahmāṇḍaśikharākrānta(ḥ) pādāṅ-guṣṭhanakhe sthitaḥ //

/ sa yi dkyil 'khor gźi yi khyon /
/ rkaṅ pa ya gcig mthil gyis gnon /
/ rkaṅ mtheb sen mo'i khyon gyis kyaṅ /
/ tshaṅs pa'i yul sa rtse nas gnon //

Standing upon the pithy spot of earth, he presses down with the sole of one foot; standing on a toenail width, he presses down up to the top of Brahmā's realm.

"Standing upon the pithy spot of earth ...": Narendrakīrti (81-2-2), this refers to the first lines drawn for the *maṇḍala* (*dkyil 'khor gyi thig btab*). [Cf. Ferdinand D. Lessing, "The Eighteen Worthies Crossing the Sea," The Sino-Swedish Expedition, Publication 38 (Stockholm, 1954), p. 126; in the initial square, one draws the East-West Brahmā Line, the North-South Brahmā Line, the Fire-Wind Diagonal Line, and the Second Diagonal Line; the center is referred to as the "pithy spot of earth."]

[5] ekārtho 'dvayadharmārthaḥ paramārtho 'vinaśvaraḥ.
nānāvijñaptirūpārthaś cittavijñānasantatiḥ//

/ don gcig gñis med chos kyi don /
/ dam pa'i don te 'jigs pa med /
/ rnam rig sna tshogs gzugs don can /
/ sems daṅ rnam śes rgyud daṅ ldan //

Having as single meaning the meaning of nontwo natures (*dharma*), the supreme that is not fearful; his object-entity of forms with diverse representation, his stream of consciousness with the [*bodhi-*] Thought and *vijñāna*-[seeds].

"Natures": Narendrakīrti (81-3-2), these are the personal aggregates, the realms, and the sense bases. "Not fearful": Narendrakīrti (81-3-4), lacking what is fearful, namely, defilement, etc. "*Vijñāna*-[seeds]": Narendrakīrti (81-3-7), which growing make the "stream of consciousness" (*santati*). "Thought": Narendrakīrti (81-3-7), the Thought of Enlightenment with the five Wisdoms not-two.

[6] aśeṣabhāvārtharatiḥ śūnyatāratir agradhīḥ /
bhavarāgādyatītaś ca bhavatrayamahāratiḥ //

/ dṅos don ma lus rnams la dga' /
/ stoṅ pa ñid dga' mchog gi blo /
/ srid pa'i 'dod chags la sogs 'das /
/ srid gsum dga' ba chen po pa //

His pleasure is in every single on-going object-entity; his pleasure in voidness is the best intelligence; having transcended the lusts of phenomenal life, his great pleasure is in the three worlds.

"Every single on-going object-entity": Candrabhadrakīrti (11-1-4), this is the voidness (gate); "pleasure in voidness," this is the signless (gate); "transcended the lusts," this is the wishless (gate).

[7] śuddhaḥ śubhrābhradhavalaḥ
śaraccandrāṃśusuprabhaḥ /
bālārkamaṇḍalacchāyo
mahārāganakhaprabhaḥ //

/ sprin dkar dag pa bźin du dkar /
/ 'od bzaṅ ston ka'i zla ba'i 'od /
/ ñi ma 'char ka'i dkyil ltar mdses /
/ sen mo'i 'od ni śas cher dmar //

Pure white like a white cloud and well shining like the rays of the autumn moon; beautiful like the orb of the rising sun, with intense red shine of his nail.

"Pure white": Narendrakīrti (81-4-3), this refers to the conventional *bodhicitta*; "rays of the autumn moon," "means (*upāya*)"-*bodhicitta*; "rising sun," "insight (*prajñā*)"-*bodhicitta*; "intense red shine of his nail," place where the *bodhicitta* is made to fall, gathered in the third (i.e., middle) channel (*rtsa*).

[8] indranīlāgrasaccīro mahānīlakacāgradhṛk /
mahāmaṇimayūkhaśrīr
buddhanirmāṇabhūṣaṇaḥ //

/ cod pan bzaṅ po mthon ka'i rtse /
/ skra mchog mthon ka chen po 'chaṅ /
/ nor bu chen po 'od chags dpal /
/ saṅs rgyas sprul pa'i rgyan daṅ ldan //

Whose sublime crest is tipped with sapphire, who wears on the top of his hair the great sapphire; having the glory of the great gem with clasp, is adorned with the Nirmāṇa (body) of the Buddha.

"Buddha": Narendrakīrti (81-5-2), the Sambhogakāya. Candrabhadrakīrti (11-1-8) explains [differently] that it is a case of the Nirmāṇa displaying on head-crest the five Buddhas. Smṛti (52-5-2) takes the verse as referring to the Knowledge Being, adorned with all the Buddhas.

[9] lokadhātuśatākampī
ṛddhipādamahākramaḥ /
mahāsmṛtidharas tattvaś
catuḥsmṛtisamādhirāṭ //

/ 'jig rten khams brgya kun bskyod pa /
/ rdsu 'phrul rkaṅ pa'i stobs chen ldan /
/ de ñid dran pa chen po 'chaṅ /
/ dran pa bźi po tiṅ 'dsin rgyal //

Who sways a hundred world-realms with the vigorous tread of his feet of magical power; whose reality maintains the great mindfulness and governs the *samādhi* of the four mindfulnesses.

"Sways ...": Narendrakīrti (81-5-6), this means the speediness on the path attended with craving; besides, there are four: (1) the feet of magical power attended with thought, i.e., with a fearless thought desiring to attain instantly [the state of] Vajradhara; (2) attended with striving, i.e., without laziness, desiring for oneself and others instantly the Buddha's wisdom; (3) attending with longing, i.e., the desire to comprehend instantly the reality; and (4) attended with analysis, i.e., to engage the *guru*'s precepts free from doubt. "Great mindfulness": Narendrakīrti (82-1-2), not forgetting the precepts; besides, the "four mindfulnesses," i.e., the four stations of mindfulness (*smṛtyupasthāna*): (1) station of mindfulness of body, the personal aggregates, etc. looked on as gods (*lhar lta ba*); (2) station of mindfulness of feelings, looking on them as great pleasure (*mahāsukha*); (3) station of mindfulness of natures (*dharma*), regarding all *dharmas* as having a "single taste" (*ekarasa*), as nonproductions; and (4) station of mindfulness of consciousness (*citta*), mindful of consciousness as identical with the "great seal" (*mahāmudrā*).

[10] bodhyaṅgakusumāmodas
tathāgataguṇodadhiḥ/
aṣṭāṅgamārganayavit
samyaksaṃbuddhamārgavit//

/byaṅ chub yan lag me tog spos/
/de bźin gśegs pa'i yon tan mtsho/
/lam gyi yan lag brgyad tshul rig/
/yaṅ dag saṅs rgyas lam rig pa//

Who has the flowery fragrance of the "enlightenment ancillaries," the ocean of Tathāgata virtues; knows the rules of the eightfold noble path, knows the path of the rightly completed Buddha.

"Enlightenment ancillaries": Narendrakīrti (82-1-8), the standard seven *bodhyaṅga*; "Tathāgata virtues," the goal, namely, the Buddha powers, confidences, etc. "Eightfold noble path": Narendrakīrti (82-2-5, 6) gives a tantric reinterpretation, (1) right views, *yoga* of one's [presiding] deity; (2) right reflection, the reflection that reality is certain; (3) right speech, diamond muttering, etc.; (4) right mindfulness, mindful that the body is a god, etc. [as in notes to verse 9, above]; (5) right *samādhi*, having as meditative object the "together-born" (*sahaja*); (6) right occupation, performing the aim of sentient beings; (7) right effort, putting one's effort in the Vajrayāna; and (8) right subsistence, subsisting on the "five fleshes or five ambrosias." "Path of the Buddha": Candrabhadrakīrti (11-2-5), the gift of the Dharma.

[11] sarvasattvamahāsaṅgo niḥsaṅgo
gaganopamaḥ/
sarvasattvamanojātaḥ
sarvasattvamanojavaḥ//

/sems can kun la śas cher chags/
/nam mkha' lta bur chags pa med/
/sems can kun gyi yid la 'jug/
/sems can kun gyi yid ltar mgyogs//

Who is highly attached to all sentient beings and is unattached like the sky; who is attuned to the minds of all sentient beings and speeds according to the minds of all sentient beings.

"Attached ... and unattached": Smṛti (53-1-1), "attached" conventionally to the aims of sentient beings, and "unattached" in the absolute sense because of voidness (*śūnyatā*). "Attuned to the minds": Narendrakīrti (82-3-7), there are two kinds of this, empowerment by the *guru* (*bla ma'i byin rlobs*) and endeavor by the disciple (*slob ma'i rtsol ba*). "Speeds": Smṛti (53-1-2), i.e., knows the make-up of the minds of all sentient beings.

[12] sarvasattvendriyārthajñaḥ
sarvasattvamanoharaḥ/
pañcaskandhārthatattvajñaḥ
pañcaskandhaviśuddhadhṛk//

/sems can kun gyi dbaṅ don ses/
/sems can kun gyi yid 'phrog pa/
/phuṅ po lṅa don de ñid śes/
/rnam dag phuṅ po lṅa 'chaṅ ba//

Knowing the senses and objects of all sentient beings, he enchants the minds of all sentient beings; knowing the goal-reality of the five personal aggregates, he maintains the pure five aggregates.

"Knowing the senses": Narendrakīrti (82-4-2), knowing them as superior and inferior; "knowing the objects," knowing what is an improper form [etc.]. "Enchants the minds": Smṛti (53-1-3), enchants the minds of candidates, teaching them the Dharma in accordance with their [respective] potentialities. "Goal-reality of the five personal aggregates": Narendrakīrti (82-4-5), the five personal aggregates [form, feelings, etc.] correspond to the five wisdoms and to the five Sugatas (= Buddhas). However, Smṛti

(53-1-3, 4) gives the nontantric list of five pure aggregates (*skandha*), of morality (*śīla*), of *samādhi*, of insight (*prajñā*) [which three according to Abhidharma subsume the eightfold noble path], and the aggregate of liberation (*vimukti-skandha*), and the aggregate of knowledge and vision of liberation (*vimukti-jñānadarśana-skandha*).

[13] sarvaniryāṇakoṭiṣṭhaḥ
sarvaniryāṇakovidaḥ/
sarvaniryāṇamārgasthaḥ
sarvaniryāṇadeśakaḥ//

/ṅes 'byuṅ kun gyi mtha' la gnas/
/ṅes par 'byuṅ ba kun la mkhas/
/ṅes 'byuṅ kun gyi lam la gnas/
/ṅes par 'byuṅ ba kun ston pa//

Who stays at the culmination of all deliverances and is skilled in all deliverances; who stays on the path of all deliverances and teaches all deliverances.

"Deliverances": Smṛti (53-1-4), mundane and supramundane; "skilled," skilled minutely in the deliverance of *śrāvakas*; "stays on the path," on the path of *pratyekabuddhas*; "teaches all deliverances," this means complete enlightenment.

[14] dvādaśaṅgabhavotkhato
dvādaśākāraśuddhadhṛk/
catuḥsatyanayākāro
'ṣṭajñānāvabodhadhṛk//

/yan lag bcu gñis srid rtsa bton/
/dag pa rnam pa bcu gñis 'chaṅ/
/bden bźi'i tshul gyi rnam pa can/
/śes pa brgyad po rtogs pa 'chaṅ//

Uprooting the life (*bhava*) of the twelvefold members, he maintains the pure twelve aspects; aspected by the rules of the four Truths, he maintains the awareness of the eight cognitions.

"The twelvefold members": Candrabhadrakīrti (11-3-5), the twelve members of dependent origination (*pratītya-samutpāda*) in their arising order attended with habit-energy (*vāsanā*), the life of this he uproots; "pure twelve aspects," the twelve members in their reversal, this he maintains. "Rules of the four Truths": Narendrakīrti (83-2-6), i.e., suffering is to be experienced, source [of suffering] is to be eliminated, cessation [of suffering] is the result to be directly realized, path [to the cessation] is the cause to be resorted to. Candrabhadrakīrti (11-3-7) and Smṛti (53-1-7), the eight are the four Noble Truths and their conforming cognitions, e.g., Suffering as a Noble Truth constitutes a cognition (*śes pa*), and "is to be realized" is the conforming cognition (*rjes su śes pa*).

[15] dvādaśākārasatyārthaḥ
ṣoḍaśākāratattvavit/
viṃśatyākārasaṃbodhir vibuddhaḥ
sarvavitparaḥ//

/bden don rnam pa bcu gñis ldan/
/de ñid rnam pa bcu drug rig/
/rnam pa ñi śus byaṅ chub pa/
/rnam par saṅs rgyas kun rig mchog//

Having the meaning of the Truths with twelve aspects and knowing the reality of the sixteen aspects; having the enlightenment of the twenty aspects and being the fully awakened one, the supreme omniscient one.

"Twelve aspects": Smṛti (53-1-8), the three turnings of the wheel for each of the four Truths to total twelve; "sixteen aspects," four aspects for each of the four Truths, thus for the first Truth the four, impermanence, pain, voidness, nonself. "Twenty aspects":

Smṛti (53-2-1, 2) denying the "twenty reifying views" (*sakkāyadiṭṭhi* in the Pāli language), namely four statements for each of the five personal aggregates (*skandha*); thus, form is not a self, self does not possess a form, form does not belong to self, the self is not in a form—which deny four of the reifying views.

[16] ameyabuddhanirmāṇakāyakoṭi- vibhāvakaḥ/ sarvakṣaṇābhisamayaḥ sarvacittakṣaṇārthavit//	/saṅs rgyas kun gyi sprul pa'i sku/ /bye ba dpag med 'gyed pa po/ /skad cig thams cad mṅon par rtogs/ /sems kyi skad cig don kun rig//	Who sends out uncountable myriads of Nirmāṇakāyas of the Buddhas; knowing all the momentary objects of the mind, realizes all the proper moments.

"Sends out": Narendrakīrti (83-3-7), the Mother Prajñāpāramitā, who is the "messenger" (*dūtī*) [sends out]. "Momentary objects": Narendrakīrti (83-4-4), the natures (*dharma*) included in the personal aggregates (*skandha*), realms (*dhātu*), and sense bases (*āyatana*). "Proper moments": Narendrakīrti (83-4-2), there are four: (1) the moment for imagining all the natures (*dharma*), (2) the moment for realizing the objects of sentient beings, (3) the moment for uncountable emissions, and (4) the moment for manifesting complete Buddhahood.

[17] nānāyānanayopāya(ḥ) jagadarthavibhāvakaḥ/ yānatritayaniryāta ekayānaphale sthitaḥ//	/theg pa sna tshogs thabs tshul gyis/ /'gro ba'i don la rtog pa po/ /theg pa gsum gyi ṅes 'byuṅ la/ /theg pa gcig gi 'bras bur gnas//	By means of the rules for the various vehicles, he constructs the aims of the world; having delivered the three vehicles, he stays in the one-vehicle fruit.

"Rules": Smṛti (53-2-4), for the diverse vehicles of *śrāvakas*, etc., i.e., their paths; "having delivered," by dint of discipline brought the *śrāvakas*, *pratyekabuddhas*, and *bodhisattvas* in their respective vehicles to their respective fruits. "One-vehicle fruit": Smṛti (53-2-6), "one-vehicle" in the absolute sense, the Mahāyoga-vehicle, or incomparable Mantra-vehicle.

[18] kleśadhātuviśuddhātmā karmadhātukṣayaṃkaraḥ/ oghodadhisamuttīrṇo yogakāntāraniḥsṛtaḥ//	/ñon moṅs khams rnams dag pa'i bdag/ /las kyi khams rnams zad byed pa/ /chu bo rgya mtsho kun las brgal/ /sbyor ba'i dgon pa las byuṅ ba//	Who having purified the realms of defilement, has made an end to the realms of *karma*; who having crossed over the ocean of floods, has emerged from the glade of praxis.

"Realms of defilement"; Narendrakīrti (83-5-6), the defilements (*kleśa*) and satellite defilements (*upakleśa*) of the three worlds; "realms of *karma*," the three realms arisen from virtuous and nonvirtuous *karma*—their habit-energies (*vāsanā*) he makes an end to. "Floods": Smṛti (53-2-7), there are four: of lust (*kāma*), of gestation (*bhava*), of [false] views (*dṛṣṭi*), and of nescience (*avidyā*). "Glade of praxis": Candrabhadrakīrti (11-5-1), like the moon—the praxis of adversary (to defilements)—emerges from the glade, wherein living beings circle, so (emerges) the spirited youth (*laṅ tsho bskyod pa*) [i.e., Mañjuśrī] of wisdom (*jñāna*).

[19] kleśopakleśasaṃkleśasuprahīṇa-
savāsanaḥ/
prajñopāyamahākaruṇā
amoghajagadarthakṛt//

/ñon moṅs ñe ba kun ñon moṅs/
/bag chags bcas pa gtan spaṅs pa/
/sñiṅ rje che daṅ śes rab thabs/
/don yod 'gro ba'i don byed pa//

Putting a final end to defilement, satellite defilement, and associate defilement, along with habit-energy; through great compassion and the insight-means, he performs the aim of living beings without fail.

"Defilement ...": Smṛti (53-3-1), the defilements (*kleśa*) are six, the satellite defilements (*upakleśa*) are twenty-four, the associate defilements (*saṃkleśa*) are seven; he puts a final end to them along with their deep-seated (*anuśaya*) habit-energy (*vāsanā*). "Great compassion": Narendrakīrti (84-1-4), this is the causal phase and is the great compassion without a particular aim. "Insight-means": Narendrakīrti (84-1-5) [referring to Anuttarayogatantra], "insight" is the nontwo stage of completion; "means" is the collection of knowable merit and the cultivation of the stage of generation; "performs the aim without fail," i.e., by that collection of merit yielding the two bodies (Sambhoga and Nirmāṇa), performs without fail.

[20] sarvasaṃjñāprahīṇārtho vijñānārtho
nirodhakṛt/
sarvasattvamanoviṣayaḥ
sarvasattvamanogatiḥ//

/'du śes kun gyi don spaṅs śiṅ/
/rnam śes don ni 'gog par byed/
/sems can kun gyi yid kyi yul/
/sems can kun gyi yid la gnas//

Having eliminated the object for every idea, his object of perception creates cessation; having all sentient beings as his mind's object, he dwells in the minds of all sentient beings.

"Object for every idea": Narendrakīrti (84-1-7), ideas attribute signs to objects, i.e., that object has such and such a mark; eliminating the object [he eliminates as well the idea]. "Object of perception": Narendrakīrti (84-1-8), this means that cognition and the knowable are nontwo.

[21] sarvasattvamano 'ntasthas taccitta-
samatāṃ gataḥ/
sarvasattvamanohlādī
sarvasattvamanoratiḥ//

/sems can kun gyi yid naṅ gnas/
/de dag sems daṅ mthun par 'jug/
/sems can kun yid tshim par byed/
/sems can kun gyi yid dga' ba//

Who has the minds of all sentient beings dwelling within (himself) and has realized sameness with their minds; who satisfies the minds of all sentient beings and gladdens all sentient beings.

"Gladdens all sentient beings": Narendrakīrti (84-2-5, 6), this is terminology for installing them in the Dharma and getting them to practice it.

[22] siddhāntavibhramāpetaḥ
sarvabhrāntivivarjitaḥ/
niḥsandigdhamatis tryadhvaḥ sarvārthas
triguṇātmakaḥ//

/grub mtha' 'khrul pa ldan pa min/
/nor ba thams cad rnam par spaṅs/
/don sum the tshom med pa'i blo/
/kun don yon tan gsum gyi bdag//

Devoid of the delusions of theory-systems he has eliminated all delusion; his mind is free from doubt in three ways, and with all entities has the nature of three virtues.

"Three ways": Candrabhadrakīrti (12-1-1), pleasure, pain, and equanimity. "Three virtues": Candrabhadrakīrti (12-1-1), of Body, Speech, and Mind.

[23] pañcaskandhārthas trikālaḥ
sarvakṣaṇavibhāvakaḥ/
ekakṣaṇābhisaṃbuddhaḥ
sarvabuddhasvabhāvadhṛk//

/phuṅ po lṅa don dus gsum pa/
/skad cig thams cad bye brag phyed/
/skad cig gcig gis rdsogs saṅs rgyas/
/saṅs rgyas kun gyi raṅ bźin 'chaṅ//

Who has the goal of the five personal aggregates in the three times, while detailing every proper moment; manifestly completely enlightened in a single moment, while maintaining the self-existence of all the Buddhas.

"Goal of the five aggregates": Narendrakīrti (84-3-6), from exchange (*parivṛtti*) of the five personal aggregates (*skandha*) there are the five Buddhas. "Three times": Narendrakīrti (84-3-1): (1) time of birth, which means the five enlightenments (*bodhi*), having such epithets as "who looks all around," "the self-originated one," "(like) the sun and moon," i.e., when born from a womb; (2) time of staying, which means acting directly for the sake of sentient beings; and (3) time of passing away, which means taking the lord and retinue as nontwo. "Proper moments": [see comment on verse 16, above]. "While maintaining the self-existence of all the Buddhas": the commentary *'Grel pa tshul gsum gsal ba byed pa'i sgron ma* (PTT, Vol. 75, p. 86-1-2), dwells in the heart of the Buddhas of the three times, as the "knowledge-body Buddha."

[24] anaṅgakāyaḥ kāyāgryaḥ
kāyakoṭivibhāvakaḥ//
aśeṣarūpasaṃdarśī ratnaketur
mahāmaṇiḥ//

/lus med lus te lus kyi mchog/
/lus kyi mtha' ni rtogs pa po/
/gzugs rnams sna tshogs kun tu ston/
/nor bu chen po rin chen tog//

Whose incorporeal body is the foremost body, "comprehender" at the apex of bodies; who exhibiting every kind of form is the "peak jewel," the great gem.

"Incorporeal body": Smṛti (54-1-8), the body of the Dharmadhātu, not an ordinary body. "Comprehender": Smṛti (54-2-1), who comprehends as the Dharmakāya, at the apex of bodies, emitting the formal Buddha bodies. "Great gem": Smṛti (54-2-1), a term for one who has been initiated as Dharma-king of the three realms [i.e., on the Tenth Bodhisattva Stage]. "Peak jewel": Narendrakīrti (84-4-4), a name of (Buddha) Ratnasambhava.

//samatājñānagāthāś caturviṃśatiḥ//

/mñam pa ñid kyi ye śes kyi tshigs bcad ñi śu rtsa bźi'o/

Twenty-four *gāthā* on Sameness Wisdom.

CHAPTER X. PROCEDURE-OF-DUTY WISDOM

[1] sarvasambuddhabodhavyo buddhabodhir
anuttaraḥ/
anakṣaro mantrayonir
mahāmantrakulatrayaḥ//

/saṅs rgyas kun gyis rtogs bya ba/
/saṅs rgyas byaṅ chub bla na med/
/gsaṅ sṅags las byuṅ yi ge med/
/gsaṅ sṅags chen po rigs gsum pa//

To be realized by all the Buddhas is the incomparable enlightenment of the Buddha; there is the nonsyllable, the birthplace of *mantras*, the three great-*mantra* families.

"Non-syllable": Smṛti (54-2-6), because in the absolute sense there is no expression. "Three great-mantra families": Smṛti (54-2-6), Vairocana as Body, Akṣobhya as Mind, and Amitābha as Speech.

[2] sarvamantrārthajanako mahābindur
anakṣaraḥ/
pañcākṣaro mahāśūnyo binduśūnyaḥ
ṣaḍakṣaraḥ//

/gsaṅ sṅags don kun skyed pa po/
/thig le chen po yi ge med/
/stoṅ pa chen po yi ge lṅa/
/thig le stoṅ pa yi ge drug//

Who generates the purposes of all *mantras*; the great *bindu* is nonsyllabled; great void is five-syllabled; the *bindu*-void is six-syllabled.

[Both Narendrakīrti and Candrabhadrakīrti change "six-syllabled" to "hundred-syllabled," as though the Sanskrit had read *śatākṣaraḥ* (cf. Narendrakīrti, 84-5-4: */thig le stoṅ pa yi ge brgya/źes bya ba*).] "Purposes of all mantras": Narendrakīrti (84-5-1), namely, the two *siddhis* (occult successes) [usually, variously mundane and the supramundane Buddhahood]. "Great *bindu* is nonsyllabled": Padma dkar-po (Derge Tanjur, *Rgyud*, Pha, f. 199a-5ff.), *nirvāṇa*, the knowledge element (*jñānadhātu*), is inexpressible; "great void is five-syllabled," the throat, etc., pronounce the mantras of the space element, etc. (going with the five personal aggregates, *skandha*), namely, (1) perception (*vijñāna*) (the space element), "A" like a *gri gug* (short crooked sword) is in the middle; (2) above it is the motivations (*saṃskāra*), wind element, "A" like a *dbyug gu* (wand); (3) at the right, feelings (*vedanā*), the fire element, "A" like a *tsheg drag* (intense crackling sound); (4) at the left, ideas (*saṃjñā*), water element ["A"] like a *thig le* (water drop); (5) below, form (*rūpa*), earth element, "A" like a *thoṅ gśol* (crooked beam); thus the five symbolize Vajrasattva as the BAM-syllable; "*bindu*-void is six syllabled," knowledge element is added to the five elements, and the six, in six directions, are associated with the consonants in six classes; when the six are "unified" they are the E-syllable, Dharmadhātu; "great void five-syllabled" is called "semen" and "moon"; "*bindu*-void six-syllabled" is called "blood" and "sun."

[3] sarvākāranirākāraḥ
ṣoḍaśārdhārdhabindudhṛk/
akalaḥ kalanātītaś
caturthadhyānakoṭidhṛk//

/rnam pa kun ldan rnam pa med/
/bcu drug phyed phyed thig le 'chaṅ/
/yan lag med pa rtsis las 'das/
/bsam gtan bźi pa'i rtse mo 'chaṅ//

Having all images and lacking all, holding the *bindu* of sixteen halved twice; when without branches and beyond calculation, holding the pinnacle of the Fourth Dhyāna.

"Having and lacking all images": Narendrakīrti (84-5-6), having all in the conventional sense and lacking all in the absolute sense. "*Bindu* divided": Narendrakīrti (84-5-7), *vajra* and *padma* divided. The *'Grel pa tshul gsum* ... p. 86-4-2 says, referring to both verses 2 and 3, that there is a sequence of *bindu* fractions or syllables in the order, five, six, eight, and sixteen. "Without branches and beyond calculation": Narendrakīrti (84-5-8), this refers to "together-born joy" (*sahajānanda*); that "branches" are "elaboration" (*prapañca*, *spros pa*) and that "calculation" is the division yielding sixteen. "Pinnacle of the Fourth Dhyāna": [this should refer to Akaniṣṭha, at the top of the Realm of Form, where according to Mahāyāna the Buddha was fully enlightened]. Candrabhadrakīrti (12-2-7) takes it in the Anuttarayoga-tantra sense of the four lights or four voids, namely [for lights], Light, Spread-of-Light, Culmination-of-Light, and the Clear Light, where the Fourth Dhyāna is equivalent to the Clear Light.

[4] sarvadhyānakalābhijñaḥ samādhikulagotravit/ samādhikāyakāyāgryaḥ sarvasaṃbhogakāyarāṭ//	/bsam gtan yan lag kun śes śiṅ/ /tiṅ 'dsin rigs daṅ rgyud rig pa/ /tiṅ 'dsin lus can lus gyi mchog/ /loṅs spyod rdsogs sku kun gyi rgyal//	Having supernormal cognition of all the *dhyāna*-branches and knowing the family and genus of *samādhi*-s; who has the best of bodies in the body arising from *samādhi*, the supremacy in the Sambhogakāya.

"Supernormal cognition": Narendrakīrti (85-1-3), knowing with certainty the four *mudrā*-s, the four moments (*kṣaṇa*), the four joys (*ānanda*), which are the branches or means (*upāya*) of *dhyāna*.

[5] nirmāṇakāyakāyāgryo buddhanirmāṇavaṃśadhṛk/ daśadigviśvanirmāṇo yathāvaj jagadarthakṛt//	/sprul pa'i sku ste sku yi mchog/ /saṅs rgyas sprul pa'i rgyud 'chaṅ ba/ /phyogs bcur sprul pa sna tshogs 'gyed/ /ji bźin 'gro ba'i don byed pa//	Who has the best of bodies in the Nirmāṇakāya, maintaining the lineage of Buddha-*nirmāṇa*; having the multifarious *nirmāṇa* in the ten directions, performing according to the aims of the living beings.

"Multifarious *nirmāṇa*": Narendrakīrti (85-2-3), adopting a materialization (*nirmāṇa*) in any one of many forms in different places.

[6] devātidevo devendraḥ surendro dānavādhipaḥ// amarendraḥ suraguruḥ pramathaḥ pramatheśvaraḥ//	/lha yi dbaṅ po lha yi lha/ /lha yi bdag po lha min bdag/ /'chi med dbaṅ po lha'i bla ma/ /'joms byed 'joms byed dbaṅ phyug po//	God of gods, Indra of the gods; master of the gods, master of the demigods; master of the immortals, *guru* of the gods; destroyer, lord of destroyers.

"God of gods": Candrabhadrakīrti (12-3-5), Brahmā. "Indra of the gods": Candrabhadrakīrti (12-3-4), Śakra (name of Indra). "Master of the gods": Candragomin (79-1-3), Viṣṇu (*khyab 'jug*). "Master of the demigods": Candragomin (79-1-3), Rāhula. "Master of the immortals": [no information]. "*Guru* of the gods": Candragomin (79-1-4), the planet Jupiter. "Destroyer": Candragomin (79-1-4), leader of the asuras, named Vemacitra; or, King of the *rākṣasa*-s, named Rāvaṇa, with ten heads. "Lord of destroyers": Candragomin (79-1-4), Mahādeva (name of Śiva).

[7] uttīrṇabhavakāntāra ekaḥ śāstā
jagadguruḥ/
prakhyātadaśadiglokaṃ dharmadānapatir
mahān//

/srid pa'i dgon pa las brgal ba/
/ston pa gcig pu 'gro ba'i bla/
/'jig rten phyogs bcur rab grags pa/
/chos kyi sbyin bdag che ba po//

Who has crossed the wilderness of phenomenal life; the single teacher who is guru of living beings; famed in the ten directions of the world as the great patron of the Dharma.

"Phenomenal life": Candragomin (79-1-6), the three realms. "Wilderness": Candragomin (79-1-6), [where] the dharmas of phenomenal life are purposeless and void. "Crossed the wilderness": Candragomin (79-1-6), not tainted by the faults of phenomenal life. "Single teacher": Candragomin (79-1-7), unrivaled (*'gran zla med pa*). "*Guru* of living beings": Candragomin (79-1-7), none higher (*goṅ na med pa*). "Great patron of the Dharma": Candragomin (79-1-8), teaches the meaning of the nonflux (*anāsrava*).

[8] maitrīsaṃnāhasaṃnaddhaḥ
karuṇāvarmavarmitaḥ/
prajñākhaḍgadhanurbāṇaḥ kleśājñāna-
raṇaṃ jahaḥ//

/byams pa'i go chas chas pa ste/
/sñiṅ rje yi ṇi ya lad bgos/
/śes rab ral gri mda' gźu thogs/
/ñon moṅs mi śes g'yul ṅo sel//

Who is girded with the girding of love and armed with the armor of compassion; who bears the sword of insight along with bow and arrow and has routed the combativeness of defilement and ignorance.

"Girding of love": Candragomin (79-1-8), "love," thinks of everyone as though an only son; and "girding," protected from hatred. "Armor of compassion": "compassion," fervently wishes that all sentient beings would be free from suffering; and "armor," the upper mantle (*stod g'yogs*) like armor that does not allow interruption of the aims of sentient beings. "Sword of insight": Narendrakīrti (85-4-5), the three insights (of hearing, pondering, and cultivation) are like a sword; "arrow" is compassion; "bow" is voidness.

[9] mārārir mārajid vīraś
caturmārabhayāntakṛt/
sarvamāracamūjetā saṃbuddho
lokanāyakaḥ//

/dpa' bo bdud dgra bdud 'dul ba/
/bdud bźi'i 'jigs pa sel bar byed/
/bdud kyi dpuṅ rnams pham byed pa/
/rdsogs pa'i saṅs rgyas 'jig rten 'dren//

The hero enemy of the Māras and tamer of the Māras, who ends the danger of the four Māras; who defeats the entire Māra army, (you) the complete Buddha, guide of the world.

"Hero enemy": Candragomin (79-2-3), the knowledge being (*jñānasattva*), who ends the danger of the four kinds of Māra, namely, "son-of-the-gods," "death" (*maraṇa*), defilement, and personal aggregate(s); and defeats all their followers, called "Māra-army."

[10] vandyaḥ pūjyo 'bhivādyaś ca mānanīyaś ca nityaśaḥ /
arcanīyatamo mānyo namasyaḥ paramo guruḥ //

/ mchod 'os bstod 'os phyag gi gnas /
/ rtag tu ri mor bya ba'i 'os /
/ bkur 'os rjed par bya ba'i mchog /
/ phyag byar 'os pa bla ma'i rab //

Who is worthy of honor, worthy of offerings, and a place of praise; who is ever worthy of trust, venerable to the highest degree, the supreme *guru* to be bowed to.

"Worthy of honor": Narendrakīrti (85-5-4), for being the hero as described in the preceding verse (no. 9); "offerings" with thanks; "praise" with joyful expression; "to be bowed to" reverently; "worthy of trust" by kings and the like.

[11] trailokyaikakramagatir vyomāparyantavikramaḥ /
traividyaḥ śrotriyaḥ pūtaḥ ṣaḍabhijñaḥ ṣaḍanusmṛtiḥ //

/ 'jig rten gsum po gom gcig bgrod /
/ mkha' ltar mtha' med rnam par gnon /
/ gsum rig gtsaṅ ma dag pa ste /
/ mṅon śes drug ldan rjes dran drug //

Who goes with single step through the three worlds, stepping forward without limits as though it were the sky; who has the three clear visions, purifies and is pure, with the six supranormal cognitions and the six remembrances.

"Single step": Candragomin (79-2-7), it means going in a single moment. "Without limits like the sky": Candragomin (79-2-8), because not tainted by faults of *saṃsāra*. "Three clear visions": Candragomin (79-2-8), of existence, nonexistence, and not-two. "Six supernormal cognitions": Candragomin (79-3-1), divine eye, divine hearing, knowing the minds of others, knowing death-transference and rebirth, magical ability, and knowing that the fluxes have been eradicated. "Six remembrances": Candragomin (79-3-2), of the Buddha, of the Dharma, of the Saṅgha, of forsaking (*tyāga*), of the gods, of the *guru*.

[12] bodhisattvo mahāsattvo lokātīto maharddhikaḥ /
prajñāpāramitāniṣṭhaḥ prajñātattvatvam āgataḥ //

/ byaṅ chub sems dpa' sems dpa' che /
/ rdsu 'phrul chen pos 'jig rten 'das /
/ śes rab pha rol phyin pa'i mtha' /
/ śes rab kyis ni de ñid thob //

Bodhisattva the great being, beyond the world with great magic power; at the limit of insight-perfection, having reached reality by insight.

"Bodhisattva": Candragomin (79-3-3), perfection of his own aim; "great being," perfection of others' aims; "with great magic power," possessing the four "feet" of magical power (*ṛddhipāda*); "beyond the world," crossed over *saṃsāra*; "at the limit of insight-perfection," has [already] the insight consisting of hearing and the insight consisting of pondering; "has reached reality by insight," has the insight consisting of cultivation (or, intense contemplation); "reached reality," realizing the diamondlike *samādhi* (*vajropama-samādhi*).

[13] ātmavitparavitsarvaḥ sarvīyo hy agrapudgalaḥ/ sarvopamām atikrānto jñeyajñānādhipaḥ paraḥ//	/bdag rig gźan rig thams cad pa/ /kun la phan pa gaṅ zag mchog/ /dper bya kun las 'das pa ste/ /śes daṅ śes bya'i bdag po mchog//	Who has all the self-knowledge and knowledge of others, the best person helpful to everyone; who surpasses all examples, best master of knowing and the knowable.

"Self-knowledge": Candragomin (79-3-6), the characteristic of that *samādhi* (i.e., the diamondlike one), the subject (*viṣayin*); "knowledge of others," the object (*viṣaya*); "surpasses all examples," unrivaled; "knowing," the evaluating knowledge (*'jal bar byed pa'i rig pa*); "the knowable," the object being evaluated (*gźal ba yul*).

[14] dharmadānapatiḥ śreṣṭhas caturmudrārthadeśakaḥ/ paryupāsyatamo jagatāṃ niryāṇatrayayāyināṃ//	/gtso bo chos kyi sbyin bdag ste/ /phyag rgya bźi po'i don ston pa/ /'gro ba'i bsñen bkur gnas kyi mchog/ /ṅes 'byuṅ gsum po bgrod rnams kyi//	Preeminent patron of Dharma, revealing the meaning of the four *mudrā*-s; best resort of living beings and of those traveling the three ways of escape.

"The four *mudrā*-s": [the four "seals" (*mudrā*) in the Mahāyāna, but nontantric sense, are presented in *Mkhas grub rje's Fundamentals of the Buddhist Tantras*, pp. 84-85, as follows: (1) the *saṃskāras* are all impermanent (*anitya*); (2) everything with flux (*sāsrava*) is suffering (*duḥkha*); (3) all natures (*sarvadharmāḥ*) are devoid of self; (4) *nirvāṇa* is tranquil and solitary. However, the three commentators, Smṛti (54-4-8), Narendrakīrti (86-2-6), and Candrabhadrakīrti (12-5-7), all take the four in the tantric sense as the *mudrā*-s called *samaya*, *dharma*, *karma*, and *mahā*, which are explained in the Yogatantra sense in *Mkhas grub rje's*, pp. 228-229. (Candragomin did not commit himself at this point of his commentary, 79-4-1, 2.)] "Three ways of escape": [the commentaries agree that these are the vehicles of the *śrāvakas*, *pratyekabuddhas*, and *bodhisattvas*].

[15] paramārthaviśuddhaśrīs trailokyasubhago mahān/ sarvasaṃpatkaraḥ śrīmān mañjuśrīḥ śrī- matāṃ varaḥ//	/don gyi dam pa rnam dag dpal/ /'jig rten gsum na skal bzaṅ che/ /dpal ldan 'byor pa kun byed pa/ /'jam dpal dpal daṅ ldan pa'i mchog//	Pure glory of *paramārtha* that is the great good fortune of the three worlds; glorious one who creates all perfection, Mañjuśrī the best of those with *śrī* (glory).

"Pure glory of *paramārtha* that is the great good fortune": Narendrakīrti (86-3-1), this is the fruit for those mentioned in the preceding verse, no. 14, who travel the three ways of escape. "*Śrī* (glory)": Narendrakīrti (86-3-2), the nontwo source for all the aims of oneself and others. "*Mañju*": Narendrakīrti (86-3-4), *mañju* (smooth), because lacking the wounds of all the "two-s."

//kṛtyānuṣṭhānajñānagāthāḥ pañcadaśa//	/bya ba grub pa'i ye śes kyi tshigs su bcad pa bco lṅa'o/	Fifteen *gāthā* on Procedure-of-Duty Wisdom.

CHAPTER XI. PRAISE OF THE FIVE TATHĀGATAS

[1] namo varada vajrāgra bhūtakoṭi namo 'stu te/
namas te śūnyatāgarbha buddhabodhi namo 'stu te//

/mchog sbyin rdo rje mchog khyod 'dud/
/yaṅ dag mthar gyur khyod la 'dud/
/stoṅ nid sñiṅ po khyod la 'dud/
/saṅs rgyas byaṅ chub khyod la 'dud//

Homage [to thee,] giver of boon, the *vajra*, the best; the true end, may there be homage to thee. Homage to thee, voidness as womb, Buddha's enlightenment, may there be homage to thee.

"Homage to thee": Narendrakīrti (86-3-5), the praise is for the Tathāgata Akṣobhya and the Dharmadhātu wisdom. Smṛti (54-5-7, 8), the praise summarizes the character of the Diamond Family. Candragomin (79-4-4), the praises in five verses amount to twenty features of homage; "giver of boon," the Dharmadhātu wisdom; "the *vajra*," the five wisdoms in the inseparable condition. (1) "The best": Candragomin (79-4-5), You, the knowledge being; (2) "the true end," not an object of intellect; (3) "voidness as womb," birth from nonproduction; (4) "Buddha's enlightenment," perfection of elimination and perfection of knowledge.

[2] buddharāga namas te 'stu buddhakāma namo namaḥ/
buddhaprīti namas tubhyaṃ buddhamoda namo namaḥ//

/saṅs rgyas chags pa khyod la 'dud/
/saṅs rgyas 'dod la phyag 'tshal 'dud/
/saṅs rgyas dgyes pa khyod la 'dud/
/saṅs rgyas rol la phyag 'tshal 'dud//

Homage to thee, Buddha passion, Buddha desire, homage to thee, bowing. Homage to thee, Buddha enjoyment, Buddha sport, homage to thee, bowing.

"Homage to thee": Narendrakīrti (86-4-2), the praise is for the Tathāgata Vairocana and the Mirrorlike wisdom. Smṛti (55-1-3), the praise summarizes the character of the Tathāgata Family. Candragomin (79-4-7), (5) "Buddha passion," for the aims of living beings. Narendrakīrti (86-4-3), besides, to assist lower beings like an abbot would; (6) "Buddha desire" that the sentient beings attain Buddhahood; (7) "Buddha enjoyment" in the "son of the family" who yearns for Buddhahood, besides, enjoyment in the aims of sentient beings; (8) "Buddha sport" in displaying the twelve Buddha acts for the aims of sentient beings.

[3] buddhasmita namas tubhyaṃ buddhabhāsa namo namaḥ/
buddhavāca namas te 'stu buddhabhāva namo namaḥ//

/saṅs rgyas 'dsum pa khyod la 'dud/
/saṅs rgyas bźad la phyag 'tshal 'dud/
/saṅs rgyas gsuṅ ñid khyod la 'dud/
/saṅs rgyas thugs la phyag 'dud//

Homage to thee, Buddha's smile, Buddha's jest, homage to thee, bowing. Homage to thee, Buddha's speech, Buddha's state of mind, homage to thee, bowing.

"Homage to thee": Narendrakīrti (86-4-6), the praise is for the Tathāgata Amitābha and the Discriminative wisdom. Smṛti (55-1-8), the praise summarizes the character of the Lotus Family. (9) "Buddha's smile": Smṛti (55-1-3), the opened lotus of the face, because he comprehends reality; (10) "Buddha's jest," emitting light rays that symbolize he has comprehended the profound, wondrous meaning and teaches the Bodhisattvas; (11) "Buddha's speech," of four kinds; (a) with fierce pronunciation, the manner of reciting in the Vajra Family; (b) with clear expression, the character of reciting in the Ratna Family; (c) with subtle, chanted tones, the way one recites in the Padma Family; (d) with "diamond letters," i.e., without sound that can be heard, the recitation in the Tathāgata Family; (12) "state of mind," either the bare nature of the Buddha's mind, or symbols of the mind, e.g., the *vajra*, the *ratna*, the *padma*, the crossed-*vajra*.

[4] abhavodbhava namas te 'stu namas te buddhasaṃbhava/ gaganodbhava namas tubhyaṃ namas te jñānasaṃbhava//	/med pa las byuṅ khyod la 'dud/ /saṅs rgyas 'byuṅ ba khyod la 'dud/ /nam mkha' las byuṅ khyod la 'dud/ /ye śes las byuṅ khyod la 'dud//	Homage to thee, arisen from naught, Buddha's arising, homage to thee, bowing. Homage to thee, arisen from the sky, source of wisdom, homage to thee, bowing.

"Homage to thee": Narendrakīrti (86-4-8), the praise is for the Tathāgata Ratnasambhava and the Sameness wisdom. Smṛti (55-2-2), the praise summarizes the character of the Jewel Family. (13) "Arisen from naught": Narendrakīrti (86-5-1), arisen from nonself (*anātman*), performing the aim of sentient beings in the manner of the twelve illusion examples; or arisen from all the Buddha merits, like the wish-granting jewel (*cintāmaṇi*); (14) "Buddha's arising": appearances without end of bodies and wisdom; (15) "arisen from the sky": not tainted by the features (*dharma*) of a birthplace; (16) "source of wisdom": refers to the Sameness wisdom itself.

[5] māyājāla namas tubhyaṃ namas te buddhanāṭaka/ namas te sarva sarvebhyo jñānakāya namo 'stu te//	/sgyu 'phrul dra ba khyod la 'dud/ /saṅs rgyas rol ston khyod la 'dud/ /thams cad thams cad khyod la 'dud/ /ye śes sku ñid khyod la 'dud/	Homage to thee, the net of illusion, Buddha's dance, homage to thee. Homage to thee, all for all, the knowledge body, homage to thee.

"Homage to thee": Narendrakīrti (86-5-3), the praise is for the Tathāgata Amoghasiddhi and the Procedure-of-Duty wisdom. Smṛti (55-4-5), the praise summarizes the character of the Karma Family. (17) "Net of illusion": Candragomin (79-5-1), inseparable bliss-void (*sukha-śūnya*); (18) "Buddha's dance": the various fierce bodies; (19) "all for all": for all of *saṃsāra* (*'khor ba thams cad*); (20) "knowledge body": the body that is bright (*gsal*) and devoid of imagination (*mi rtog pa*).

//pañcatathāgata jñānastutigāthāḥ pañca//	/de bźin gśegs pa lṅa'i ye śes kyi bstod pa tshigs bcad lṅa'o/	Five *gāthā* on Praise of the Five Tathāgatas.

CHAPTER XII. EXHIBITION OF MANTRAS

[1] OṂ sarvadharmā 'bhāvasvabhāvaviśuddhā vajra [cakṣu] A Ā AṂ AḤ/

OṂ. All natures are intrinsically pure like the *abhāva*. O diamond (vision)! A Ā AṂ AḤ.

Candrabhadrakīrti (14-4-6), this is the *upahṛdaya* (near-heart-mantra) of Vajratīkṣṇa. Narendrakīrti (86-5-8), OṂ is the benediction (*śis pa brjod pa*); "all natures" are all the *dharmas* included in the personal aggregates (*skandha*), realms (*dhātu*), and sense bases (*āyatana*); how "intrinsically pure"?—"like the *abhāva*," i.e., unsubstantial (*abhāva*), appearing like the moon in the waters; "O diamond (vision)," the inseparable appearance and void, the extraordinary seeing by the Buddha eye; as to the method: A is the means (*upāya*), Ā is insight (*prajñā*), arising from these two is AṂ, the conventional (*saṃvṛti*) *bindu* (*thig le*), and AḤ, the absolute unsubstantial.

[2] prakṛtipariśuddhāḥ sarvadharmā yad uta sarvatathāgatajñānakāyamañjuśrīpariśuddhitām upādāyeti A ĀḤ/

All natures are intrinsically pure, to the extent one takes on the purity of Mañjuśrī, the knowledge body of all the Tathāgatas. A ĀḤ.

Candrabhadrakīrti (14-4-6), this is the *upahṛdaya* of Duḥkhaccheda. Narendrakīrti (87-1-5), "intrinsically" means "nonartificial" (*ma bcos*); "to the extent one takes on" (*yad uta ... upādāyeti*) means "[assumes] the rank in the sense of body"; A is means (*upāya*) and ĀH is insight (*prajñā*), and with these two one may assume the rank that is given the name "Mañjuśrī the knowledge body."

[3] sarvatathāgatahṛdaya hara hara OṂ HŪṂ HRĪḤ/

O, heart of all the Tathāgatas. Remove, remove! OṂ HŪṂ HRĪḤ.

Candrabhadrakīrti (14-4-7), this is the *upahṛdaya* of Prajñājñāna. Narendrakīrti (87-2-2), "heart" means "knowledge body," abiding in the heart of all the Tathāgatas; "remove, remove" (*hara hara*) means asking their heart, the heart of Body, Speech, and Mind, to remove all the defilements of the ordinary body, speech, and mind; OṂ HŪṂ HRĪḤ, thus becoming the Body, Speech, and Mind.

[4] bhagavan jñānamūrte/

O Bhagavat, the knowledge body.

Candrabhadrakīrti (14-4-7), this is the *upahṛdaya* of Jñānakāya. Narendrakīrti (87-2-4), to whom belongs the previously mentioned Body, Speech, and Mind.

[5] vāgīśvara mahāpaca/

O lord of speech, the great cooking.

Candrabhadrakīrti (14-4-7, 8), this is the *upahṛdaya* of Vāgīśvara. Narendrakīrti (87-2-6), who while cooking changes the colors in the knowledge body of everything nontwo (*thams cad gñis su med pa'i ye śes kyi skur 'tshed ciṅ kha dog bsgyur bar byed do*).

[6] sarvadharmagaganāmaḷasupariśuddhadharmadhātujñāna-garbha ĀḤ//

O womb (*garbha*) of the pure Dharmadhātu Wisdom where all natures are pure like the sky! ĀḤ.

Candrabhadrakīrti (14-4-8), this is the *upahṛdaya* of Arapacana. Narendrakīrti (87-2-7, 8), ĀḤ means dissolves into nonarising [the absolute].

//mantravinyāsa//

Exhibition of Mantras.

CHAPTER XIII. THE SUMMING UP

[1] atha vajradharaḥ śrīmāṃ hṛṣṭatuṣṭaḥ kṛtañjaliḥ/
prāṇamya nāthaṃ saṃbuddhaṃ bhagavantaṃ tathāgataṃ//

/de nas dpal ldan rdo rje 'chaṅ/
/dga' źiṅ mgu nas thal mo sbyar/
/mgon po bcom ldan de bźin gśegs/
/rdsogs saṅs rgyas la phyag 'tshal te//

Then Vajradhara, ecstatic, with folded hands in homage to the glorious one (*śrīmat*), and bowing to the *nātha*, Saṃbuddha, Bhagavat, Tathāgata;

[2] anyaiś ca bahuvidhair nāthair guhyendrair vajrapāṇibhiḥ/
sa sārdhaṃ krodharājanaiḥ provācauccair idaṃ vacaḥ//

/rnam maṅ mgon po gźan rnams daṅ/
/gsaṅ dbaṅ lag na rdo rje de/
/khro bo'i rgyal por bcas rnams kyis/
/gsaṅ bstod nas ni tshig 'di gsol//

He, Vajrapāṇi, attended by many other *nāthas* and *guhyendriyas*, as well as by the Fury Kings with their intense praise (*provāca-ucca*), offered these words,

[3] anumodāmahe nātha sādhu sādhu subhāṣitaṃ/
kṛto 'smākaṃ mahānāthaḥ samyaksaṃbodhiprāpakaḥ//

/mgon po bdag cag rjes yi raṅ/
/legs so legs so legs par gsuṅs/
/bdag cag yaṅ dag rdsogs pa yi/
/byaṅ chub thob pa'i don chen mdsad//

Well-expressed: Lord (*nātha*)! We sympathetically rejoice. Excellent, excellent! We have made the attaining of right complete enlightenment our chief goal.

[4] jagataś cāpy anāthasya vimuktiphalakāṅkṣiṇaḥ/
śreyo mārgo viśuddho 'yaṃ māyājālanayoditaḥ//

/'gro ba mgon med rnams daṅ ni/
/rnam grol 'bras bu 'tshal ba yi/
/rnam dag legs pa'i lam 'di ni/
/sgyu 'phrul dra ba'i tshul bstan pa//

For the world without protector, longing for the liberation-fruit, there was promulgated this pure and excellent path, as the method of the "net of illusion."

"Pure and excellent path": Candrabhadrakīrti (14-5-8), "pure" means "good in the beginning"; "excellent" means "good in the middle"; "deep" (next verse, no. 5) means "good in the end."

[5] gambhīrodāravaipulyo mahārtho jagadarthakṛt/
buddhānāṃ viṣayo hy eṣa samyaksaṃbuddhabhāṣitaḥ/

/zab ciṅ yaṅs la rgya che ba/
/don chen 'gro ba'i don byed pa/
/saṅs rgyas rnams kyi yul 'di ni/
/rdsogs pa'i saṅs rgyas kun gyis bśad//

For the Samyaksambuddhas have promulgated this field of the Buddhas that is deep, broad, and immense—the great goal created for the sake of the world!

Final summing up by Candrabhadrakīrti (15-1-2): Mañjuśrī is the main body of the six Families. The six original Buddhas are "knowledge beings" (*jñānasattva*). In the absolute sense, there are six knowledge bodies. The rehearsal of names (*nāma-saṃgīti*) is the rehearsal of the meaning of contemplating the names in his six *maṇḍalas*. The Bhagavat Śākyamuni is Vairocana; it was in a future time that, materializing as Śākyamuni, there was the [phenomenal] Śākyamuni.

//upasaṃhāragāthāḥ pañca//

[Tibetan missing here.]/

Five summary *gāthā*.

//bhagavat-tathāgata-Śākyamunibhāṣitā bhagavato Mañjuśrī-jñānasattvasya paramārthā nāmasaṃgītiḥ parisamāptā//

/bcom ldan 'das 'jam dpal ye śes sems dpa'i don dam pa'i mtshan yaṅ dag par brjod pa/bcom ldan 'das de bźin gśegs pa Śā-kya thub pas gsuṅs pa rdsogs so/

Finished is the supreme rehearsal of names of Mañjuśrī the knowledge-being Lord, as promulgated by the Lord Tathāgata Śākyamuni.

Index of Sanskrit First Pāda-s

Index of Tibetan First Lines

Index to the Translation and Annotations